An Introduction to Psycholinguistics

Learning About Language

General Editors:
Geoffrey Leech & Mick Short, Lancaster University

Already published:

For Jinwen

1894 Chautauqua New York
Alexander Graham Bell (47 years), inventor and teacher of the deaf, with Helen Keller (14 years), seated, and Anne Sullivan Macy (28 years), standing. Keller is touching Macy's mouth with her left hand.

An Introduction to Psycholinguistics

Danny D. Steinberg

Longman
London and New York

Longman Group Limited,
Longman House, Burnt Mill,
Harlow, Essex CM20 2JE, England
and Associated Companies throughout the world.

Published in the United States of America
by Longman Publishing, New York

© Longman Group UK Limited 1993

First published 1993
Third impression 1995

ISBN 0–582 05982.8 PPR

British Library Cataloguing-in-Publication Data

A catalogue record for this book is available from the British Library

Library of Congress Cataloging-in-Publication Data

Steinberg, Danny D.
    Introduction to psycholinguistics/Danny D. Steinberg.
       p. cm.
    Includes bibliographical references and index.
    1. Psycholinguistics.   I. Title.
P37.S77 1993
401'.9—dc20   92–38645
                                           CIP

Set 8U in Linotron Bembo 11/12 pt
Produced through Longman Malaysia, ACM

Contents

PART 3: SECOND LANGUAGE 201

Preface

With this book I wish to introduce the interested reader to Psycholinguistics, that field of inquiry where language is regarded from a psychological perspective. As such, Psycholinguistics inevitably intersects with psychology, linguistics, philosophy, education and other disciplines, as well. While this is an introductory book, the reader is nonetheless taken to the heart of matters and contemporary controversy. This is so whether the issues are of a theoretical or a practical nature.

Prior knowledge of any discipline is not presupposed. I have tried my best to introduce readers to the essential concepts of the constituent subfields with a view to gaining knowledge and understanding issues so that readers may be able to think for themselves and conduct enquiries on their own.

The book is divided into three parts: *First Language*, *Language and Mind* and *Second Language*. While every chapter in the book is self-sufficient and can be read directly, I would recommend that, for full advantage, chapters within each part be read in order. While the parts themselves may be read in any order, it would be best that *First Language* precede *Second Language* since so many of the problems and issues relevant to *Second Language* are introduced and elaborated on in *First Language*. Then, too, because *Language and Mind* involves rather challenging topics and issues, I would suggest that readers deal with *First Language* before doing *Language and Mind*. *First Language* is designed to provide ideas, raise questions and stimulate the kind of thinking that will make *Language and Mind* engaging to read.

The reader may wonder why I selected the group

photograph of Alexander Bell, Helen Keller and Anne Sullivan Macy for the frontispiece. Besides being great heroic people who served the cause of humanity, their lives and work bring to the fore so many of the fundamental problems facing Psycholinguistics: *What is the origin of language? What is the origin of thought? Does one depend on the other? What is the nature of language? How may language be acquired?* As I hope the reader will discover during the course of this book, Bell was a true psycholinguist both in thought and deed long before that word was invented.

Tokyo   D.D.S.
July 1992

Acknowledgements

I would like to acknowledge my great debt to Mr Jeff Matthews of Naples, Italy. He made substantial contributions to earlier drafts of a majority of the chapters of the book. I would also like to express my gratitude to Ms Armene Modi of the Language Institute of Japan and Dr Yasuaki Abe of Nanzan University for their helpful suggestions concerning earlier chapter drafts and to Prof Geoffrey Leech for his many useful editorial comments.

We are grateful to the following for permission to reproduce copyright material:

Cambridge University Press and the author David Crystal for our Figure 4.1 'Finger Spelling: the one-handed American method and the two-handed British method' and the top illustration in Figure 9.1 being an overhead view of the brain, from pages 223 and 258 in *The Cambridge Encyclopedia of Language*, 1987; Croom Helm for Figure 4.2 from M. Brennan, 'Marking Time in British Sign Language' in J.G. Kyle and B. Woll (eds) *Language in Sign: An International Perspective on Sign Language* (1983); Mouton de Gruyter for Figure 4.3 'American sign language sentences' from Scott K. Liddell (1980) *American Sign Language Syntax*; Prentice Hall, Englewood Cliffs, New Jersey for lower illustration (side view of the brain) in Figure 9.1 from I. Taylor and M. Taylor *Psycholinguistics: Learning and Using Language* © 1990, p. 364; Princeton University Press for Figures 9.2 and 9.3 from W. Penfield and L. Roberts *Speech and Brain Mechanisms* (1959).

We have been unable to trace the copyright holder for the frontispiece photograph and would appreciate any information that would enable us to do so.

PART 1

First language

CHAPTER 1

How children learn language

We have minds and in our minds we have language. But how did language get there? How did we learn to produce and understand speech? At birth we cannot speak, nor can we understand speech. Yet, by the age of 4 years we will have learned the basic vocabulary, syntax (grammatical rules and structures) and pronunciation of our language. This is true of children the world over, whatever the language of their people may be. And, while they still have passives and other elaborate syntactic structures to learn (along with a never-ending stock of vocabulary items), nevertheless, by that age they will have overcome the most difficult obstacles in language learning. Indeed, the language proficiency of the 4- or 5-year-old is often the envy of the adult second language learner who has been struggling for years to master the language. It is one of the fundamental tasks of the field of psycholinguistics to explain how all of this has occurred.

For reasons that will become more apparent later, language learning must be separated into two distinct, but related, psychological processes: that of speech production and that of speech understanding. I shall deal with each in turn and then consider how they are related.

1.1 The development of speech production

1.1.1 Vocalization

While babies a few months old do not speak, they do make sounds through their mouths. In fact, they make quite a variety of sounds. They cry, they coo like pigeons, they gurgle, suck, blow, spit and make a host of other virtually indescribable noises. However, while these are not speech sounds their production gives the child exercise in articulation and control. Importantly, too, the child gets practice in coordinating breathing with the making of sounds. These same sounds (crying, cooing, etc.) are made by infants all over the world. Even deaf children make them. Deaf children, however, do not progress to babbling, the next level of vocalization that has some resemblance to speech.

Babbling is a type of vocalization where the child uses speech sounds, mainly vowels and consonant–vowel syllables, e.g. 'a', 'u', 'ma', 'gi', 'pa'. The child's repetitive uttering of these sounds give them a speech-like quality, e.g. 'mama', 'gigi', 'papa', especially when these sounds are involved with the features of the intonation pattern of their language, as they tend to be. As the period of babbling progresses, the more it sounds like the speech of the language to which the child is being exposed. Around 6 months of age, Japanese-exposed children start to sound somewhat Japanese, English-exposed children start to sound somewhat English, Chinese-exposed children start to sound somewhat Chinese, and so on. By 10 or 11 months children will often babble in pseudo non-word 'sentences' using declarative, question and exclamatory intonation patterns.

That babies should first acquire the intonation patterns of their language, even before producing any words, is not so surprising. After all, when any of us hears a new language for the first time, what we tend to hear first is its rhythm, pitch and stress patterns. We don't know how to cut the flow of a sentence into words, and neither does the child. We become familiar with the melody, so to speak, before we get to the words. It is this melody, this intonation pattern, that the infant learns first to recognize and then to imitate.

1.1.2 The one-word utterance

When do children start to say their first words? It may surprise you to learn that research on this question is not at all conclusive. Actually this not an easy question to answer, not only because there is a very wide range of individual differences but also because the precise determination of just when a word has been learned is not easy to make.

First words have been reported as appearing in normal children from as young as 4 months to as old as 18 months, or even older. On the average, it would seem that children utter their first word around the age of 10 months. Some of this variability has to do with physical development, such as the musculature of the mouth and throat, which is necessary for the proper articulation of sounds. Undoubtedly, too, certain brain development is also involved since the creation of speech sounds must come under the control of speech areas in the cerebral cortex.

The advice columnist Ann Landers once stated, in response to a query, that children would not be able to speak until well after 6 months of age. She had cited the opinion given to her by a leading paediatrician. A flood of letters immediately poured in from parents who disagreed with her (really with the paediatrician!) on the basis of experience with their own children. A great many parents claimed that their children uttered words as young as 4 and 5 months of age. At 4½ months one boy was saying 'Mama', 'Daddy' and 'no' while at 5½ months one girl was saying 'bottle', 'Daddy', 'bath' and 'byebye'. Even granting the tendency of parents to exaggerate their children's accomplishments, such observations have a ring of truth about them given the large number of responses which Ann Landers received. (I myself remember one little girl who lived next door and was fluently producing sentences when only 8 months of age!)

Despite such great differences in the onset of speech, by the time children are around 3 years of age, differences have largely disappeared. The slower ones catch up and the early speakers no longer seem to have an advantage. Incidentally, it might be noted, too, in this regard that there is no known relationship between intelligence and the onset of speech for normal children. As a matter of fact, many very famous people, including Albert Einstein, are reputed to have been slow to talk. One should not infer from this, however, that these people were also slow to *understand* speech. The contrary is more likely to have been the case. (Discussion of the relationship between speech production and understanding is presented later in this chapter.)

To determine just when a word has been learned is generally not an easy matter. Simply the saying of sounds that correspond to a word in the language is not enough. A parrot can do a good job of mimicking but we do not attribute language knowledge to it. Along with the researcher and the eager parent, what we look for is the *meaningful* use of sounds. If the child says 'banana' or some approximation of those sounds, and does so only when seeing or touching that object (and not other objects such as people or cars), then we might consider that the child knows that word. (Often only a parent can identify the sounds the child makes because of the peculiarity of the child's speech.) In order to do a thorough scientific study to determine when children learn their first word, the dedicated researcher would have to be on call every day for almost two years in order to check out parents' claims. And even this may not be enough since some parents may miss the signs of when the first word has been learned! Little wonder then that solid data on this issue are hard to come by.

The many uses of a single word

A single word, even the same one, can be used for many different purposes. A word can be used to **name** an object, e.g. 'mama' for 'mother', 'nana' for 'banana'. These same words can also be used to **request** something, e.g. 'mama' for 'I want my mother' and 'nana' for 'I want a banana'. A word can also be used to **emphasize actions** such as in greeting, e.g. 'hi' with a wave of the hand, or in leave-taking, e.g. 'bye-bye' with a different wave of the hand. Single words can even be used to **express complex situations**. One researcher, for example, noted a child saying 'peach' + 'Daddy' + 'spoon' in a situation where her father had put a piece of a peach onto a spoon. It is believed, for the following reasons, that the child here was using a series of three single-word utterances rather than one three-word sentence: there was a slight pause between words, there was no sentence intonation, and the child had only been at a single-word stage of production. Other researchers have documented the same phenomenon.

When one reflects on the multiple uses to which a child

puts single words, one can only conclude how reasonable it is of the child to do this. Lacking the knowledge and ability to form proper sentences, the child uses to the utmost the limited resources that it has, i.e. single words without any syntax. Actually that is what we all tend to do in a foreign language situation when we have only single words at our disposal. Even with such limited language we can do some shopping, order food in a restaurant, take trains and so on. This use of a single word to express a whole sentence (technically, a 'holophrastic' use, in the child language literature) can be effective when the situation is simple and obvious enough so that the listener can guess the intended meaning. But, when more complex or precise communications are required, single words do not suffice. Speakers will need a greater linguistic command of the language to achieve such purposes.

1.1.3 Two- and three-word utterances

At 18 months or so, many children start to produce two- and three-word utterances. Again the reader is cautioned that this is but an average and that there is great individual variation in this regard. Table 1.1 shows a typical list of such utterances along with what a mature speaker might say in the same circumstances (a 5-year-old could be considered a 'mature' speaker in this regard!) and the possible purposes that the child may be using the utterances for (technically, 'speech acts').

The most striking features about the dozen or so very ordinary utterances shown here are the variety of purposes and the complexity of ideas which they exhibit. At only a year and a half, children use language to request, warn, refuse, brag, question, answer and inform. In order to gain these ends the utterances that they use express such ideas as *quantity* ('more'), *possession* ('my'), *negation* ('no sleep'), *location* ('banana table') and *attribute* ('big', 'red').

Even such a small sample of utterances as this demonstrates how advanced the child is from a cognitive point of view. The thinking and conceptual abilities of the very young child are quite remarkable. Actually it was just until the past few decades, when the study of child language intensified, that the true conceptual abilities of the young child began to be

Table 1.1   Some two-word utterances and their purpose

Child's utterance	Mature speakers' equivalent	Purpose
Want cookie	I want a cookie	Request
More milk	I want some more milk	Request
My cup	This cup is mine	Warning
Mommy chair	This chair belongs to Mommy	Warning
Mommy chair	Mommy is sitting in the chair	Answer (to question)
Big boy	I am a big boy	Bragging
Red car	The car is red	Inform
No sleep	I don't want to go to sleep	Refusal
Where doll?	Where is the doll?	Question
Daddy bring	Daddy will bring pizza	Inform
Give candy	Give me some candy	Request
Banana table	The banana is on the table	Inform/answer

appreciated. In the past those abilities were greatly underestimated. And yet, the child's speech, in all likelihood, must reflect only a small part of what the child knows and is thinking. For, the child already can *understand* much more speech than he or she can produce (more detailed discussion on this later) and undoubtedly has thoughts and concepts that are well in advance of the attained level of speech understanding.

Returning to Table 1.1, we may note that in terms of a grammatical analysis of the utterances, one principal characteristic is the infrequent appearance of function words such as articles, prepositions, auxiliaries (be, have) and modals (will, can). Mainly it is nouns, verbs and adjectives which appear in the utterances. This is not surprising when one considers that it is these classes of words which carry the most information (which is why they are often referred to as *content* classes) and would be the first that children would learn to understand. It would be strange indeed to find a child whose first words were anything like 'is', 'with', 'can' or 'the'.

The child uses combinations of content words with the expectation that the listener will understand the relations between items, such as in 'Banana table' for 'The banana is *on* the table'. In time the child does learn to use function words properly such as in '*to* Mama', '*with* John', '*the* truck', 'candy *and* cake'. However, the functions of such words could never be discovered if nouns, verbs and adjectives were not understood first. Only a child who already can understand words like 'banana' and 'table' is in a position to guess what a preposition like 'on' might mean when someone says 'The banana is on the table', and, the banana is on the table for the child to see.

Another important grammatical characteristic of the child's utterances is the lack of inflections, inflections being changes in the forms of words. Thus, we see 'dog' instead of 'dogs', 'sit' for 'sitting', 'jump' for 'jumped', and 'John car' for 'John's car'. Rarely do plurals, verb endings, tense markings and other inflections appear. Again, this makes good sense. When listening to speech, the child seeks out the essence of words, discarding extras which are burdensome to figure out. Later the child will learn to add inflections but this refinement must wait until basic words are learned first.

It is because two- and three-word utterances are mainly formed of content words, lacking function words and inflections, that this stage of development in a child's speech is often referred to as the *telegraphic* stage. Being short in length and with content words predominating, such utterances have the essential characteristics of a telegram message.

1.1.4 Function words and inflections

Once two- and three-word utterances have been acquired, the child has something on which to elaborate. Function words like prepositions, the article and auxiliaries are then acquired, as are inflections like the plural and tense markings. The best single study on this topic was done by the noted psycholinguist, Roger Brown. In a long-term and very detailed study with three children, Brown focused on the acquisition of different function words and inflections, hereafter referred to as grammatical morphemes. A morpheme is a root word or a part of a word that carries a meaning. Thus, for example, the word 'elephants' consists of two morphemes, 'elephant' and Plural ('s'), as does the word 'ran', consisting of 'run' and Past.

Ten basic morphemes from the Brown study are shown in Table 1.2 in the order in which they were acquired. (Actually the number is 11 if the Third Person Regular and Irregular are counted separately.) Sample child utterances illustrating these morphemes are also shown. Thus, we see that Present Progressive, Prepositions ('in' and 'on') and the regular Plural were learned well in advance of morphemes like the Article, Third Person (Regular and Irregular), and the Auxiliary 'be' in both its Regular and Contracted forms.

Table 1.2   Morpheme acquisition order and explanatory variables

Order	Morpheme	Examples	Environmental observability	Sound change difference
1	Present Progressive	Girl play**ing**	High	High
2	Prepositions: in, on	Ball **in** water	High	High
3	Plural	car**s**, boy**s**, fish**es**	High	Low
4	Past Irregular	came, f**ell**, **went**	Medium	High
5	Possessive	Jack'**s**, Ann'**s**, Liz'**s**	High	Low
6	Articles	**a** dog, **the** dog	Medium	High
7	Past Regular	jump**ed**, hugg**ed**, want**ed**	Medium	Low
8	Third Person:			
	Regular	talk**s**, sing**s**, watch**es**	Low	Low
	Irregular	do**es**, ha**s**	Low	High
9	Auxiliary *be* Regular	I **am** playing, You **are** playing, She **is** playing	Low	High
10	Auxiliary *be* Contracted	I'**m**, You'**re**, She'**s**	Low	Low

Why these morphemes should have been acquired in this order has been the subject of much speculation. Some, like Dulay, Burt and Krashen, for example, intimate that there is a sort of predetermined order in the child's mind governed by, as yet, unknown mechanisms, and that the morphemes appear in the order they do because of this. My own explanation of this ordering is more direct and simple.

It involves psychological learning principles that are of a universal and well-understood nature. As such, they will hold for children learning the grammatical morphemes of any language.

Even though Brown's morpheme data are based on only three children and the order would probably not be exactly the same for all English-speaking children, nonetheless the general order *does* fall in with what we would expect. A very different order would be quite counterintuitive. By posing important questions raised by the data and then providing answers to these questions, I hope that I may demonstrate this to the reader's satisfaction.

1. Why might the Plural and Possessive be learned before the Third Person? Since all three regular suffix morphemes of Plural, Possessive and Third Person have exactly the same sound forms /s/, /z/ and /iz/ and the selection of any of these suffixes are governed by the same sound rules, the reason for the ordering must be attributable to some factor other than the sound system.
2. Why might the Present (Progressive) be learned before the Past (Regular or Irregular)?
3. Why might the Past Irregular be learned before the Past Regular?
4. Why might the Auxiliary 'be' be learned in the Regular form before the Contracted form?

Let us now consider possible answers to these questions:

1.   Plural and Possessive before Third Person

The Plural and Possessive are much more involved with meaning and information, including physical situations and objects that are readily observed in the environment. Thus the child can easily discern one versus two cookies, one versus two or three cats, his or her toys versus another child's toys, etc. On the other hand, the Third Person is more involved with grammatical requirements and serves less vital communicative needs. The same is true for the Auxiliary, as well.

So, even though the child learns the sound rule for applying /s/, /z/ and /iz/ and uses it for the Possessive and

Plural, only later does the child use the rule for constructing the Third Person. Undoubtedly this is due to the concept of Third Person being of little importance as compared to those expressing ideas about plurality and possession.

2. Present before Past

For the present tense, the child will hear speech involving that tense (the mother says, 'The dog is barking') at the same time that objects, events and situations in the world are experienced (the child hears the dog barking). However, for the past, the child hears speech ('The dog barked') when the object, event or situation is no longer there to be directly experienced. This being the case, in order to identify the speech sounds which signal the past, the child must remember the environmental event which occurred in the past and then realize that the sound change is an indication of a past event, e.g. 'barked' as opposed to 'barking'.

Clearly, a great deal of thought and analysis is required for the child to learn the past. First, the child must acquire the morpheme structure for the present. Then, on the basis of that, the child can learn the past. If the child does not first learn the present morpheme, it is inconceivable that the child would ever learn the morpheme structure for past. When listening to people speak, a child who knows no language can only begin with an analysis of the present. If people spoke only of things past, the child would not likely learn any language since there would be nothing in the immediate environment to relate their speech to. The present tense must be the basis for the child's learning the past tense.

3. Past Irregular before Past Regular

Since the idea of past is involved with both the irregular and regular past, the explanation for the order of acquisition of these two past forms must lie elsewhere. Suppose we compare the present forms of verbs with the past forms.

Past Irregular: come/came, fall/fell/, **go/went**, sing/ sang, break/broke

Past Regular: jump/jump**ed**, jog/jogg**ed**, want/want**ed**

We can see that the sound changes from present to past are much more noticeable for the irregular verbs than the regular ones. Since a sound difference must be first noticed before it can be learned, and since the irregular ones are more noticeable, we would expect them to be learned earlier. Another factor here is that the irregular verbs tend to be ones that are especially important in everyday life. This, too, might give these often-called 'strong verbs' an additional advantage.

4.   Auxiliary 'be': Regular before Contracted

Let us compare the regular (uncontracted) and contracted forms: am/'m, is/'s, are/'re. In all cases the uncontracted form constitutes a complete syllable and word while the contracted forms do not. Not only is a syllable easier to hear than a non-syllable but the syllable word will be given some degree of stress and pitch which will further make it easier to hear.

Based, then, on the above analysis of the four questions, we can say that two variables account for the order of acquisition: Meaningfulness or Ease of Observability in the Environment and Sound Change Difference (noticeability), with the first playing the predominant role. ('Predominant role' meaning here that values on the Environmental Observability are given more weight that those on the Sound Change Difference variable.) A morpheme that is high on both, such as Present Progressive, will be learned before Contracted Auxiliary which is low on both. If we assign in the table a **high**, **medium** or **low** value on each of the two variables for all of the morphemes, we see that more highs are at the top of the list and more lows are at the bottom. Such an outcome provides support for our theory in explaining the acquisition order of the morphemes.

But what of the prepositions 'in' and 'on' and the rating of 'high' that I gave them in the table? The reason I rate these function words as highly meaningful is because the physical relations which they signal are important in terms of communication, e.g. 'The **apple** is *on* the **box**', 'The **apple** is *in* the **box**'. Although, as compared to the content classes of nouns, verbs and adjectives, their meaningfulness is lower, once the child has learned content words, the meaningfulness of these prepositions becomes quite high. Then, too, they have the advantage of their relations being directly observable in the physical environment; these relations involve objects that are stationary with respect to one another. Such clearly observable object-plus-object relations, it seems to me, make these prepositions relatively easy to learn. Other prepositions like 'to', 'at' and 'with' perhaps lack all these advantages.

A footnote on morpheme knowledge

Back in the 1950s, a fascinating piece of morpheme research was done by Jean Berko Gleason. She tested young children with respect to their knowledge of certain morphemes, such as the Plural, by means of a simple but ingenious procedure.

For example, she showed a child a drawing of an unusual little creature. She said to the child, 'This is a "wug".' Then while pointing to a drawing of two of the creatures, she said, 'Now there are two of them. These are two —', and waited for the child to offer the completion word. A child who produced 'wugs' could be said to know this aspect of the plural. Other aspects of the Plural were also tested, again using strange creatures with names that the child would have never heard before, e.g. 'niz'. Gleason's research not only serves to remind psycholinguists how important and useful the principle of productivity can be in establishing what children know, but it also illustrates how, with imagination, good research can be done with young children.

1.1.5 Developing complex sentences

With longer utterances, simple structures typically develop into more complex ones. Children start to make negatives, questions, relative clauses and other complex structures. As an example of how such structures may be acquired, the detailed development of sentence negation is instructive in this regard.

The acquisition of negation, according to Bellugi and Klima and others who later replicated their research, develops in three main periods. An outline of each of these periods along with sample sentences follows.

Period 1

'No money'; 'Not a teddy bear'; 'No play that';
'No fall'; 'No singing song'; 'No the sun shining'

In this first period , generally a negative marker (Neg) of some sort, 'no' or 'not', is placed at the front of an affirmative utterance (U). Thus we see utterances of the typically of the form, *Neg + U*. Children everywhere seem to do much the same thing. French children, for example, place *non* or *pas* before *U* while Japanese children place the Japanese negative marker *nai* after the *U* (*U + Neg*) in accord with the observed structure of their language.

Period 2

'I don't want it'; 'I don't know his name';
'We can't talk'; 'You can't dance'; 'Book say no';
'Touch the snow no'; 'That no Mommy';
'He no bite you'; 'I no want envelope';
'There no squirrels'

We see in this second period, that the negative marker tends to appear internally within utterances. The auxiliary 'do' begins to appear although in combination with the negative marker (don't). Utterances are still of a rather crude nature, though, and negative imperatives, 'Touch the snow no', are as poorly formed as they were in the previous period ('No play that', 'No fall').

Period 3

'Paul can't have one'; 'This can't stick'; 'I didn't did it';
'You didn't caught me'; 'Donna won't let go';
'I am not a doctor'; 'This not ice-cream';

'Paul not tired'; 'I not hurt him';

'Don't touch the fish'; 'Don't kick my box'

The child has now a good idea of when 'do' must be inserted ('You didn't caught me', 'Don't touch the fish', Don't kick my box') and when 'do' is not inserted ('I am not a doctor', 'Donna won't let go'). The child still makes errors but seems to grasp the basic notion that 'do' is not added when there is a modal ('can', 'will': 'This **can't** stick [adhere?]', 'Donna **won't** let go') or when 'be' is the verb ('I **am** not a doctor'). After this period, it is only a matter of months before most of the problems in negative making are successfully dealt with.

Bellugi and Klima found that the three children in their study (the same three who were in the Brown morpheme acquisition study) all took about 6 months to pass through the three periods. Still, there were great individual differences as to when they began the negative productions of the first period: one of the children began as early as 1½ years of age while the others didn't begin until they were around 2½ years.

While such wide differences in speech production are typical of very young children, by 4 or 5 years of age it seems that most differences level off. And, while there are still passives and other complex structures for children to master, by this age they are able to produce most of the essential structures of their language (this is evidently a worldwide phenomenon, whatever the language). It is perhaps by 9 or 10 years of age that all of the structures of the language have been acquired.

1.2   Speech understanding and its importance

1.2.1   Speech understanding, the basis of speech production

We have seen how children develop the ability to produce sentences. But, what is the source of that ability? Consider such typical children's utterances as 'Want banana', 'No sleep', 'Why it's not working?' and 'Where I can find them?'. Since children are not born with the knowledge of any particular language, it is necessary that they *be exposed* to the language in order to learn it. It is further necessary that the speech to which children are exposed *be related* to objects, events and situations in the environment and to experiences in their minds.

Children will not learn speech, if they are exposed only to speech sounds. Even if the child hears a spoken word a thousand times, e.g. 'dog', there is no way for the child to discover the meaning of the word unless some environmental clue is provided – in this example, a dog or a picture of a dog. Even abstract words (discussed later) must be learned in some such way.

While the ability to utter speech sounds, such as 'dog', in appropriate situations (when a dog is present or is barking, for example), is a good indicator that the child knows the word, simply being able to utter the sound form is of no significance. This is like someone being able to repeat the Japanese word *inu*. Anyone can do this but unless that person knows the meaning of that word, which is 'dog', we would not say the person knows that word. A parrot can learn to utter many words and sentences but we do not regard the parrot as having knowledge of language in any significant sense. What is critical is that the child know the meaning of what is uttered. Even if a child learns to imitate some words, we would not say that the child knows those words unless the child demonstrates in some way that he or she knows the meaning of the word. We can judge this if the child uses the word correctly, or if the child responds appropriately in some behavioural way, such as by looking, pointing or following some command.

Now, in order for a child to learn the meaning of the sound form of a word, the child must first hear that word spoken by others. (The child cannot know beforehand that one object has the name of 'mama' while another has the name of 'dog'.) At the same time that the word is spoken some relevant environmental experience must occur (the appearance of the child's mother, for example). These being the necessary conditions for learning, it is clear that the child must learn to understand speech before he or she is able to produce it (meaningfully). It is necessarily the case that speech understanding precedes speech production. Speech production, therefore, is dependent on speech understanding and its development follows that of speech understanding.

Aside from the above considerations, there is empirical evidence that speech comprehension develops in advance of speech production. Parents have always noted that children are able to respond appropriately to speech that is more complex than what they (the children) are able to say. Besides parental observations, findings from research studies which were especially designed to compare understanding and production also demonstrate the primacy of understanding. Huttenlocher, for example, studied four children and found that they were able to understand speech at a level well beyond that to which they had progressed in production. The children were able to respond appropriately to commands even when these commands involved vocabulary and structures that they had never used in their own speech. One young boy, for example, responded appropriately (by pointing) to such distinctions as 'baby's diaper' versus 'your diaper', and 'baby's bottle' versus 'your bottle'. (The 'baby' here referred to was the boy's younger sister!)

Similarly, in another study, Sachs and Truswell found that children who could say only single words ('kiss', 'smell', 'ball', 'truck', etc.) could understand speech structures composed of more than a single word. The children provided appropriate responses when given commands consisting of novel two-word syntactic combinations, such as 'Kiss ball' and 'Smell truck'.

There is the observation, too, that some children completely skip over earlier stages of speech production to more advanced stages. The physicist Einstein and the British writer Carlyle are reputed to have been slow in starting to speak, but when they did they spoke in sentences. Such a phenomenon is completely understandable when one considers that children first acquire knowledge of language through speech understanding and that delay occurs only with the expression of such knowledge, i.e. production. Without the language knowledge acquired through speech understanding, Einstein, Carlyle or anyone else for that matter would not have been able to utter even a word meaningfully, let alone a sentence.

Evidence with handicapped children perhaps provides

that he has told a lie (he can review this by comparing what he said with what he knows to be the actual situation, and note this discrepancy – the discrepancy between saying and situation being the concept of lie), and then assign this concept to the sound form. Whether this hypothesis is accurate or not is something the child will test when he hears the word 'lie' again.

1.2.3 Memory and language acquisition

Underlying all of the remarkable accomplishments of the child in language acquisition is one crucially important psychological factor, that of memory. For, in the course of learning to identify the words of the language, devising rules for their use, and relating speech to the environment and mind, the child utilizes a phenomenal memory capacity. The child must remember a multitude of particular words, phrases and sentences, along with the contexts (physical and mental) in which they occurred. Such data provide the basis for structural analyses.

If, for example, children did not remember many of the words, phrases and sentences that they heard, they would have little basis for discovering abstract meanings and rules. The various syntactic structures that were mentioned and discussed earlier, negation for instance, requires that the child remember many negative sentences. If the child could not remember negative sentences that had been experienced previously, the child would have nothing with which to compare a presently occurring sentence, and, thus could not make significant inferences as to its structure. Without a good memory, language learning would not be possible.

Aside from the common observation that children often remember, word for word, stories which they are told, children also learn a host of idioms in phrase and sentence form. There is no reason, therefore, not to believe that children also store in memory a multitude of ordinary phrases and sentences, which can serve them for analysis later. Such a prodigious memory capacity, it is worth noting, is not unique to language. For, in many other areas of life – in remembering faces, objects, music, past events and vast quantities of knowledge in a variety of fields – the extent of a child's memory is similarly remarkable.

1.3 Parentese and Baby Talk

1.3.1 Parentese

Parentese (a term which I use to replace the oft-used 'Motherese') is used to refer to the sort of speech that children receive when they are young. The speech which parents and others use in talking to children has a number of distinctive characteristics. For example, parents generally talk to their children about what is happening in the immediate environment and not about abstract or remote objects and events. A sentence like 'The dog wants water' rather than 'I might start reading that psycholinguistics book tomorrow' is what a 1- or 2-year-old is likely to hear. Also, sentences tend to be short and the structures simple, e.g. 'The dog wants water' rather than 'The dog which has been running a lot wants to drink some water'. Vocabulary, too, tends to be simple, 'see' rather than 'notice' and 'hard' rather than 'difficult'. When sentences are spoken to children, the speech tends to be slower, the pitch higher and more pauses inserted than would occur if the same sentences were spoken to mature speakers. Also, more words are given stress and emphasis. Such exaggerations undoubtedly serve to highlight and to focus the child's attention on important sentence constituents. (More on this on page 143.)

Parents, too, use grammatical speech when talking to their children. Research by Newport, Labov and others show that few of the sentences are ungrammatical in nature. Such consistency undoubtedly is useful to the child who is searching to discover the structures which underlie sentences. Incidentally, the findings that sentences are mainly grammatical lays to rest Chomsky's mistaken claim that the child receives sentences which are largely ungrammatical, 'degenerate' being the term he uses.

It is interesting that not only adults, but children, too, tend to use Parentese when talking with younger children. It has been found, for example, that 4-year-olds produced simplified speech when talking to 2-year-olds but not to adults (some of the 4-year-olds even did not have younger siblings). Although much of this research has been done with English, there is good reason to suppose that such a phenomenon is universal since the same has been observed in many language communities. People who wish to communicate will naturally use speech that is at a linguistic level they think the hearer will understand. The characteristics of Parentese evidently are ones which serve to make the acquisition of language understanding and production easier for a learner. This is not to say that if parents did not use Parentese, their children would not learn language. Undoubtedly they would learn language anyway. But, given the obvious facilitating nature of Parentese and the way it naturally arises, it may well be that children who receive such language input learn to understand speech faster than children who do not.

1.3.2 Baby Talk

Baby Talk is different from Parentese. While Parentese uses regular vocabulary and syntax, Baby Talk involves the use of vocabulary and syntax that is overly simplified and reduced. Curious though, from a psycholinguistic view, is the fact that most of the features which Baby Talk adopts are those which have their basis in the early speech of children. Parents and others evidently believe that those features, when reintroduced back to the child, serve to foster communication.

Most Baby Talk involves modifications in vocabulary. There are already established words like 'bow-wow' (dog), 'pee-pee' (urine) and 'choo-choo' (train) in English and, in Japanese, 'wan-wan' (dog: the standard word for which is *inu*), 'shee-shee' (urine) and 'bu-bu' (car: the standard words for which are *jidosha* or *kuruma*). From such examples, we can see that the main sound structure of such words tends to be dominated by a Consonant + Vowel syllable unit which is repeated (duplicated).

Another construction principle for many Baby Talk words, is that they represent (somewhat) the sounds which various things make. Thus, 'bow-wow' and 'wan-wan' are simulations of the barking of dogs, 'bu-bu' is supposed to be the sound made by a car engine, and 'choo-choo' the sound made by a train. That such a sound as 'choo-choo' is meant to approximate to now largely extinct steam locomotives bothers neither parent nor child. Here the word has become part of standard Baby Talk vocabulary.

Besides standard Baby Talk vocabulary ('standard' in the sense that the item has already been coined and adopted by others), it is not uncommon for a family to create and use its own words, words which are not used outside of the family. Often these words derive from mispronounced words which their child produces. For example, in attempting to imitate the word 'vomit', one child I know said 'vompo'. After that the parents used 'vompo' instead of vomit in talking to the child. Sometimes a few such vocabulary items might be retained by parents for sentimental reasons.

In English Baby Talk, it might be mentioned in passing, it is common to add the 'iy' sound to words ending in a consonant, e.g. 'birdy' for bird, 'horsie' for horse, 'kitty' for kitten. This provides the vowel for the completion of the paradigmatic Consonant + Vowel syllable. Since the 'iy' suffix also serves a diminutive and affectionate function in English, this may also serve to promote its usage.

Syntax plays a less prominent role in Baby Talk than does vocabulary. Parents seem only occasionally to use Baby Talk syntax. When they do, their utterances are strikingly similar to those in the children's telegraphic stage of speech production. A mother might say, for example, something like 'Mommy give Tony banana' instead of the syntactically proper 'I will give you a banana'. In such an utterance, neither the modal 'will' nor the article 'a' has been included. And, the proper names 'Mommy and 'Tony' have been substituted for the personal pronouns 'I' and 'you'. Certainly, fixed proper names are easier for the young child to understand than are items involving shifting speaker–hearer relations. It is later that the child learns to cope with the complexities of 'I' and 'you'. Such proper name substitutions, it should be noted, also occur in Parentese and thus are not solely features of Baby Talk.

Whether Baby Talk should or should not be used is sometimes a concern of parents, with intensity of concern varying greatly from country to country. In Canada and the US, there seems to be little such concern, while in Japan there seems to be a lot. Since Baby Talk is a transition phase, in that it is not continued for very long (children themselves will soon replace it rather than being regarded as babies by older children), and since Baby Talk (like Parentese) appears to be a universally occurring natural phenomenon, it would seem to me that Baby Talk could be beneficial to some small degree for the child in learning language. Certainly, there is no good reason to think of it as being harmful. That most parents (and grandparents) derive special enjoyment from using Baby Talk with their children might well serve to reinforce social solidarity.

1.4 Imitation and correction

1.4.1 The role of imitation

It was once widely believed by theorists that children acquire language entirely through imitation, i.e. by copying the speech that they hear. It is undoubtedly true that children do imitate a great deal of what they hear. They do learn to say such words and phrases as 'dog', 'Papa', 'run', 'happy', 'no', 'Why not?', 'bread and butter', 'Not now', etc. They do imitate the intonation patterns and sounds of their language, and they do tend to approximate the proper order of words in a sentence.

On the other hand, while some language learning does involve imitation, this principle is inadequate to explain the fundamentals underlying the acquisition of language. Because imitation involves the reproduction of speech, it therefore cannot explain how speech is understood, the knowledge of which is the basis of speech production. Nor can it explain the child's acquisition of morphemes such as the Plural or Past Tense, or structural manipulations such as those of Negation and Question.

To illustrate how imitation cannot account for rules, let us consider, in some detail, errors that children make. English children commonly produce words like 'mouses', 'sheeps', 'gooses', 'goed', 'comed', 'falled' and 'breaked'. Why do children produce such words? Clearly, this cannot be due to imitation since children generally do not hear people say such words. The most satisfactory answer is that children have formulated rules in their minds, and construct such words on the basis of these rules. The same must be said for children saying things like 'No heavy', 'No the sun shining', 'When we can go?' and 'He is doing what?'. Since these are not utterances made by adults, and since they regularly appear, they cannot be ones that children have imitated. They must be ones created on the basis of rules which the children have devised.

While exceptions to rules must be learned, such as in pluralizing nouns ('mice' and not 'mouses') and in making the Past Tense ('went' and not 'goed'), and while further aspects regarding negation and question-making must be developed, the errors in themselves provide strong evidence that rule-learning (Regular Plural, Regular Past) has taken place. Rules, by their very nature, cannot be imitated. Rather, they are abstract constructions of the mind. Rules do not appear in the physical environment – only speech sounds representing words and sequences of words do. It is on the basis of these observables that abstract and non-observable principles and rules are created in the mind and then applied later in production. Thus, while imitation does play an important role in language acquisition, it is a limited one – limited to certain aspects of speech production.

1.4.2   The role of correction

Like imitation, the role of correction in language acquisition has been widely misconceived. Correction is *not* an important factor in that process. While it used to be thought that correcting children's speech is essential for improvement, research has shown that such is not the case. In actual fact, parents pay little attention to the grammatical correctness of their children's speech. Rather than correcting the child's grammar, parents are more interested in responding to: the *truth value* of what is said (they will scold a child who says 'I didn't doed it' when he or she is lying), the *social appropriateness* of what is said (a child who says to a visiting aunt, 'Daddy no like you' will be given a talking to later but not on syntax) or *the cleverness* of what the child says (the parent will praise the child).

When parents do attempt to correct their children's speech, the results are often fruitless and frustrating. Consider the following exchange between a mother and son (noted by McNeill):

Son: *Nobody don't like me.*
Mother: *Nobody likes me.*

The above sequence is repeated by mother and son seven more times.

Mother (in desperation): *Now, listen carefully. Nobody likes me.*
Son: *Oh! Nobody don't likes me.*

While some progress was achieved (the son added 's' to 'like'), the major concern of the mother, the improper occurrence of the auxiliary 'do', was not noticed by the child as needing correction.

Undoubtedly, there are instances where a parent's correction does result in improvement. Still they are not great in number. In any case what serves typically as correction is the mere repetition of the child's utterance in corrected form. The child is really given no direct clue as to exactly what is wrong with the utterance that he or she has produced. And, to give the child a direct explanation (even if a parent were able to formulate the problem) would often be absurd. The mother in the example above could hardly say to the child, 'Now, Johnny, you don't add "do" in that sentence to make it negative because the sentence is already negative; the word "nobody" is the negative of "somebody".'

Children naturally correct their own mistakes over time, without the intervention of others.

1.5 Discussion questions

1. Which is primary: speech production or speech understanding? Why?
2. How is it possible for children to begin by speaking whole sentences without going through the one- and two-word production stages?
3. Why do children produce 'telegraphic' speech?
4. Why are some morphemes, such as the Possessive and the Past, learned faster than others, such as the Third Person Singular and the Auxiliary 'be'?
5. What is the sound rule that governs the use of adding

's', 'z' or 'iz' to make regular plurals, possession and the third person?

Hint: Consider whether the final (last) sound in the word to which the suffix is to be added is a consonant or a vowel, and what type of consonant it is. You might use the following words as examples: crow, crows; Bob, Bob's; cat, cats; Chris, Chris'; piece, pieces; judge, judges.

6. A child says, ' I no want some candy.' What must the child still learn in order to make a proper negative sentence?

7. How might a child learn the meaning of 'idea' as in 'That's a good idea!'?

8. Do you know some words in Baby Talk of a language other than English? Generally, what is the form of the sound structure of these words? Does it agree with what has been said in the chapter?

9. Would you recommend the use of Parentese or Baby Talk in speaking to a child?

10. What evidence is there that children learn rules when they learn language? In your discussion present data concerning one morpheme, such as Plural or Past, and also one sentence structure rule, such as negation.

11. Can rules be learned by imitation?

12. How might a child get rid of errors without being corrected by others?

Suggested readings

Brown, R. (1973) *A First Language: The Early Stages.* Cambridge, Mass.: Harvard University Press.

De Villiers, J. G. and De Villiers, P. A. (1978) *Language Acquisition.* Cambridge, Mass.: Harvard University Press.

Dulay, H., Burt, M. and Krashen, S. (1982) *Language Two.* Oxford: Oxford University Press.

Goodluck, H. (1991) *Language Acquisition: A Linguistic Introduction.* Oxford: Blackwell.

Ingram, D. (1991) *First Language Acquisition.* Cambridge: Cambridge University Press.

Reich, P. A. (1986) *Language Development.* Englewood Cliffs, NJ: Prentice-Hall.

Slobin, D. (ed.) (1986) *The Crosslinguistic Study of Language Acquisition*, vol. 1: *The Data*. Hillsdale, NJ: Lawrence Erlbaum.

Taylor, I. and Taylor, M. M. (1990) *Psycholinguistics: Learning and Using Language*. Englewood Cliffs, NJ: Prentice-Hall.

Journals

Journal of Child Language
First Language
Journal of Psycholinguistic Research
Child Development

CHAPTER 2

Animals and language

Human beings have language, but what about animals? Do chimpanzees, dolphins or other creatures have language and use it to communicate with one another as we do? Are the minds of higher animals similar to our minds? And what if they don't have their own language, can we teach them some sort of human language? But if they can't learn language, would this mean that they are lacking in intelligence, or would it mean that they lack a specific language ability that only humans are born with?

The study of animals and language is, of course, interesting for its own sake, but it is interesting too in how animal research findings may relate to a better understanding of fundamental psycholinguistic conceptions and processes. Let us begin our inquiry with a review of research which attempts to teach language to animals.

2.1 Teaching language to the chimpanzee, gorilla and dolphin

An animal researcher's dream:

I had . . . incredible fantasies about the possibilities of ape language. One of them was that I could go to some section of Africa where there are chimps in the wild and have Nim [the chimp to whom I taught sign language] serve as an interpreter for kinds of communication that are unknown to humans. That is, I would ask Nim, 'what is that chimp over there saying to the other chimp' and Nim would explain it to me in sign language.

Herbert Terrace

2.1.1 Vicki: the speaking chimp

The first known comprehensive scientific attempt to teach language to our nearest evolutionary relations was carried out in the 1940s by a husband and wife team of psychologists, Cathy and Keith Hayes. The Hayes raised a baby female chimp, Vicki, along with their own baby son, Donald, with the hope that Vicki would learn speech as Donald would. Vicki was treated as a full member of the family; she ate her meals at the table, played games at home and went on outings. However, despite all their efforts, after three years Vicki had only learned to utter four words: 'mama', 'papa', 'up' and 'cup', and these were so poorly pronounced they were hard to understand. Yet during the same amount of time, Donald had become fluent in the language. In the face of such disappointing results, the Hayes felt obliged to abandon the project.

2.1.2 Washoe: the signing chimp

In 1966, another husband and wife team of psychologists, Allen and Beatrice Gardner, attempted to teach sign language to a baby chimp, a female they called Washoe (rhymes with 'show'). They reasoned that any attempt to teach chimps to speak was doomed to failure because of the simple fact that chimps do not possess the necessary vocal apparatus for human speech. Vicki's failure to learn to talk could plausibly be said to be due to a simple physiological failure and not a mental one. Since chimps are so adept at using their hands, the Gardners conceived of the idea of teaching them a modified form of American Sign Language (ASL), a language used by the hearing-impaired in the United States.

It might be noted here that ASL is a genuine and complete language, as are many other sign languages, such as British Sign Language and French Sign Language. It has a vocabulary and a syntax just as an ordinary speech-based language does; anything that can be said in English can be expressed in sign language. However, it differs from linear speech in that it involves three dimensions with facial and other body movements as well as hand movements. A whole word can be expressed by a hand configuration. ASL is not based on finger spelling, which is a letter-by-letter system, nor is its grammar very similar to English grammar. (For a more detailed discussion of sign language, see Chapter 4.)

One of Washoe's early signs was 'open', which is expressed by a throwing out of the arms. After about four years with the Gardners, Washoe learned a vocabulary of about 130 signs and, according to the Gardners, displayed two- and three-word utterances, such as, 'Go sweet', when she wanted to be taken to the raspberry bushes, and 'Open food drink', when she wanted something out of the refrigerator. The two- or three-word length of utterance is similar to that produced by human children around the age of 2 years.

The Gardners give the impression that the language of the signing ape and that of the signing child is very similar and that differences can only be found through close analysis. In one study, they go so far as to claim the ape to be superior to the child. However, as Premack and other researchers have noted, after three years Washoe's achievement never advanced beyond its very elementary level. In contrast, by the age of 3, ordinary children have learned thousands of words and construct sentences on the basis of an abstract syntax, including the making of such complicated negatives as, 'I don't know his name', 'Paul can't have one' and 'I am not a doctor'. (Whether or not to add 'do' in a negative sentence or where a negative marker like 'not' is to be placed is not a simple matter.) Hearing-impaired children who have learned ASL from infancy also acquire a similarly high level of linguistic knowledge.

Despite the Gardners' claims that Washoe's early acquisition of signs is analogous to the development of language in human children, the truth of the matter is that Washoe never progressed beyond the linguistic level of the average 1½- or 2-year-old child. The many years of training and exposure to sign language which Washoe experienced could not advance her beyond the most elementary level of human achievement.

2.1.3   Son of Washoe and a chimp signing community

After a number of years, Washoe was moved to a facility in the state of Washington and became part of the research conducted by Roger and Debby Fouts (another couple), who were working with a number of chimps. The Fouts regard their chimp subjects fondly and are currently involved in a project to establish a primate reserve in that state, where chimps would be given some of the rudiments of human culture, such as tools, for example, so that they could start their own community.

The Fouts' primary interest is in looking at how language may or may not develop in the social context of that community. One of their major focuses is on Washoe's 'adopted' son, Loulis, who, they say, is acquiring signs not only from Washoe but from the other chimps. The Fouts have witnessed Washoe demonstrating signs for Loulis and even helping to mould Loulis' hands into the proper configurations. They say, too, that they have observed three-way chimp conversations. For them, all of this demonstrates that language in the chimpanzee can advance, once given a start, without the intervention of humans. To date, though, little further progress has been made in this regard.

2.1.4   Lana: the computer chimp

The Rumbaughs (another husband and wife team!) taught the chimp Lana a simple artificial language called Yerkish (after the Yerkes primate centre). This language consisted of seven colours and nine geometrical shapes which represented mainly objects and actions. These items were displayed on a large keyboard. Lana had to press certain keys in the right sequence to make requests, like 'Please machine give milk' or 'Please Tim give ball'. Lana learned hundreds of sentences in this fashion. She had names for people, food, objects and even a special phrase 'that-which-is' to name things she did not know the name of. Once she even asked the trainer to leave the room (with a polite 'please'!) after he had purposely mixed up one of her sentences to test her reaction.

Sue Savage-Rumbaugh herself believes that apes have but a limited language acquisition ability. She has expressed the opinion that perhaps the media raised hopes too high for animal language research, although it might be said that animal researchers themselves have hardly been modest or cautionary in the claims they have made. She says it is not likely that chimps might be able to talk about their dreams or tell us about how it feels to be a chimp. However, still an optimist, she goes on to say that it is not possible yet to state what chimps might or might not be able to do, and that 'It is possible that chimpanzees might communicate novel ideas to us'. Her hope lies in improving teaching techniques. However, the fact the human children learn language *without* being taught, simply through being exposed to meaningful speech, suggests to me that the search for better teaching techniques is not likely to yield much better results.

2.1.5   Nim Chimpsky and the Chimpskyan revolution

The optimism of the 1960s turned sour in the 1970s when Terrace, a psychologist who was an early enthusiast of chimps being able to learn sign language, worked with a chimp which he named Nim Chimpsky. Terrace taught Nim a modified form of American Sign Language.

In discussing his results, Terrace said,

Our initial findings were very positive. I felt that I had the best evidence of anyone that in a very primitive sentence a chimpanzee could combine two or more signs according to a particular grammatical rule very much as a young child might.

Examples of Nim's two-, three- and four-sign sequences are 'more drink', 'tickle Nim'; 'banana Nim eat', 'banana eat Nim'; 'eat drink eat drink', 'banana me eat banana'.

By the time the project ended, Terrace had changed his mind about Nim's grammatical abilities. After studying the research video tapes, Terrace concluded that Nim, knowing that he had to sign in order to get what he wanted, would take some of what the teacher signed and give the appearance of producing structured two- or three-word utterances, without producing, however, any consistent subject–verb or verb–subject word order. When Nim made longer utterances, Terrace says that all he was doing was mainly imitating what the teacher signed and adding words almost at random until he got what he wanted. (Terrace's examples above rather bear this out.) Terrace came to the conclusion that chimpanzees were capable of learning only a few of the most elementary aspects of language. The most important clue as to why a chimpanzee does not advance to producing a long utterance, Terrace feels, is that its demands can adequately be taken care of with single words. However, as child language acquisition research shows, even though many of the demands of a small child can also adequately be taken care of by single words, they do advance beyond that stage rather quickly. There must be more involved in the process of language acquisition than the simple satisfying of demands.

Critics of Terrace's conclusions say that the negative results of his experiments are not due to the limitations of the chimpanzees, but rather are due to inadequacies in Terrace's experimental procedures. Nim was kept in a room and drilled intensively for 3 to 5 hours a day by hundreds of different tutors. Such an approach, critics such as the Fouts say, fails to get at the spontaneity of a good relationship between a researcher and an animal. According to Roger Fouts, 'We talk to people we like – and people we like don't ask us the same dumb questions 50 times in a row. We converse about things.' However, here we may note that even in the case of children who are badly treated by their parents, such children generally learn language. (Nim was treated with affection by his tutors.) It seems likely to me that, even given the restricted language-learning situation in which Nim was placed, a child would have mastered most or all of what was presented during the training sessions. Whether the Fouts can really get much better results with their chimp community remains to be seen.

It seems that one of Terrace's original motives in doing his research was to prove that Noam Chomsky, the famous linguist, was wrong in his belief that animals could not learn language. Clearly, Chimpsky was named after Chomsky. Ironically, though, as it turned out, it was Terrace and not Chomsky that was made a chump of by Chimpsky.

2.1.6 Sarah: the magnetic token chimp

Another prominent piece of research involving a symbol-using chimp is that with Sarah, the ward of David Premack of the University of Pennsylvania. Rather than using sign language or electronic keyboards, Premack gave Sarah 130 magnetic symbols to manipulate directly. These included ones for the names of colours such as 'red' and 'blue', for different fruits such as 'banana' and 'peach' and for actions such as 'wash', 'cut' and 'take', and some functions such as 'QUESTION'. A typical sentence might be 'QUESTION banana red' (Is the banana red?), to which Sarah accurately would answer 'no'.

Premack's research with Sarah makes it very clear that such animals are intelligent creatures. For example, Sarah had little trouble dealing with a feature once thought to be characteristic only of human language: displacement – i.e. the ability to talk about things that are not present. She was easily able to use her plastic tokens to request items that were not present, such as asking for fruit, e.g. 'Give banana'. When told 'brown colour of chocolate' (Brown is the colour of chocolate), she was able to learn the new word 'brown' thereby demonstrating that she could learn new vocabulary items by means of language instruction. (She had already acquired the meaning of the abstract word 'colour', which is, in itself, a notable achievement.)

Other apes in Premack's research were also able to distinguish between strings of words differing only in word order, such as 'red on green' and 'green on red'. This clearly demonstrates that some syntax has been acquired, although this syntax is obviously of an elementary nature, since it involves only the order of nouns. Premack himself has taken the view that little more syntax than this can be learned by apes.

2.1.7   Koko: the signing gorilla

Francine Patterson (a single 'parent'!) has claimed remarkable results with the gorilla Koko, born in 1971, whom she has trained in American Sign Language. One interesting fact she discovered was that Koko could be productive in her sign language, making new words to describe new objects by combining previously known ones. Koko, for example, created 'eye-hat' for mask, 'white-tiger' for zebra, and 'finger bracelet' for ring. Human languages include these same word-making characteristics; for example, 'blackbird' in English, 'white bird' for 'swan' in Japanese, and 'finger bracelet' for 'ring' in Chinese.

After four-and-a-half years of instruction Koko had learned 132 words. After 10 more years that total came to 500. Koko's syntax, however, did not progress beyond the same elemental level as that of the other language-taught chimpanzees. Patterson also reports that Koko uses her signs for such purposes as to swear, rhyme, joke and lie, although she does not provide strong evidence in this regard.

Koko is friendly and apparently tries to start up sign language conversations with strangers. Sometimes she signs to herself when she is alone. For example, on a videotape of Koko that I have seen, Koko spontaneously made the sign for smoking while browsing through a magazine and on coming across an advertisement for cigarettes. On the same tape, Koko also used signs to tell Patterson that someone was hiding behind a tree. Such events, seem to contradict Terrace's claim that apes will sign only when they want something. Another of Terrace's claims, that apes will not attempt to give names to objects on their own, is also contradicted by Patterson's data, since Koko did create words such as 'eye-hat' and 'white tiger' to describe newly encountered objects. On the other hand, all in all, I am sure Terrace would point out, Koko's language achievement, like that of the chimpanzees, is quite rudimentary.

2.1.8 Dolphins: teaching through sight and sound

There is much anecdotal lore about the intelligence of dolphins and whales. However, until the 1960s no scientific attempt had been made to determine their potential to communicate with human beings. In 1964, in one of the first such studies, Lilly tried to teach a dolphin to force air through its blow-hole in such a way that it would allow the dolphin to imitate human speech sounds. A young male dolphin named Elvar reputedly produced approximations of the word 'squirt', which Lilly had been trying to teach him to pronounce. Lilly also claimed that Elvar interchanged human sounds with dolphin sounds 'as if to translate for us' but provided no scientific substantiation in this regard. In fact, pronunciation difficulties were so great that Lilly was obliged to discontinue the study. He then moved on to investigate the means by which dolphins communicate with one another. Lilly's extravagant claims to the contrary (including claims that dolphins have an intelligence and a religion that is superior to those of humans), such research has yet to show that these animals use anything as complex as what we would call language.

Radically different and more scientific approaches to the teaching of language to dolphins were later initiated by Louis Herman (my friend and colleague) at the University of Hawaii. Herman conducted experiments using two different types of artificial languages, one involving sounds, the other involving gestural signs. He wanted to see if, or how well, dolphins could learn to understand language.

In 1979, a teaching programme was begun with two dolphins, *Phoenix* and *Akeakamai* (the latter's name meaning 'lover of wisdom' in the Hawaiian language). Each dolphin learned one of the two artificial languages. Akeakamai was taught the gesture-based language, while Phoenix was taught the sound-based language. Each was taught a vocabulary of about 30 words, mainly names of objects, actions and modifiers. The sound-based language had its sounds projected underwater into the dolphin tank. These sounds were controlled by Herman and his assistants from their underwater laboratory, which had a window view into the tank. The visual language of gestures (invented by Herman and his colleagues) involved the use of the trainer's arms and hands. The trainer stood by the side of the tank out of the water where he or she could be seen by the dolphin. To avoid their unconsciously giving the dolphins cues for direction, the trainers wore opaque goggles so that the dolphins could not see their eyes.

The two dolphins learned correctly to carry out a number of commands in the water. The commands consisted of two-, three-, four- and even five-word sequences, each constructed on the basis of object and action words. Thus, 'window tail touch' is to be interpreted as 'Touch a window with your tail'.

Of special interest are Herman's results which show that generally the dolphins correctly responded to what are often called 'semantically reversible sentences', sentences for which the subjects and objects cannot be interpreted by meaning alone but by the use of syntactic knowledge. For example, the English sentences 'Jack pushed Tom' and

'Tom pushed Jack' describe two different events, one in which Jack is doing the pushing and the other in which Tom is doing the pushing. Given our knowledge of the people involved and the action taken (which in this case is virtually zero) we probably would feel that either event is equally likely to occur in the world. Such reversibility would not be so easy, however, with sentences like 'The cat chased the mouse' and 'The mouse chased the cat' since, based on our knowledge of the world, we would generally expect the cat rather than the mouse to be doing the chasing.

Our expectations for certain events or situations can influence the interpretation we give to words. For example, how would you interpret the words 'struck', 'nail' and 'hammer' in a sentence? Probably you would think of the hammer striking the nail. Thus, even without the words being in the proper grammatical order, based on your life experience, you can predict certain relationships between hammer and nail and the action of striking. In the same way, an animal such as the dolphin might be able to respond appropriately to a string of words, not on the basis of their word order, but on the basis of their life experience. A proper test for grammatical knowledge must take this phenomenon into account.

Herman was aware of this problem, so as part of his research he presented the dolphins with commands involving semantically reversible structures. He gave them, for example, both 'pipe hoop fetch' (take the hoop to the pipe) and 'hoop pipe fetch' (take the pipe to the hoop). Since generally the dolphins responded appropriately to both commands, Herman was able conclude that the dolphins had acquired a syntactic aspect of grammar, word order. Since word order in these commands indicates different semantic or meaning relationships, it is reasonable to claim that the dolphins had acquired at least the rudiments of such syntactic relational notions as direct object and indirect object. Thus, in 'person frisbee fetch' (Take the frisbee to the person), 'frisbee' is the direct object and 'person' is the indirect object.

The dolphins, Herman emphasizes, also do new things on the basis of understanding the words and their relations in a command structure. Once the structure and relations are learned, then all new sentences with those characteristics should be understood, providing, of course, that the meaning of particular words are already known. Thus, after acquiring the notions of direct and indirect object, Akeakamai responded correctly on her first exposure to the sentence 'person left frisbee fetch' (take the left frisbee to the person). Herman rejects the criticism that the dolphins are merely carrying out the same kind of stimulus–response-shaped behaviour as do many marine park dolphins and whales. He correctly points out that it could not be simple stimulus–response-shaped behaviour because the dolphins respond appropriately to specific commands which they have never received before.

It might be noted here that although the dolphins responded to commands, this cannot be taken as evidence that they have learned the grammatical structure for command. This is because *all* dolphin 'sentences' had the meaning of commands. In other words, the dolphin does not know the syntactic difference between an imperative, a question or a declarative sentence form because there is nothing which marks a sentence as being a command or not a command. All sentences were of one form. There is, therefore, nothing of a command syntactic form for the dolphins to learn.

Besides the learning of other syntactic structures, it also remains for further research to demonstrate whether dolphins would be able to express in production what they already have learned in terms of language understanding. Given what we know about child language acquisition and the relationship of speech understanding and speech production, we might expect that the dolphins would develop the production capacity with little difficulty, provided they are given a convenient means for physical expression.

2.2 Animal communication in the wild

Human speech is only one small part of the communicative inventory of chirps, hisses, growls, snorts, whistles, gestures, barks and buzzes which we find in the rest of the animal kingdom. Animals communicate through a wide variety of means, and though not everything coming from animals is communicative in nature, at a basic level animals have many of the same reasons as we do for passing information: to get food, to find a mate, to warn and threaten others, etc.

Many animals use sound signals, but many also use other modalities. Substances involving smell may be used as signals, as in the case of ants, which leave chemical trails for nestmates to follow in finding food. Visual signals may, for example, be used by dogs to threaten or attract; the baring of teeth and tail-wagging serves to convey such intentions.

The most complex type of communication in the wild, unsurprisingly, involves that of the higher primates. Richard Seyfarth and Dorothy Cheney report that wild vervet monkeys make specific sounds that are more complicated than hitherto believed. For example, these monkeys' alarm calls seem to be predator-specific. Thus, while one type of grunt indicates 'Beware, here comes an eagle!', another type of grunt indicates 'Beware, here comes a leopard!'.

The calls of birds can announce, among other things, a readiness to mate, give alarm and defend territory. As researchers have determined, the bird calls and songs of particular species are largely inborn, although there are certain aspects of these calls and songs which will not develop unless the young bird is exposed to the voice of the adult bird. Of some interest to the student of language is the ability of certain species of birds, most notably the parrot and the mynah bird, to imitate human speech with amazing clarity. One bird can have a repertoire of a number of phrases and sentences, such as, 'Hello, how are you?' and 'Get away from there!'. Rarely though does the bird produce an utterance in a relevant context. It can produce speech, but has no understanding of it, nor does it ever produce utterances other than those it has been specifically trained on.

Of great interest, too, is the way honey bees inform other bees of the presence of food in the vicinity. They use both vision and touch. A bee reporting back to the hive will go through a series of movements, a kind of dance, to tell other bees if a nectar source is near or distant, and, moreover, if it is distant, just how far away and in what direction. Other bees can get the message not only by seeing these movements but by touching, that is, by approaching the scout bee and feeling its movements with their own antennae. Interestingly, scout bees which have been out looking for food do not automatically perform the dance upon returning to the hive. Knowing the value of relaxation, they only perform the dance when they have an audience. The dance they do is quite specific, for it can tell the other bees at just what angle they must orient themselves with respect to the sun as they leave the hive.

Princeton University ethologist James Gould has found that not only is the bee dance accurate in its ability to inform other bees where food has already been found, but, in a series of experiments involving laying out food at regular intervals, the bees could anticipate the new location of the food. 'You find that some of the bees are flying past you to the next place – and are waiting for you when you get there!' Are the bees creating maps in their 'minds'? As yet, no adequate explanation has been provided for this apparent foresight in bee behaviour.

2.3   Animal communication and human language

Can the natural communicative signs of animals in the wild be regarded as language? In order to answer this question, let us look at what characterizes human language and compare it to the communicative signs of animals. The single most important characteristic of human language is its creativity. Using individual words we create simple structures, such as 'The man ran'. We can make more complex sentences where we can include an object: 'The man played the guitar'. We can add to make relative clauses: 'The man who bought the bicycle played the guitar'. We can ask questions: 'Does the man who bought the bicycle play the guitar?' We can make passives: 'The guitar was played by the man who bought the bicycle'. We can make abstract conditional structures about events which have not occurred: 'If it had rained yesterday, I would have bought an umbrella'. In this last sentence, what is truly remarkable is that none of the events talked about – the rainfall and the buying of an umbrella – had actually occurred.

When we look at animal communication, it is clear that whether it is prompted by hunger, anger, danger, attraction, submission or the need to congregate or disperse, one signal has a fixed meaning and combinations of signals to form more complex structures do not occur. Even the elemental three- and four-word novel utterances produced by 2-year-old children have no counterpart in animal communication. Although animals do have ways of adding information, these means are essentially quantitative and not qualitative. Thus, a louder sound might mean more danger, a faster tail-wag might mean more excitement, and the bee's altering the angle of its dance can refine its direction-giving. Animal communication is quite specific and stereotyped. The animal calls or signs or scents have a fixed meaning, and whatever the means an animal might use for communicating, it does not involve creative recombination or the complex structures that are typical of human language.

This lack of language creativity and complexity is true even of animals who have been taught language by humans. The studies with Vicki, Washoe, Sarah, Lana, Koko and the dolphins demonstrate only a minimal degree of achievement. At best, they can make or understand only simple combinations, e.g. 'QUESTION banana red', 'put pipe net', or coin a few new words, such as 'white-tiger' for zebra. Neither in its natural state nor in its 'research educated' state has any animal been able to demonstrate a linguistic ability beyond that of the ordinary 1½- or 2-year-old human child.

Perhaps the apes could have demonstrated a higher level of linguistic achievement had the focus of the teaching been as much on the understanding of language as on its production. As we know from child language acquisition, comprehension and not production is primary; comprehension occurs before and is the basis of production. It is probable that the comprehension level of the apes was greater than their production levels. Nevertheless, I would guess that the apes' language understanding probably was not greatly in advance of their production. If it had been, the researchers would probably have noticed it.

2.4 Pygmy chimp reheats debate

In October of 1990 it was reported in the press that a pygmy chimpanzee by the name of Kanzi had learned words and learned to use grammatical rules. This started up the whole animal and language controversy once again. In an article in the book *'Language' and Intelligence in Monkeys and Apes*, UCLA psychologist Patricia Marks Greenfield and Sue Savage-Rumbaugh (of Lana fame – see above) claim that tiny Kanzi, when around 5 years old, learned over a period of 5 months to use grammar equal to that of a 2-year-old human child. According to Greenfield, 'He makes short, telegraphic sentences talking about relationships between actions and objects, objects and locations, and so forth' and has acquired grammatical rules that allow him to produce an infinite number of sentences and even invent his own symbols and use them consistently. All communication is done with hand gestures and symbols on a computer keyboard. Kanzi is said to have a vocabulary of about 250 printed words.

Even complex relations are said to be differentiated by Kanzi. If Kanzi were going to bite his sister Mulika playfully, he might sign 'bite Mulika', but if his sister bit him, he would sign 'Mulika bite'. Thus, order, an important syntactic feature, would signal a difference in meaning.

Well, as might be expected, neither Herbert Terrace nor Noam Chomsky have been much convinced by these results. Terrace says,

We've had claims like this before and on closer scrutiny the animals were found to be responding to cuing (subtle, inadvertent gestures by caregivers) or rewards. That kind of response is not terribly pertinent to language.

Chomsky is less gentle in his criticism. A chimpanzee using grammar 'is not a logical impossibility, but it is so outlandish that I don't know of any biologist who has taken the possibility seriously'. He persuasively argues that if pygmy chimps really had the ability to use grammar in millions of years past, they surely would have used it by now because language is so biologically advantageous. 'It's completely unknown biologically that any organism could have a capacity that would be highly valuable for survival but would not use it'. It does indeed seem rather odd to think that an animal would have evolutionarily developed the highly complex capacity for language but would not have used that capacity, until humans from some universities came along to show them how.

2.5   Conclusions regarding animals and language

The research with animals clearly shows that animals have only a rudimentary language ability, whether in the wild or through training. What is puzzling and requires explanation is why their language ability is so low when their overall intellectual ability is so much higher. Apes exhibit, for example, intelligent complex behaviour regarding social organization, food acquisition and problem solving. Why, then, are they not able to learn more of the sign language taught to them? After all, human children learn sign language in all of its complexity. And why couldn't they at least learn to *understand* human speech given that they have a hearing acuity which is as good as or better than human hearing? After all, there are human beings who are born without the ability for speech production, yet they can learn to understand human language in all of its complexity.

And why, too, cannot otherwise intelligent chimps be able to deal with numbers and do elementary arithmetic? The chimp Ai at Kyoto University's Primate Research Institute was able to escape from her padlocked cage (taking her oran-utan friend with her!) by finding a hidden key and opening the lock. Yet, after years of ingenious and dedicated training by psychologist Matsuzawa, she could only count and understand numbers up to six. She couldn't handle seven, nor could she do elementary subtraction. Yet documented studies with apes going as far back as the First World War (the research of the renowned Wolfgang Kohler) demonstrate that they are creative and inventive in solving other types of problems.

Contemporary theorists basically offer two types of explanations on the issue of animals vs humans in the acquisition of language. (These are considered in detail Chapter 7.) Piaget, Putnam and other empiricists hold that animals lack certain aspects of general intelligence which are needed for learning complex language. Chomsky, on the other hand, argues that the effect is due to animals being born without a special language ability, an ability that is little related to intelligence. Whether animals lack intelligence or lack a special language ability is related to the fundamental issue of how human beings, themselves, acquire language. Do we acquire language through intelligence or through a special language ability? Despite much argument, dispute and even a little objective inquiry, this question as yet remains unresolved. In any case, whether it be special intelligence or a special innate language ability, it seems evident that animals do not have it.

2.6   Discussion questions

1. Does a parrot that speaks have language?
2. The typical child by 4 years of age has learned over 2000 words. Why do you think that Washoe could learn only about 130 signs after over three years of training and not many more afterwards?
3. Among the various means described in this chapter for teaching language to animals, i.e. human speech sounds, sign language, plastic tokens, etc., which do you feel is the best, and why? Can you think of another method which might be better?
4. If apes are so intelligent, as some people say, why have they never developed a sign language on their own similar to human sign language?
5. When a dog responds to commands, like 'Fetch' and 'Sit' has the dog learned the syntactic notion of the imperative?
6. Is there a way of expanding on Herman's experiments with dolphins to involve a variety of syntactic structures? Consider, for example, trying to teach a question structure through getting responses to questions which require a simple 'yes' or 'no' answer. Or, you might consider the teaching of the conditional if/then structure.
7. In what ways is the linguistic creativity exhibited by the animals which were discussed similar to or different from human linguistic creativity?

Suggested readings

Cheney, D. L. and Seyfarth, R. M. (1982) How vervet monkeys perceive their grunts: Field playback experiments. *Animal Behaviour*, **30**, 737–51.

Gardner, B. T. and Gardner, R. A. (1975) Evidence for sentence constituents in the early utterances of child and chimpanzee. *Journal of Experimental Psychology: General*, **104**, 244–67.

Greenfield, P. M. and Savage-Rumbaugh, S. (1990) Article in K. T. Parker and K. R. Gibson (eds), *'Language' and Intelligence in Monkeys and Apes*. Cambridge: Cambridge University Press.

Hayes, C. (1951) *The Ape in Our House*. New York: Harper.

Herman, L. M., Richards, D. G. and Wolz, J. P. (1984) Comprehension of sentences by bottlenosed dolphins. *Cognition*, **16**, 129–219.

Hockett, C. F. (1959) Animal 'languages' and human language. In J. N. Spuhler (ed.), *The Evolution of Man's Capacity for Culture*. Detroit: Wayne State University Press.

Matsuzawa, T. (1985) Use of numbers by a chimpanzee. *Nature*, **315**, 6014, 57–9.

Patterson, F. (1978) Conversations with a gorilla. *National Geographic*, **154**, 438–65.

Premack, D. (1971) Language in the chimpanzee? *Science*, **172**, 808–22.

Premack, D. (1986) *Gavagai! or the Future History of the Animal Language Controversy*. Cambridge, Mass.: MIT Press.

Savage-Rumbaugh, E. S. and Rumbaugh, D. M. (1978) Symbolization, language, and chimpanzee: A theoretical reevaluation based on initial language acquisition process in four young Pan-23 troglodytes. *Brain and Language*, **6**, 265–300.

Terrace, H. S., Petitio, L. A., Sanders, R. J. and Bever, T. G. (1979) Can an ape create a sentence? *Science*, **206**, 891–900.

CHAPTER 3

Wild children and language

It seems that people have always wondered about whether language is instinctive, something that is as natural to humans as walking and smiling. They have also wondered too whether, even without experiencing language, children would be able to produce it on their own. Even as recent as the sixteenth century, we have such a brilliant thinker as Montaigne saying,

I believe that a child brought up in complete solitude, far from all intercourse (which would be a difficult experiment to carry out) would have some kind of speech to express his idea, for it is not likely that nature would deprive us of this recourse when she has given it to many other animals.

Some have even thought that children who had not been exposed to speech, would speak in the original language of humankind. Montaigne believed this too, and he also believed that many animals have language. As the chapters in this book on child language and on animals and language testify, people are still very much interested in these and in other related questions as well, such as whether there is an age beyond which a person would be unable to learn language.

3.1 Legends, evil kings and emperors

According to legend, some experiments have already been carried out to determine what language, if any, children would develop if they had never been exposed to speech. The ancient Greek historian Herodotus wrote of a story which he heard from priests in Egypt about one of their kings, Psamtik I, who reigned in the seventh century BC. According to the tale (which was already more than 300 years old when Herodotus heard it), Psamtik gave two infants to a shepherd with the instruction that they be raised without anyone speaking in their presence. The king assumed that, without outside interference, the children would eventually speak the original human language. The children's first word (and perhaps only word!) was reported by the shepherd to have been *becos*, or something sounding like it. After inquiring of his learned advisers as to what what language that word might be in, the king was told that such sounds meant 'bread' in the Phrygian language, a language then spoken in what is now central Turkey. Psamtik felt that he had his answer regarding original language, although sceptics have suggested that the sounds could have come from the children imitating sheep or goats!

Akbar the Great, the Mogul Emperor of India in the sixteenth century, is also reported to have carried out a similar experiment. However, in this instance, after years of confinement, the infants did not speak at all. Likewise it is said that James IV of Scotland also conducted such an experiment with infants. When he heard their first utterings, the king declared that they were in perfect Hebrew!

After the passage of centuries and even millennia, there is no way of knowing whether these monstrous experiments were really done in the way that is reported or that the results claimed were what was really found. Whatever the case they do reflect an overall human fascination with language and the form that a supposed 'natural' language would take. Mediaeval European scholars, too, spent much time talking about and even trying to reconstruct the language that they believed was spoken by Adam and Eve. 'Natural man' was one of the topics of the Enlightenment, too, and from Rousseau's 'noble savage' to Edgar Rice Burroughs' 'Tarzan' we have been drawn to the idea of a human being untouched by civilization. Although educated people today do not believe that a child deprived of language from birth would start speaking the original language of humankind, or any language at all for that matter, there is great scientific interest in original language(s) and in the effects of language deprivation. Deprivation or isolation cases may be able to tell us something about the nature of human language, how it is learned, and when it is best learned.

Since ethical considerations deter scientists from conducting language deprivation experiments with children, scientists have been on the lookout for cases which occur naturally, so to speak, i.e. without their intervention, such as through peculiar circumstances or the perversity of human behaviour. Over the past few centuries there have been a number of reported cases of children raised by wolves, pigs, sheep and other animals. (A fascinating collection of such cases is described in Malson's book *Wolf Children*.) Then, too, there are children who have apparently survived on their own for years in the wild; growing up even without the aid of animals. On a different level, there are the cases of children who have been kept in confinement or isolation by their parents or others, and consequently were not exposed to language. But there are also a great number of children who have been cared for by loving parents, but who, because of a physical disability, such as deafness, have nonetheless been deprived of language. Studying the deaf, too, therefore might also provide us with insight into certain psycholinguistic questions in much the same way as does the study of children who have grown up in the wild or in isolation.

Unfortunately, as far as the cases involving wild children are concerned, most of the reports are not adequate for serious scientific analysis. Too often they are based on fragmentary data usually with no details other than that such and such a child had been found in such and such an environment. The exact nature of their language when found, and the children's subsequent language development, were not properly studied, most having lived in an age before there was widespread scientific psychological and linguistic interest in the matters raised by their condition. However, some cases *have* been well documented, and it is the most important of these that will be presented here.

3.2   Victor: the Wild Boy of Aveyron

Scientific investigation into the matter of wild children increased dramatically in January of the year 1800 when a boy was captured in the woods near the village of Saint-Sernin in the Aveyron district of France. He appeared to be 11 or 12 years old, was naked except for what was left of a tattered shirt, and he made no sounds other than guttural animal-like noises. *His general appearance and behaviour were typical of the wild men of popular legend and he seemed to have survived on his own for years in the wild. Probably he had been abandoned originally but at what age or by whom could not be ascertained. Attempts to trace his personal history failed and nothing could be uncovered of his life before his being discovered.

Fortunately for the boy, the France of 1800 was alive with a spirit of scientific inquiry and a sympathy for lost children. When Sicard, the noted director of the Institute for Deaf-Mutes in Paris, heard of the boy, he made efforts and was successful in getting custody of him. Sicard's mission in life was the education of the deaf and he had already had considerable success with deaf children, many of whom had been discarded as retarded by the community. He demonstrated that, to a significant degree, many such children could be taught to communicate in sign language and could also learn to read and write. Sicard delighted in showing off the children, for they proved themselves quite capable of engaging (through writing) in intelligent and often witty banter with his scientific colleagues.

Sicard perceptively noted that there seemed to be strong similarities between this newly found wild child who had been deprived of language by isolation and those children who had been deprived of language and normal social contact because of deafness. He was eager, therefore, to apply to the Wild Boy (as he was then called) some of the methods he had developed in educating the deaf.

It was not long, though, before Sicard's optimism faded in the face of the lack of progress with the Wild Boy of Aveyron. Not only did the boy fail to learn any language but his behaviour was quite unlike that of the other children in the institute. After only a few months, the institute issued a report stating that there had been no progress with the boy and that none could reasonably be expected. They regarded him as being unteachable and gave up on him. Fortunately, however, the boy's education was then taken over by another eager educator, the creative and dedicated,

Jean-Marc Gaspard Itard. Itard set up an ambitious programme for the boy, with goals which included social as well as language training. Itard's success with the boy clearly shows that the assessment made by Sicard and the others at that institute had been quite incorrect.

The Wild Boy was given the name Victor by Itard and his education began with intense work that involved a variety of games and activities which Itard designed to socialize Victor and make him aware of the world around him. These had a dramatic effect. Victor took pleasure in long walks, taking baths, dressing himself and setting the table. Where, at the time of his capture, Victor had, for example, been virtually insensitive to temperature and ate with his hands, he now insisted on the bath water being just right and having utensils when eating. While earlier he had not reacted at all to the passing countryside during a carriage ride, he now took obvious pleasure in the changes of scenery. He enjoyed guessing games, especially of the shell game variety, such as where one tries to follow the quick movements of the hand in which a chestnut is held and then guesses under which of three cups the chestnut is hidden. He expressed a wide range of emotions and desires through movement, or 'action language' as Itard called it. His senses appeared normal, from his reaction to the world around him.

Speech training with Victor, however, proved to be very frustrating for Itard. It centred around simply trying to get Victor to repeat some words and speech sounds. This he consistently failed to do, and Itard concluded that it was unrealistic to expect speech from an adolescent who had just spent virtually his entire life in the wild. Nevertheless, Victor could distinguish speech sounds from other sounds in the environment and he was even able to differentiate the sounds of normal speech from the poorly pronounced speech sounds made by the deaf children in the institute where he now resided.

Victor's speech training first resulted in his being able to repeat the sound 'li', apparently his personal contraction of the name Julie, the name of the daughter of an assistant at the institute. In addition, he would repeat the phrase 'Oh Dieu!' ('Oh God'), which he picked up from one of Itard's assistants, Madame Guérin. He also learned to say the word for 'milk' (*lait*, in French). With regard to this word, however, Itard noted that Victor would generally just repeat it when given milk, but not really use the word in a communicative sense, such as in asking for milk.

Itard decided to abandon attempts to teach Victor language by speech imitation and moved on to another of his goals, to sharpen the boy's perceptual abilities. He embarked on a programme of having Victor learn to match colours and shapes, and then match drawings with the objects they represented. Following an insightful idea, he then set about teaching Victor the letters of the alphabet using cut-out letters. The boy learned the milk word *lait* again, but this time in the form of alphabetic letters. Victor was able to spell it out, at first upside down, since that is how he had first seen it from across the table. Of his own accord, he later picked out those letters and used them to spell out a request for milk when he was taken on a visit to someone's house. Clearly, Victor had learned the relation between written symbol and object. In its own way, this accomplishment may have been as exciting and as dramatic for Victor as it was for Helen Keller when she first realized that the movements made on her hand (a symbol) represented water (an object).

At first, Victor took written words such as <book> to mean a specific object, a particular book, but eventually he learned to associate the words with classes of objects, in this example, all books. [Note: words enclosed in angle brackets will indicate that a written form is being described. Also, although the words are written in English, it is French spelling that is implied.] He also went through some of the same problems of overgeneralization that ordinary children go through in learning language, classifying, for example <knife> with <razor>. He learned adjectives such as <big> and <small>, <hot> and <cold> and a variety of colour words. He also learned verbs such as <eat>, <drink>, <touch> and <throw>. Each of these words was written on a card for him. In the beginning, he communicated with others using the word cards. Later he was able to write the words himself, from memory. (As is noted in Chapter 4, I rediscovered the same idea and applied it to teaching language to deaf children in the US and Japan.)

Thus, in less than a year after the boy was given up as practically being an imbecile, Itard was able to issue a report stating, in effect, that Victor's senses, memory and attention were intact, that he had the ability to compare and judge, and that he could read and write to a significant extent. As far as Victor's continuing lack of speech was concerned, Itard concluded that isolation and age might have caused that particular language ability to weaken. Correct or not, this conclusion regarding speech anticipated, by over a century, modern theorizing concerning the existence of a 'critical age' for language learning! Unfortunately, Itard did not consider written language (as evidenced by Victor's ability to read and write) as a language accomplishment equal to that of speech. (In Chapter 4, it will be shown that language in the written or sign mode is in no way inferior to that in the speech mode.)

Itard could not explain why Victor could acquire reading and writing but not speech. Neither can anyone else, for that matter, since whether or not Victor suffered from brain damage or a congenital brain disorder such that his speech comprehension and production were both affected is something that can never be known. Itard had none of the brain-imaging devices we now have for examining the condition of the brain (see Chapter 9) and no post-mortem was performed on Victor's brain. It is unfortunate, too, that Victor's brain was not preserved, for, if it had been, there would be the possibility of examining it today for abnormalities. [This is not as wild as it may sound. Recently a brain that had been preserved for over one hundred years – that of a language-damaged patient of Broca (the eminent nineteenth-century French neurologist) – *was* analysed for abnormalities by computer imaging (Chapter 9). The results clearly confirmed Broca's hypothesis concerning the cause of the patient's language disorder!]

During the last of the five years he had devoted to Victor, Itard tried once again to teach the boy to speak. He used laborious methods that had been used with some success on the deaf using the sense of sight and touch to make them understand just how the vocal cords vibrate, where the tongue is placed, how the facial muscles move, etc. Once again these attempts failed; soon afterwards

Itard decided to end his work with Victor. Itard arranged for Victor to live nearby in a house with Madame Guérin, Itard's assistant. Victor lived there for 18 years, continuing to be mute until his death in 1828.

Victor's case greatly interested French scholars and he became a focal point of the philosophical debate between the followers of Descartes, who believed that humans were born with certain ideas in their minds, and the followers of John Locke, who believed that humans had no ideas in their minds at birth. Itard's conclusions were couched within a Lockeian philosophical framework, offering Victor's accomplishments as evidence that human beings are almost 'blank slates' to be written upon by our experiences in the environment and society. (A detailed consideration of the views of Locke and Descartes are presented in Chapter 7.)

3.3   Genie: raised in solitary confinement

The case of the Wild Boy of Aveyron may have been a case of simple child abandonment, something which was not and still is not uncommon in some parts of the world, especially where a child is considered in some way to be physically or mentally unfit to survive. Although Victor seems to have grown up alone in the wild, at least he did develop considerable survival skills over time and was free. Enforced isolation, however, is another matter. There are cases of children being isolated from even the outside environment and mistreated to an extent that it is difficult to talk about dispassionately. A girl called Genie is one such case.

Genie (a pseudonym) was discovered in the late 1970s in a city in the United States. She was 13½ years old and had been locked in a small room in her house by her father for the preceding 12 years! During the day she had been kept naked except for a harness which held her to an infant's toilet seat. At night she was put into a restraining sleeping bag and placed in a crib which was in effect a cage. She was fed but never spoken to. Her father beat her frequently with a wooden stick and growled at her like a dog while doing so. She heard no human voices, according to her mother, and her only contact with another human was when being fed and beaten. Other than a few pieces of plastic or paper that she was given to play with, she had nothing to look at, nothing to touch, nothing to do. Genie's mother, who lived in the house, eventually escaped taking the child with her. It was in this way that the case was discovered by the authorities. The father committed suicide on the day he was to be put on trial for mistreating the child.

At the time of her discovery, Genie was in a pitiful physical condition. Furthermore, she had been beaten into virtual silence and appeared to have no language. Based on information later provided by her mother, the girl had already begun to acquire language just prior to her confinement, which was when she was 20 months of age.

Like Victor, during her first few weeks of freedom, Genie was alert and curious. But, unlike Victor, she displayed some ability to understand and even imitate (although poorly) some individual words, such as 'mother', 'red' and 'bunny'. She could not understand a simple sentence, however. Generally, she responded only to gestures and to the intonation of words. Batteries of psychological tests indicated that her cognitive abilities were little more than those of a 2-year-old, with her language displaying many of the same characteristics of 2-year-olds as they go through the initial stages of language learning.

After just a few months of care, however, Genie changed considerably. She grew, gained weight and strength and was able to go on long walks. While her original speech production had been limited to a few utterances such as 'no-more' and 'stoppit', by the end of a few months she had acquired the words for hundreds of objects! She had an intense curiosity about the names of things in the world around her. Soon she began to understand some of the language used in her presence. For instance, when another child was asked how many balloons he had, and he had answered 'three', although he really had only two, Genie, observing the exchange, gave the child another balloon. (Thus he would have three, so that what he had said would be true.) Other incidents, too, indicated that she was beginning to learn to understand more than the single word utterances that she would use.

Although Genie understood many things said to her,

she often gave a delayed response to simple commands. Sometimes she delayed as long as 5 or 10 minutes before carrying out such a simple request as to open a door. Whether this was due to the persistence of the memory of being beaten by her father or due to some other cause is something which could not be determined. Her own speech nonetheless progressed to longer utterances. These often began with routine items like 'Give me' and 'May I have' and her speech was generally composed of such expressions. Thus, Genie had proceeded, as most children do, from the one-word to the multi-word telegraphic stage. The difference is that while ordinary children are typically around 1½ or 2 years when they make this transition, Genie was 14 years old.

During the first five years after her liberation, Genie was cared for by an affectionate foster mother and was given much attention by concerned researchers. As a result, she developed well socially. She enjoyed going to stores, walking about, playing games and became quite fond of music. She was attentive to the conversation around her and seemed to understand much of it. However, the quality of her speech showed little advancement; her utterances remained simple and often ungrammatical. (The proper use of tense, the article and prepositions, for example, were absent from her speech.) Still, she was able to convey complex meanings such as when she recalled some details of her own terrible past, producing such utterances as, 'Father take piece wood. Hit. Cry'. And, she did use speech to do many of the same things that other children do, to make requests, play games which require using words, and even tell lies.

After about a year had passed since she was first discovered, Genie was evaluated again on her language ability. She was tested, for example, on a variety of syntactic structures such as her understanding of simple negation, being required to respond correctly to sentences like 'Show me the bunny that *does not have* a carrot' as opposed to 'Show me the bunny that *has* a carrot.' She was tested on her understanding of simple adjectives, such as 'big' and 'little' ('Point to the *big* circle'). She was required to place objects 'in', 'under', 'next to', 'behind', etc., with respect to other objects to see if she understood the relationships expressed by those prepositions. She had to distinguish singular from plural ('Point to the *balloon*' as opposed to 'Point to the *balloons*'), the difference between 'and' and 'or' ('Point to the spoon *and* the pencil' versus 'Point to the spoon *or* the pencil'). The tests included pronouns, tenses, superlatives ('big', 'bigger', 'biggest'), active/passive ('The dog chased the boy' versus 'The boy was chased by the dog'), WH-questions (Who . . .?, What . . .?, Where . . .?, etc.), relative clauses ('The boy *who is tall* took the book') and complex negations ('The book that is red is *not* on the table'). Genie showed good comprehension for most test items although she had difficulties with disjunction (either/or), tense, and subject and object pronouns. Clearly her ability to understand speech had improved quite rapidly.

Although Genie made good progress in speech production, that progress was very slow. It took a few years for her to advance to the telegraphic stage and then some to go on to longer and more mature utterances. In spite of the fact that her speech was often deficient and ungrammatical, she was able to use language to express complex relationships. Utterances like 'Father take piece wood. Hit. Cry' show this quite clearly.

Genie generally spoke very little, mainly speaking only when spoken to. There were no spontaneous outbursts of the language play that one finds in normal children as they learn language. The after-effect of years of being beaten for making the slightest sound may have resulted in a much greater gap than is found in normal children between speech understanding and production. Normally, with time the gap between the two abilities decreases as speech production progresses until children get to the point where they can say most of everything that they can understand. In Genie's case, however, the difference remained great.

Genie's language acquisition was studied for about eight years, after which time she made little progress. Her language ability, both in terms of understanding and production, remained below normal and her speech continued to be ungrammatical. Genie, like Victor, was not able to acquire a normal level of language despite receiving a great amount of care and attention.

3.4   Isabelle: confinement with a mute mother

In 1942, Marie Mason reported a case that concerned a
child, Isabelle (a pseudonym), who, because of her confinement with a mute mother, did not begin learn to acquire
language until she gained her freedom at 6½ years of age.

The mother of Isabelle had sustained a brain injury at
the age of 2, and as a result never developed speech.
According to Mason, 'She could neither talk, nor read, nor
write . . . she was totally uneducated . . . [and] communicated with her family by means of crude gestures of her
own origination.' At the age of 22, the woman had a child,
Isabelle. During the period of her pregnancy, and for six-
and-a-half years after the child's birth, the mother and child
had apparently been locked in a room behind drawn shades.
The mother finally escaped, taking Isabelle with her, which
was when Isabelle's case was brought to the attention of
authorities. This led to Isabelle's admittance at the age of
6½ to the Children's Hospital in Columbus, Ohio, in
November of 1938. Mason was Assistant Director of the
Speech Clinic of the hospital and she undertook the task of
trying to help Isabelle.

After overcoming an initial shyness, the child displayed
curiosity about her environment, pointing and gesturing to
objects which interested her. It was determined that
although Isabelle had no speech production ability ('. . . she
made no attempt to reproduce these concepts orally'),
nonetheless '. . . she distinctly indicated a comprehension of
their meaning'. Isabelle had readily grasped the fundamental
linguistic principle that speech sounds were symbols for
objects.

Although the child displayed normal hearing, initial
psychological tests were discouraging as to the potential for
linguistic development.

. . . gesture was her only mode of expression. . . . She revealed
the performance of a three-year old child with complete failure on
any test involving linguistic skill . . . . The general impression
was that she was wholly uneducable, and that any attempt to
teach her to speak, after so long a period of silence, would meet
with failure. In spite of this, I decided to make the attempt on my
own assumption that Isabelle's failure to speak was due to the six
and a half years of isolation with a mute and deaf mother.

Isabelle made her first attempt at vocalization just *one week* after Mason's first visit with her. The child's first spoken sounds were approximations of 'ball' and 'car' in response to being shown a ball and a toy car and being prompted by Mason through gestures to try and say the words. Subsequently,

. . . Isabelle's acquisition of speech seemed to pass through successive developmental changes. While it is true that her earliest vocal utterances were those of a child of a year and a half or two years, it is also true that she passed through each successive stage more rapidly than the normal child whose speech maturation begins at two or before and extends over a longer period of time.

In less than three months after her entrance to the hospital, Isabelle was producing sentence utterances! We find this entry in Mason's journal:

Feb. 8, 1939. Says the following sentences voluntarily: That's my baby; I love my baby; open your eyes; close your eyes; I don't know; I don't want; that's funny; at's [that's] mine (when another child attempted to take one of her toys).

After just one year, 'Isabelle listens attentively while a story is read to her. She retells the story in her own limited vocabulary, bringing out the main points.' After a year and a half, the report of a student teacher working with Isabelle noted that the child's questions now included complex structures such as, 'Why does the paste come out if one upsets the jar?' and 'What did Miss Mason say when you told her I cleaned my classroom?'. We find represented in these sentences WH questions (why, when, etc.)with the auxiliary 'do', embedded sentences, conditional conjoining and proper tensing!

Thus, after only 20 months, Isabelle '. . . had progressed from her first spoken word to full length sentences . . . [and] . . . intelligent questioning'. Concluding her article, Mason states:

Here is a little child now eight years old, who in a period of less than two years, has made striking social adjustments to a living and hearing world after six years in a world of silence, fear, and isolation; a child who can communicate with others in speech after six and a half years of primitive gesturing to a mute and deaf mother . . . .

Truly this was a remarkable achievement. How different from the outcomes with Victor and Genie!

3.5   Helen: the famous deaf and blind girl

Any discussion of language deprivation must include the case of Helen Keller, a person who was blind and deaf since infancy. Actually Keller was born normal then, due to illness, she became deaf and blind at the age of 19 months. Thus, before tragedy struck, she had already had experienced the initial stages of language acquisition. That, however, was the extent of language exposure until six years later, at age 7, when Anne Sullivan Macy was engaged by Keller's parents to teach her language. In spite of Keller's seemingly overwhelming sensory handicaps, Sullivan Macy's efforts to teach Helen language through the sense of touch were successful. Helen learned language through touch and later even learned to speak, by directly touching the voice articulators (mouth, lips, vocal chords through the throat, etc.) of Sullivan Macy and others. (See frontispiece.) However, because she was unable to hear and thus could not receive any auditory feedback, her own speech was somewhat strange; she spoke in a high-pitched somewhat monotone, voice. She further learned to interpret and produce Braille. To crown these accomplishments Keller went on to graduate from Radcliffe (Harvard University) *with honours* and to become an acclaimed lecturer and writer in the service of handicapped people.

I would like to mention in passing here that Sullivan Macy was recommended as Helen's teacher to Keller's parents by none other than Alexander Graham Bell. Before becoming famous as the inventor of the telephone, Bell was a noted educator and researcher of the deaf, as was his Scottish father before him. Since, too, Bell's mother and his own wife were deaf, Bell was, therefore, quite familiar with deafness and the problems involved in deaf education.

Keller's autobiography, *The Story of My Life*, is fascinating to read. That dramatic moment when she learned her first word is movingly described in it:

One day, while I was playing with my new doll, Miss Sullivan put my big rag doll into my lap also, spelled 'd-o-l-l' and tried to make me understand that 'd-o-l-l' applied to both. Earlier in the day we had had a tussle over the words 'm-u-g' and 'w-a-t-e-r'. Miss Sullivan had tried to impress it upon me that 'm-u-g' is mug and that 'w-a-t-e-r' is water, but I persisted in confounding the two. In despair she had dropped the subject for the time, only to renew it at the first opportunity. I became impatient at her repeated attempts and, seizing the new doll, I dashed it upon the floor. I was keenly delighted when I felt the fragments of the broken doll at my feet. Neither sorrow nor regret followed my passionate outburst. I had not loved the doll. In the still, dark world in which I lived there was no strong sentiment of tenderness.

I felt my teacher sweep the fragments to one side of the hearth, and I had a sense of satisfaction that the cause of my discomfort was removed. She brought me my hat, and I knew I was going out into the warm sunshine. This thought, if a wordless sensation may be called a thought, made me hop and skip with pleasure. We walked down the path to the well-house, attracted by the fragrance of the honeysuckle with which it was covered. Someone was drawing water and my teacher placed my hand under the spout. As the cool stream gushed over one hand she spelled into the other the word 'w-a-t-e-r', first slowly, then rapidly. I stood still, my whole attention fixed upon the motions of her fingers. Suddenly I felt a misty consciousness as of something forgotten, a thrill of returning thought; and somehow the mystery of language was revealed to me. I knew then that 'w-a-t-e-r' meant the wonderful cool something that was flowing over my hand. That living word awakened my soul, gave it light, hope, joy, set it free!

How is it that Keller was able to attain the level of language excellence that she did? It might be argued that Keller's success in language acquisition was beneficially affected by the relatively brief encounter she had with speech in her infancy. However, the fact that after the lengthy six-year period of not being exposed to language, it took as long as it did for her to learn her first word – when she had to realize that a sense experience (the feeling of something being drawn in her hand) symbolized an object (water) in the world – may indicate that her pre-illness exposure to language was of minimal benefit. Still, it is possible that her early language experience in infancy did have a beneficial structural effect on her brain and mind which served to assist her later.

3.6   A critical age for first-language acquisition?

Why is it that Isabelle and Helen learned language to the full but Victor and Genie did not? Why didn't Victor and Genie learn more than they did, particularly considering their teachers' dedication to their welfare and evidently sound educational ideas? One thing is certain, and that is: without exposure to language, children will not acquire any language, let alone any supposed original language of humankind. Children need some form of exposure, be it in the form of speech, signs, writing or touch before language learning can occur.

In reviewing the details of the cases of Victor, Genie, Isabelle and Helen, we can identify three major factors which could have operated to influence their varying success in language acquisition: (1) the age at which the onset of non-exposure to language occurred; (2) the duration of non-exposure to language; and (3) the extent of any physical, psychological and social trauma prior to being discovered and taught language.

As far as Victor is concerned, we do not know why he had been roaming alone in the wild, nor do we know whether he had experienced any language prior to his capture. It may be that for most, or all, of the estimated 11 or so years of his life, his exposure to language and to ordinary human life had been minimal. On the other hand, he may have had some exposure to language before his abandonment. Why he was abandoned is not known, but there is the possibility that he could have been regarded as retarded. Barring the unlikelihood of his being raised by animals, Victor must have been raised by humans, at least in infancy, for some period of time. But because we have no information regarding such crucial circumstances, there is no way we can state with any assurance why Victor was not able to attain full competence in speech or written language.

Nonetheless, it is of importance to note that he progressed more in written language than in speech. This finding suggests that the motor skill of speech production is more affected by age than general language ability. This may be so. However, because we do not know whether or not Victor had suffered from a speech disorder prior to his discovery, we cannot be sure of this. Still, while we see that exposure to written language was rather effective, it is not clear why Victor was unable to fully master this mode of communication. Certainly he never achieved in written language the equivalent of Genie's level of speech comprehension, let alone the advanced levels of Isabelle and Helen.

Genie, at 13 years, was about Victor's age (11 or 12 years) before she was exposed to language. Nevertheless, despite over 11 years of isolation, she *was* able to develop a much higher level of language than Victor, her achievement mainly in the area of speech comprehension. Genie's accomplishment in this respect establishes that if there is a critical age for acquiring the fundamentals of a first language, grammatical structures, grammatical rules and vocabulary, the limiting age could not be very young, for Genie was over 13 years old when she began to learn language.

That Genie's speech production ability was faulty in terms of pronunciation may be related to factors which operate in the acquisition of second-language pronunciation by ordinary people (see Chapter 10), where it has been found that the ability to control certain muscles of the body, in particular the articulators of speech (the tongue, mouth, vocal chords, etc.), generally begins to decline around 10 to 12 years of age. The fact that Genie had not used speech from infancy until she was 13 years old probably put her at a disadvantage more than would be the case for a typical second-language learner of the same age. At least the ordinary second-language learner would, in using his or her first language, have had the benefit of exercising the articulators of speech for over a decade. Even so, we cannot be sure that Genie's poor speech ability was not the result of some negative psychological influence due to her mistreatment. After all, she had been punished severely for years just for making any sort of sound.

The language achievements of Isabelle and Helen contrast sharply with those of Victor and Genie. Why were these two girls able to do so well? The fact that Helen had been exposed to language during her first 19 months of life could not have been the deciding factor because Isabelle had had no such exposure. What they have in common, however, is the age at which, after the period of deprivation, language exposure and teaching began: Isabelle was 6 years old, while Helen, at 7 years, was almost the same age. Victor and Genie were almost twice as old as these girls in this regard. It could well be – as some theorists, such as Lenneberg, suggested – that the biological ageing of the body, particularly the brain, is a principle factor governing various aspects of the language acquisition process.

In any case, whatever the underlying cause might be, can we conclude that the critical age for full first-language learning lies somewhere under Victor and Genie's ages of 12 and 13 years ('under' because they had difficulty learning) but over Isabelle and Helen's ages of 6 and 7 years ('over' because they did learn)? Perhaps so. However, we cannot at all be sure since the poor performance of Victor and Genie may have been the result of other factors. We do not know how Victor (assuming he was not congenitally retarded or had some brain dysfunction) and Genie would have fared if, during their period of language deprivation, they had not been isolated but instead been socially accepted. What if they had been cared for and loved? After all, Helen was given special and tender care by her parents and even Isabelle, although shut away in a small room, had the love and companionship of her mother.

It is clear from our consideration of the cases of wild children that the ideal experimental situation for studying the problem of a critical age for first-language learning has not yet presented itself. Let us hope for humanity's sake that it never does.

3.7 Discussion questions

1. Why might Isabelle have progressed more rapidly than Genie in both speech understanding and production?
2. Genie learned to speak but Victor did not. Why do you think it happened this way?
3. Why do you think Helen Keller did so much better in language and other aspects of life (becoming an honours graduate from a renowned university and becoming a lecturer and writer) than the other children who suffered language deprivation?

4. At what age do you think it would be too late for a person to learn any significant part of a first language?
5. If the perfect experiment regarding language deprivation were done, what do you think the results would be and why?

Suggested readings

Curtiss, S. (1977) *Genie: A Psycholinguistic Study of a Modern-Day 'Wild Child'*. New York: Academic Press.

Keller, H. (1972) *The Story of My Life*. New York: Collier Macmillan International. Originally published in 1903 by Doubleday.

Lane, H. (1976) *The Wild Boy of Aveyron*. Cambridge, Mass.: Harvard University Press.

Malson, L. (1972) *Wolf Children and the Problem of Human Nature – with the Complete Text of the Wild Boy of Aveyron*. New York: Monthly Review.

Mason, M. K. (1942) Learning to speak after years of silence. *Journal of Speech and Hearing Disorders*, **7**, 4, 295–304.

CHAPTER 4

Sign language, written language and the deaf

4.1 Soundless language

Can language exist in the mind without speech? How can a soundless language like sign language be acquired? Odd as such questions may appear, there are good psycholinguistic reasons for asking them, for an inquiry into such questions will prove to be quite revealing with regard to the psychological nature of language and the various sensory mediums by which it may be acquired. Furthermore, in the course of such an inquiry, a number of controversial issues will arise, issues which are of great practical importance for deaf people in terms of communication and education. It will become clear that, without a firm grounding in psycholinguistic concepts, attempts to deal sensibly with such practical language problems will result in confusion.

4.2 Language without speech

By now most of us have had the opportunity to experience sign language, if only to see it occasionally in the corner of our TV screens. There we can see a person translating speech into sign for the benefit of deaf and less severely hearing-impaired viewers. You may wonder, and quite justifiably, whether those signs truly are part of a language or are just a collection of gestures that lack the sophistication of a language based on speech.

How can we judge whether persons who use 'sign language' truly have language? While some might attempt to present a lengthy treatise on the nature of language and then use that as a criterion, I would rather like to offer a simpler, and, I believe, more effective, criterion. Can we not agree that *a person has a language if that person can communicate by signing whatever can be communicated by speech*? This seems reasonable because we can all agree that people who communicate in speech do have language. Of course, this criterion must allow for a difference in the physical means of communication: signing rather than speech. This is not a critical concession, for, just as we regard the physical acts of producing and hearing speech as being different in some way from language (which exists in our minds), so, too, can we regard the producing and seeing of signs as being similarly different from language. Language, of course, does depend on some physical mode for its acquisition and use, but the point here is that the mode need not be limited to sound. Even touch can be used as a mode by persons who are both deaf and blind (as it was by Helen Keller).

What we are really interested in here is whether a sentence like 'If the weather had been fine so that Mary's uncle could have come to give her the money, then she might have bought that new stereo' could be conveyed through signing? Such a communication expresses a variety of complex semantic functions and relations (question, conditional, time, etc.) and involve a number of events and situations, none of which, interestingly enough, had occurred. (According to the sentence: the weather was not fine, the uncle didn't come to give Mary money, and Mary did not buy a stereo.) A person who could produce and understand communications such as this, even though they are through sign rather speech, surely can reasonably said to have language.

Well, research does show that signers of such sign languages as American Sign Language, French Sign Language, British Sign Language, and certain others can indeed communicate in sign whatever is expressed in speech. However, this may not be true though of other sign languages which are incomplete syntactically or are limited in terms of vocabulary. Incomplete sign languages are typically found in developing countries, although in even some developed nations, sign language may suffer from deficiencies. In Japan, for example, where the national government prohibits the teaching and use of sign language in public schools, standardization and vocabulary are problems. (The rationale for this anti-sign position is considered in a later section.)

Returning to the language criterion, not only can a fluent signer of a complete sign language such as American Sign Language (ASL) sign whatever a speaker can say, but the signer communicates at the same speed as a speaker does. The speed at which signers produce sentences (more precisely the propositions which underlie sentences) in a sign conversation tends to be the same at which speakers produce sentences in a speech conversation. This occurs even though a signer, as does a speaker, has the ability to exceed this speed. There seems to be an optimum speed at which humans are able comfortably to process language information, whether that information is in the form of speech or sign.

Before considering the essentials of sign language, it will be useful, and interesting, to examine a related means of communication that is used by hearing persons: gestures. Although gestures may be complex, they are but collections of signs and do not form a true language; there is no grammar with which gestures may be combined to form the equivalent of sentences, except of the most rudimentary sort ('You come', 'I hungry'). Nevertheless, they do play an important part in communication both in conjunction with speech and as an alternative for speech.

4.3 Gestures and signs

4.3.1 Gestures without speech

People use a variety of body movements to convey messages. Most of these movements, called gestures, mainly involve the face and hands although the posture of the body is important as well. We use gestures to communicate a variety of types of messages, as, for example: greetings (hello, goodbye – by moving the hands and arms); requests and commands (come, go, stop – by moving the hands); insults (the sticking out of the tongue by children, the raising of the middle finger by adults); answering (yes, no, I don't know – by moving the head), evaluating (good/perfect – by making a circle with the thumb and index finger; and victory/success – by making the V sign); descriptions (tall, short, long – by use of the hands and arms), referring (self, other, this one, that one – by pointing) and scolding (a facial scowl). These are only some of the categories for which we have gestures that may be used for communication independently of speech.

Some gestures are almost universal, such as the moving of the hand or arm towards the body to indicate 'come' (Americans make a sweeping motion of the arm from the elbow towards their own body with the hand held in a vertical position while Japanese have their arm outstretched horizontally but move only their hand with the palm facing downwards), or in pointing to one's body to indicate 'self' (Americans point to their chest while Chinese point to their nose – to my knowledge no community points below the waist). Most gestures, however, are specific to cultural, linguistic or geographic areas. Thus Sri Lankans shake their head in a way which, while indicating 'yes' or 'agreement' for them, indicates 'no' or 'disagreement' for English speakers. (I once was the adviser of an MA student from Sri Lanka, and even though I knew that her shaking of the head indicated agreement with what I was saying, I never could get used to it.) And, while the Japanese place their index fingers sticking upwards on the sides of their head to indicate that someone is 'angry', a person from France visiting Japan might, in searching for a meaning, interpret the gesture as indicating 'cuckold', after the French language expression 'wearing of the horns'.

Facial movements, in particular, are used everywhere to express a wide range of emotions and feelings. We do not need actually to utter the words 'I am . . . {happy, surprised, disgusted, disappointed, excited, angry, etc.}' when we have in our non-verbal repertoire the amazing flexibility to roll our eyes in exasperation, contract our brow in consternation and haughtily raise our eyebrows (from which, by the way, we get another haughty sort of word, 'supercilious', meaning, from Latin, 'raised eyebrow'). States of aversion, confusion, attention, distress, love, annoyance, superiority, belligerence, doubt, stupidity, bewilderment, determination, and so on, can all be conveyed by various combinations of facial expression, hand movement and body posture.

In examining gestures, it becomes obvious that some gestures are more related to, or suggest, the ideas that they are intended to represent than are others. The hand and arm gesture for 'come', pointing to your own body for 'self' or a smile gesture for 'friendliness', for example, have a certain closeness. These kinds of gestures having a close relationship between gesture and meaning are called *iconic* gestures. These iconic gestures contrast with ones that are more abstract, such as the shaking of hands to signify agreement in the closing of a business deal. This would be a non-iconic gesture. It gives less clue as to meaning than the iconic gesture. Such being the case we would expect iconic gestures to be easier to acquire than non-iconic ones. Some gestures, however, are not so easy to categorize. Would you be able to guess that a listener's noisy sucking in of breath while the eyes look upwards signals 'deep consideration for what the speaker has said' in certain segments of Japanese society? I was baffled when I first came upon it!

Besides the general gestures used in a culture, there are also restricted gestures which are known and used by small groups. These are typically to be found in specialized fields of work.

Stock trading   We have all seen pictures of stocks being bought and sold on the floor of an exchange. With those furious hand and finger signals, stocks are named, prices quoted and deals are closed.

Betting   At a race-track in Britain, you might see a man putting one right finger in his left ear. He is not relieving an itch but, as a bookmaker (a bet taker), he is indicating that the odds on a certain horse are 6 to 4.

Music   A symphony conductor often pulls the palm back towards the body to request less volume from the orchestra.

Sports   Referees and judges use elaborate hand and arm gestures to indicate the state of play and the assignment of points and penalties.

Television   If you were an announcer presenting the

news, and the person in charge drew his or her index finger across the throat, you would bring your talking to a close. On the other hand, if you were on a dark deserted street in a dangerous part of town with two rough-looking characters approaching you, and one signalled the other with that gesture while looking your way, you would start running.

4.3.2   Gestures with speech

Despite the great number of gestures which are available for use, it is clear that most of the gesturing that people engage in when they communicate are coordinated with speech. While some of these gestures have an iconic sign function – i.e. can be used by itself to convey a meaning – others do not. A good example of the latter is *beat*, where one's hand or finger is kept in motion and is synchronized with what a person is saying.

Beats are constant in form and do not change with the content of the sentences. In making beats, people will move their hands up and down or back and forth. This tends to be done in the periphery of gesture space, such as to the side, not in the central portion. The purpose of beats, according to McNeill in his insightful analysis of gestures, is basically to emphasize the discourse function of concurrent speech. Beats do not add to the content of a description or story but rather serve to emphasize the introduction of new characters, the setting of a scene, the occurrence of some event, and the like. McNeill presents the following case example. A person (*A*) has been shown a film and is asked to talk about it. *A* says that the character in the film has a girlfriend, and as *A* says 'his girlfriend' he makes a beat. *A* then says that her first name is Alice and, as he says 'Alice', he makes another beat. *A* then goes on to say that her family name is White and, as he says 'White', he makes another beat. Three beats were performed successively in this little bit of narrative, one beat per piece of new information. However, it should be noted that many beats may occur with a single sentence and that new information is not always involved. For example, McNeill describes one 5-year-old child saying, in response to being asked what something is, 'It's something else.' As he was saying this the child's hand rose up and down three times on the armrest of the chair he was sitting in. Thus, even young children acquire quite early the gestures which accompany the speech of their language.

The use of beat, however, is more pronounced in some cultures than in others. Italians and Jews, for example, seem to do it more than Japanese and Britons. One Jewish man talking to another man might even tap the other on the stomach. (I doubt that a Japanese could even be trained to do this!)

Besides beats, people make another, perhaps more important type of gesture along with speech. This is the iconic or content gesture which, according to McNeill and his colleagues' research, occurs just once within each clause. Such gestures occupy the central gesture space and can add to or make more explicit some part of a description or a story line. Thus, for example, when people are asked to describe something they see and they utter sentences like 'He is trying to go *up the inside of the drainpipe*' and 'He is going *up through the pipe* this time', in both cases the speakers make an upward gesture, either with the finger or the hand. The gesture is made while that important portion of the sentence (italicized) is being uttered.

Making note of what people do when they talk, such as their production of icon and beat gestures that they make, can be a very interesting pastime. You will be surprised at what you learn, if you can stifle that urge to smile or laugh aloud.

4.4 Sign languages

4.4.1 Types of sign language

Sign languages use hand, face or other body movements in a three-dimensional space as the physical means of communication. Principally, there are two types of sign language and these differ as to whether or not the signs represent ordinary (speech-based) languages. Thus, there are sign languages which represent the words (through signs) and their order as they appear in ordinary languages, such as Swedish, English and French, and there are sign languages such as American Sign Language and British Sign Language which have their own words and grammatical systems for the generation of sentences.

4.4.2 Sign languages representing spelling or speech

Sign language based on ordinary language can be of two different kinds. One such kind represents words by spelling them out in terms of individual signs, where each sign represents a letter of the alphabet. Hand and finger configurations are used to indicate letters, such as making a V with the index and middle fingers or an O with the thumb and index finger. Thus, a word such as *enough* would be signed letter by letter, *e*, *n*, *o*, *u*, *g* and *h*, following English spelling. Words and entire sentences are communicated in this letter-by-letter method. The order of letters is exactly the one that occurs in the writing of the ordinary language.

There are both one- and two-hand systems of finger spelling (Figure 4.1). The Americans and Swedes, for example, use one hand, while the British use two. Users of

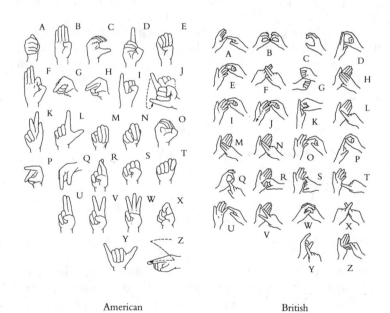

American   British

Figure 4.1 Finger spelling: 1 and 2 handed

both systems can sign relatively quickly but both processes are rather laborious. The two-handed system is faster and provides more easily identifiable letters but it does not allow a hand free for other uses. Only a few deaf schools (like the Rochester School in America) rely wholly on finger spelling to express all communications. (The sentence 'The boy coughed' is expressed as the series of individual letter signs: t, h, e, b, o, y, c, o, u, g, h, e, and d.) Signers of all systems, though, must learn to use finger spelling since most proper nouns like Manila, Caroline and Kensington, do not have their own special individual signs. Such proper nouns must be finger spelled.

More popular than The Rochester Method of finger spelling is a kind of sign language which uses whole signs for each speech word or meaningful word part (morpheme). For 'coughed', for example, there would be one whole sign for 'cough', and another for the past tense. *Seeing Essential English* and *Signing Exact English* are typical of such sign systems. These language systems, which, for want of a name, I shall call Signing Ordinary Language (**SOL**), follow in signs the exact linear flow of spoken words. Thus, 'I asked John for the cards' would have a sign for each English morpheme in that sentence, signed in the same order as the spoken sentence: *I* + *ask* + *PAST* + *John* + *for* + *the* + *card* + *PLURAL*. The word 'asked' has a separate sign for the root 'ask' and a separate sign for the suffix marking past tense. Similarly, 'card' and a sign which marks the plural have separate signs. These systems are relatively new, having been devised by educators in the past 40 years.

A SOL system has certain important advantages for the learner. By learning it, not only will the person be able to communicate with other hearing-impaired persons (who know the system) but the learner will have knowledge of the syntax and vocabulary of the ordinary language as well. The ordinary language would then not have to be learned as a remote second language (as far as vocabulary and syntax is concerned) by persons whose native language is an independent sign language. For the same reason, too, learning to read will not be as difficult. In addition, the SOL system has the advantage of being easier for hearing persons to learn than independent sign languages since SOL is based on the grammar which hearing people already know through speech. This is particularly advantageous to the parents of deaf children who naturally want to establish a means for communicating with their children as quickly as possible. Most deaf children, it is worth noting in this regard, are born to hearing parents.

Despite its many advantages, SOL suffers from one serious, perhaps fatal, disadvantage. Deaf signers generally do not like it. They find it more cumbersome and less natural to use than a sign language that has evolved through extensive use in the deaf community.

4.4.3   Independent sign languages (SL)

Some characteristics of SL

The signs of a sign language that is independent of a speech-based language (hereafter, SL) can be broken down into three basic components: *hand configuration*, how the hand is formed; *place of articulation*, where the hand is formed; and *movement*, how the hand moves. At the word level of an ordinary language, there are not only words which differ completely in meaning from one another, but also words which are very much related, differing only in morphology, or their sound form. For example, in English from the word 'compare', words like 'compared', 'compares', 'comparing' and 'comparison' are derived. Such morphological changes also have their equivalents in SL. Adjusting the movement of a sign by changing the speed or tension or rate of repetition, gives an SL the ability to derive nouns from verbs, such as 'comparison' from 'compare', as well as produce derivations which are unique to the SL. For example, in ASL the signs for 'church', 'pious', and 'narrow-minded' (!) differ only in the manner of movement involved. There are, then, uninflected forms of signs which can be defined by the features of place, configuration and movement, with variations in movement providing the means for morphological variation and changes in aspect. SL words and morphemes are manipulated in much the same way as are spoken words so as to provide variation in grammatical classes and meaning.

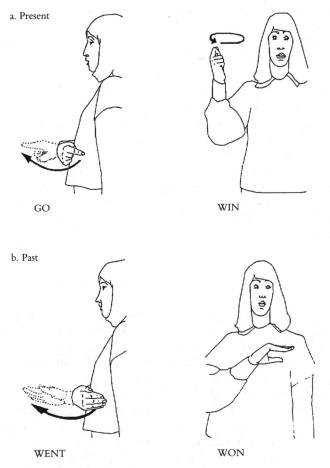

a. Present

GO   WIN

b. Past

WENT   WON

Figure 4.2 British sign language verbs

Just how signs tend to be made when comparing ASL to say, Chinese Sign Language (CSL), we find not unexpectedly that not only are the signs themselves completely different, but, also, that ASL uses a slightly more pinched hand configuration, with the fingers curling under, fist-like, into the palm, much more so than in CSL. If a signer of CSL learned to sign ASL with all the correct features of articulation mentioned above, yet kept his or her hand configuration in the less pinched CSL fashion, the result would be perfectly understandable to a signer of ASL, yet there would be something different about it. It would be the sign language equivalent of speaking with a foreign accent!

Incidentally, this might be a good place to emphasize that, contrary to common expectation, there is no universal sign language. There are even strong dialectic differences within a language. For example, signers from Paris have difficulty in understanding signers from Lyon, and vice versa. You may be surprised to know, too, that American Sign Language and British Sign Language (Figure 4.2) are not mutually comprehensible. American Sign Language (Figure 4.3) actually has more in common with French Sign Language than with British Sign Language because it (ASL) was derived from French Sign Language in the nineteenth century. Sign languages, like speech-based languages, have their own historic origins around the world and develop along their own individual lines.

The syntax of sign language

In a speech-based language, individual words are structured together into sentences according to syntactic rules, the heart of the grammar of a language. SL, too, has rules which govern the relationship between individual signs in a sentence. While the words and morphemes of sentences in languages such as Signing Exact English are signed in the air on a sort of imaginary two-dimensional blackboard, in a word-by-word (and morpheme) linear sequence, SL sentences are radically different. They are not linear sequences but three-dimensional creations. Such a space allows for combinations of meanings and the simultaneous blending of a number of meaning elements that cannot be produced linearly. As a result, signed sentences can be produced quickly and with a minimum of effort.

The proper indexing or apportionment of space is crucial to producing grammatical sentences in SL. For example, nouns, pronouns and verbs have to be assigned points in the speaker's space. These points have to be differentiated throughout a sentence and remain as reference points such that the component relations of the sentence, the

(a) The sequence of signs 'woman–forget–purse' is used as a statement, *The woman forgot the purse* (the articles are not separately signed).

(b) The same sign sequence is accompanied by a forward movement of the head and shoulders, and the eyebrows are raised: this would express the yes–no question, *Did the woman forget the purse?*

Figure 4.3 American sign language sentences (captions added by Danny D. Steinberg)

noun phrase subject, the verb, and the noun phrase object, are related to one another in a coherent fashion. The area in front of a speaker's torso is a field in which, for example, pronoun references can be signed – a 'he' or 'she' left hanging in space, as it were – and referred back to as 'relative pronouns'. Verbs of movement follow paths through this space from point to point, their start and end points indicating subject and object relations. Variations of movement can occur within this space to show time and aspect, and spaces can be built within spaces to embed one sentence within another, to contrast one event with another or to refer to something further back in time. Violation of the rules which govern the relationship between signs will lead to confusion, with the occurrence of poorly formed and ambiguous sentences, very similar to what happens in speech when rules of grammar are broken.

The parallels between the acquisition of language through speech and sign language are very striking. In acquiring SL as a first language, deaf children go through stages of language acquisition which are similar to those of hearing children. Their signing goes through a single-sign stage and even a telegraphic stage of simple sign productions where inflections and function signs are not included. However, there are linguistic problems, which deaf children must face and overcome, that are unique to SL, such as the proper indexing of space. While young signers at the age of 3 will not yet have fully differentiated their signing space correctly, this will have been accomplished by the age of 5. It is by this age that all of the essentials of the formal language system will have been acquired.

4.5   The sign language struggle in deaf education

4.5.1   SL out of the closet and into respectability

As recently as the 1970s some theorists denied that a sign language could be a genuine language. Such scholarly denial reflected the biased opinion of many hearing persons, as well. Much of the original bias against SL stemmed from a poor understanding of the nature of language. Until the mentalist revolution in linguistics and psychology, which was spearheaded by Chomsky in the 1960s, language was generally equated with speech in a behaviouristic type of conception. With the advent of mentalism, language began to be widely perceived as a kind of knowledge in the mind that is related to but is independent of its physical manifestation in speech. Such a conceptual separation was just what sign language researchers needed for pursuing their investigations into SL. They were then able to formulate an abstract SL grammar for the mind, a mental grammar that was similar in essence to those that hearing people were believed to have.

The strong belief held by many deaf educators and the general public that speech was necessary for one to be human could be challenged. Signers could now, like speakers, be said to have language; although they did not have speech. Language and not speech could be regarded as the true distinguishing human characteristic. The change started slowly in the 1960s but soon gathered momentum and by the middle of the 1970s the proponents of SL began to succeed. Soon SL was actively taught in a large number of schools for the deaf in the US, Sweden, and other countries.

It was during this same period that, with the boost given to SL by educators and researchers, the SL deaf community came out of the closet, so to speak. Signers began to gain confidence and pride and to communicate such feelings to the public at large. No longer did the SL deaf and their hearing friends and relatives feel embarrassed as they once did.

When some 20 years ago actress Louise Fletcher (a hearing person) made her acceptance speech for an Academy Award for her role in the film *One Flew Over the Cuckoo's Nest*, she caused quite a stir when she simultaneously interpreted her own speech into ASL for the benefit of her deaf mother and father who were at home watching the show on television. It is now commonplace in many countries to see various TV programmes, meetings and special events with simultaneous interpreters present for the benefit of the deaf. The problems of deaf people and of deaf education even became a major theme in another well-known film, *Children of a Lesser God*. This award-winning film also served to dispel some of the misconceptions held by the public. Then, too, just a few years ago, an incident occurred which also served in some degree to make the hearing community more aware of the deaf and SL. A hearing woman was appointed dean at America's only college for the deaf, Gallaudet College in Washington, DC. Because she could not communicate in ASL – the language in general use by students and faculty on campus – the students began protest demonstrations, which were reported on all the major news networks. This publicity, and the ensuing sympathy for the aims of the students, forced the university directors to back down and appoint a dean who was bilingual in spoken English and ASL. I might mention here that Thomas Gallaudet (1787–1851), after whom the college is named, contributed significantly to the creation of the original ASL on his return to America after study in France.

SL sign language has become so widespread that most people in the deaf community in the United States and Canada now use ASL in communicating with one another. SL allows them to communicate in a highly efficient way with a means that is most congenial to them. Even in Japan, where sign language of any sort is prohibited in the public schools, deaf people manage to learn Japanese SL outside of the regular schools. Often the social welfare department of a city will offer SL courses. (I attended one such evening course when I lived in Hiroshima.) SL has naturally become a part of the deaf community despite the national govern-ment's opposition to it. Even at a school for the deaf in Hiroshima where sign language was banned, I saw students signing to one another when their teachers weren't looking. Actually, since their speech and writing abilities were minimal, there was no other effective means for them to communicate with one another. There is no stopping people from learning SL from others if that is how they wish to communicate.

How deaf people are to communicate with members of the dominant hearing community is a different problem, and remains so. Barring the unlikely event that hearing people will learn SL on a mass scale, it is necessary for the deaf to acquire some means of communication with hearing persons. In this regard two main approaches are available. One is the traditional Oral Approach. The other, little known, is the Written Language Approach.

4.6   The Oral Approach

The general public aside, just who is it that the SL people have been struggling with for recognition over the years? Well, these have been the proponents of the teaching of speech, generally called the Oral Approach. The Oral Approach has a worthy aim, to teach the hearing-impaired to produce and understand speech so that they can communicate with the hearing community. Unfortunately, historically, its supporters, who controlled education in the schools, advocated the use of speech *to the exclusion of any other means of communication.* The use of SL was proscribed even for communication among deaf persons. While the Oral Approach advocates, such as Daniel Ling and the Ewings, may even admit that sign language is a language, they argue not only that the learning and use of sign language negatively affects the acquisition of speech but that without speech there will be defective thinking. (The teaching of reading and written language are attacked for similar reasons, which is why the teaching of reading in so many deaf schools was – and often still is – delayed until children are beyond the second or third grade.) These contentions, which have no basis in empirical observation or psycholinguistic theory, are false. If anything, knowledge of SL and reading *facilitate* the acquisition of speech. And, as far as thought is concerned, deaf people without speech are found to test nearly as highly in intelligence as hearing people. It is unfortunate that such erroneous ideas continue to be held in so many places.

The Oral Approach focuses on the teaching of speech production. Children from the the age of 2 or 3 years onwards are specially trained in the skill of articulating speech sounds. Also, it is not uncommon at present to have some computerized equipment that displays sounds and assists in the teaching. Many children do respond and do acquire a fair ability to speak. For the most part, however, these are children who have only a moderate hearing loss. Those with profound impairment typically do poorly.

The understanding of speech is usually fostered through both exploiting any residual hearing that learners may have and the teaching of 'speechreading', commonly known as 'lipreading.' With speechreading, an adept person can interpret about half of what is said, which, given the great amount of redundancy in ordinary speech, is enough to guess most of the content. Many sounds, however, are particularly difficult to differentiate visually; these include most vowels, e.g. 'a', 'e', 'u', 'i', and many consonants such as 'k', 'g', 'l', 'r', 's', 'sh', 'ch' and 'j.' In addition, in certain languages, such as Japanese, which exhibit relatively little lip and facial movement, the articulation of speech is especially difficult to deal with.

As was noted above, a great problem with the Oral Approach is that it tends only to work for a portion of the hearing-impaired population. Research shows, unsurprisingly, that the less people can hear, the less they will be able to produce and understand in terms of speech. Thus, relatively few children who are born with a severe or profound hearing loss (over 75 or 80 decibels in their better ear) acquire any significant degree of speech. Even those with a lesser hearing loss often do not acquire sufficiently clear pronunciation such that they are understood by ordinary hearing persons. As a result of a pure Oral Approach education, many hearing-impaired persons are not only unable to communicate with the hearing community but are unable to communicate adequately with their hearing-impaired colleagues. It was this tragic situation, one that continues in many places today, that convinced many educators of the deaf, that educational programmes should include sign language in their curriculum along with speech training. These programmes, which generally go by the name of Total Communication, spread in the 1970s in the US, Canada and other countries. While Total Communication is now widely accepted in many countries, nevertheless, there is still great resistance (as in Japan) to admitting sign language into the educational curriculum for the hearing-impaired.

4.7 The Written Language Approach

4.7.1 The importance of literacy and essentials of the approach

Although Total Communication has improved the lot of the deaf in a significant way by providing sign language in addition to speech training, one great educational problem remains, that of literacy. On the average, hearing-impaired persons, still (even after a Total Communication education) graduate from high school with a reading level equivalent only to that of a hearing child in Grade 5 of elementary school. (Their writing ability is poorer.) This is true for the US, Japan and other developed countries and is even lower in less-developed countries. The problem is that reading and writing are dependent on knowledge of ordinary speech-based languages; we use our knowledge of the grammar of the ordinary language both to understand what we read and to produce what we write. Since the hearing-impaired person's knowledge of speech-based language is usually quite limited, the ability of that person to acquire literacy based on that knowledge is similarly limited.

Given the overwhelming necessity of being able to read and write in order to function well in modern society, it is not surprising that we find that most hearing-impaired people are able to secure only low-level jobs, when they are able to secure jobs at all. A high level of literacy is essential if the hearing-impaired are to realize their potential. Towards this end, I believe that an approach, one that I call the Written Language Approach, can be of benefit.

The essential idea of this approach is that the meaningful written forms of an ordinary speech-based language such as English or Spanish (its words, phrases and sentences) are acquired through direct association with objects, events and situations in the environment. Thus, just as hearing children learn language by initially associating the speech sounds that they hear with environmental experiences, hearing-impaired children can learn language in a similar way, but through an association of written forms with environmental experiences. As a result, hearing-impaired children will acquire essentially the same vocabulary and syntax of the language of hearing children because, in the writing of a language such as English, Danish or Chinese, virtually all of the vocabulary and syntactic structures that appear in speech also appear in writing, e.g. subject–verb relations, object–verb relations, negation, question, relative clause formation, passives.

This is not to say that there are no differences in speech and writing. Essentially, though, one basic grammar underlies both forms of expression. And, because virtually any sentence or idea that can be expressed in speech can be expressed in writing, we can say, by analogy, that written language can be regarded as a complete language. Its main difference with speech concerns the physical means of transmission – writing involves light, while speech involves sound.

4.7.2   Historical perspective

Actually, the ideas which I propose here are by no means new. Further, they have a remarkable history although few in deaf education are aware of them. When I first conceived of these ideas, I truly believed they were original with me. It was only after successfully completing original research with American and Japanese deaf children using this approach, did I discover that a hundred years earlier, none other than Alexander Graham Bell had taught written language to a 5-year-old deaf boy with some success and that 200 years before him a thinker by the name of Dalgarno had, in 1680, formulated the same approach at Oxford! Bell was well aware of Dalgarno's conception, for, in 1883 Bell stated,

I believe that George Dalgarno . . . has given us the true principle to work upon when he asserts that a deaf person should be taught to read and write in as nearly as possible the same way that young ones are taught to speak and understand their mother tongue. We should talk to the deaf child just as we do to the hearing one, with the exception that words are to be addressed to his eye instead of his ear.

Perhaps Itard may have been aware of Dalgarno's ideas, for he, too, used a written language approach with the Wild Boy of Aveyron and was quite successful in that approach as compared to his efforts in using speech (Chapter 3).

Somehow in the 1970s the idea of the Written Language Approach began to sprout once again. It came to me and it came to Shigetada Suzuki, a deaf educator in Japan; I have heard rumours of some work in Europe but have not been able to verify these. Other than my work with English and Japanese, and Suzuki and his colleagues with Japanese, no other serious research as been done under this conception. In fact, to my knowledge (and dismay), it seems that no one even talks about these ideas.

4.7.3   Written language and reading distinguished

At this point it would be well to consider the distinction between written language and reading. The main difference is that written language is learned directly from the environment without the use of any prior linguistic medium, such as sign language or speech. Reading, by contrast, is learned through a linguistic medium. Thus, when we say that a hearing person has learned to read, we presume that that person already had language prior to learning to read. We furthermore presume that reading was taught through the medium of that language, i.e. speech. Typically we point to a written word and say it ('dog'). And, in reading a book we point to written words and say them ('The little dog ran to the girl'). The child interprets the written words by means of the vocabulary and syntax which the child has already learned in speech. This is the essence of reading.

However, suppose we consider a hearing-impaired child who does not know speech or sign, and we point to the written word 'dog'. That child will not be able to understand the meaning of this word. If, however, a picture of a dog is placed alongside the written word, then the child will have the opportunity of learning the meaning of the word. A child who learns language in this way can be said to have learned written language. The writing itself is the primary medium for language concepts. The child must discover the meaning of the written vocabulary items and then induce the syntactic relations that pertain to those items, just as hearing children do with speech.

Learning to read is a much easier process than learning to interpret written language, since, in learning to read one will not have to acquire the grammar of the language. The grammar is already known before the first reading lesson begins. To learn to read, one simply has to learn how visual written forms correspond to known speech sound forms. To learn written language, however, the vocabulary, morphology, syntax and other aspects of the grammar must all be acquired on the basis of the visual written forms and their relationship to meaningful objects, situations and events. The hearing-impaired child must undergo the same process of language learning that the hearing child did in acquiring language. Such a process can be expected to be more time-consuming than learning to read.

4.7.4   Assessment of the Written Language Approach

There are a number of distinct advantages to the Written Language Approach:

1.   *The learning medium is appropriate.* Perception of written items depends on vision, a medium in which the normal hearing-impaired have full capability.

2.   *Written language knowledge need not be acquired by the instructors.* Parents and teachers of the hearing-impaired do not have to learn the written language in order to teach it; they already know the writing system and how to use it. (Hearing parents who wish to acquire sign language which they can pass on to their children must spend years in learning it, just as they would any other second language.) Only relatively simple instructional methods and techniques need be acquired.

3.   *Instruction can begin early.* Parents of hearing-impaired children can teach their children written language at home during the children's most formative years. Children as young as 6 months can be exposed to written language in a natural way, and learn in the supportive comfort of their own home. Children of hearing parents need not have to wait for two or three years before their parents learn some sign language which can be passed on to them. Nor would children have to wait at home before they can be taken to school for what is necessarily a limited amount of sign language or speech instruction, given the number of hours that the child can spend in school.

4.   *All hearing-impaired children can benefit.* Effort devoted to teaching written language is never wasted since whatever is learned will improve the child's level of literacy in the future, whether the child learns speech or sign language.

5.   *Written language acquisition is compatible with other approaches.* Written language can be taught in conjunction with other approaches, with speech or sign language, without any detriment to the integrity of these approaches.

6. *Written language knowledge can facilitate speech.* In learning written language, the syntax and vocabulary that underlies the speech of an ordinary language are also learned. Acquisition of such knowledge will reduce the burden of oral speech instruction and facilitate the acquisition of speech.
7. *Written language can raise intellectuality.* Being able to interpret written language will allow the person access to books, magazines and a variety of other written materials, materials which are essential for personal intellectual growth and provide an entry to higher education.

While understanding written language presents no special obstacle to the young child, producing written language does. It is difficult for a young child to write. For, until a child reaches 4 years of age, or so, he or she does not have adequate neuromuscular control to be able to write, and to write for long periods. There is little the young child can do to communicate with others in writing, except to carry around an alphabet board or word cards (like those Itard made for Victor). Advancing technology, however, may provide a solution to this problem in the form of a laptop keyboard and display screen which a young child could carry around. There is no good reason not to make written language a part of every hearing-impaired child's education. Of course, the Written Language Approach cannot solve all of the communication problems of the hearing-impaired, but it can solve some important ones.

4.8   A parting note on deaf education

A number of different approaches to deaf education have been discussed, Sign Language, the Oral Approach, Total Communication, and the Written Language Approach. In my opinion, the hearing-impaired would benefit by the application of all of these approaches. While some approaches may be more beneficial than others, depending on the degree of hearing loss, it is a matter of justice that every hearing-impaired person should be given the opportunity to expand their linguistic skills through each and every one of them.

4.9   Discussion questions

1. Can there be language without sound or speech?
2. Why is a sign language, such as American Sign Language, a true language?
3. How do the gestures used by ordinary persons as they speak differ from sign language?
4. How does the gesture of 'beat' function in speech?
5. What are some characteristics of the American Sign Language system?
6. Do you think that Signing Exact English or Seeing Essential English should replace American Sign Language?
7. What do you think about the dispute in deaf education concerning the Oral Approach and the Sign Language method?
8. How does written language as a first language differ from reading?
9. Why do hearing-impaired people generally have low-level jobs? How may the Written Language Approach benefit the hearing-impaired in this regard?
10. Suppose your child were born deaf. What sort of language education would you want for your child?

Suggested readings

Anthony, D. (1971) *Seeing Essential English*. Anaheim, California: Educational Services Division, Anaheim Union High School District.

Bell, A. G. (1883) Upon a method of teaching language to a very young congenitally deaf child. *American Annals of the Deaf and Dumb*, **28**, 3, 124–39.

Conrad, R. (1979) *The Deaf School Child: Language and Cognitive Functions*. London: Harper & Row.

Dalgarno, G. (1971) *Didascalocophus, or the deaf and dumb man's tutor*. Menston: Scolar Press. (Originally published by Theater in Oxford, Oxford, 1680).

Ewing, A. and Ewing, E. C. (1964) *Teaching Deaf Children to Talk*. Manchester: Manchester University Press.

Furth, H. G. (1971) Linguistic deficiency and thinking: research with deaf subjects, 1964–1969. *Psychological Bulletin*, **76**, 58–72.

Garretson, M. D. (1976) Total communication. In R. Frisina

(ed.), *A Bicentennial Monograph on Hearing-Impairment Trends in the USA*. Washington, DC: A. G. Bell Associates.

Gustason, G., Pfetzing, D. and Zawolkow, E. (1975) *Signing Exact English*. Los Alamitos, CA: Modern Signs Press.

Kyle, J. G. and Woll, B. (1985) *Sign Language: The Study of Deaf People and Their Language*. Cambridge: Cambridge University Press.

Liddell, S. (1980) *American Sign Language Syntax*. The Hague: Mouton.

McNeill, D. (1987) *Psycholinguistics: A New Approach*. New York: Harper & Row.

Meadow, K. P. (1980) *Deafness and Child Development*. London: Arnold.

Moores, D. F. (1978) *Educating the Deaf: Psychology, Principles and Practice*. Boston: Houghton Mifflin.

Steinberg, D. D. (1984) Psycholinguistics: the writing system as a native language for the deaf. *Annual Review of Applied Linguistics*, **5**, 4, 36–45.

Steinberg, D. D. and Harper, H. (1983) Teaching written language as a first language to a deaf boy. In F. Coulmas and K. Ehlich (eds), *Writing in Focus*. The Hague: Mouton.

Suzuki, S. and Notoya, M. (1984) Teaching written language to deaf infants and preschoolers. *Topics in Language Disorders*, **3**, 10–16.

Journals

American Annals of the Deaf
Journal of Speech and Hearing Disorders
Sign Language Studies
Volta Review

PART 2

Language and mind

CHAPTER 5

Mental grammar

5.1 Grammar and psycholinguistics

5.1.1 How do speakers produce and understand sentences?

How do we produce and understand sentences? What role does a mental grammar, the grammar we have in our minds, have in such essential communicative processes? These questions lie at the heart of psycholinguistics and some understanding of them is essential, despite the high degree of complexity and abstractness which the subject matter presents.

In this regard linguists have long puzzled over what the main goal of linguistics should be. Is it to describe a language? Or, is it to describe what speakers know about a language? There is a distinction here, one that has important implications for psycholinguists.

5.1.2 Linguistics as psychology

In the first half of the twentieth century, linguists were divided on the issue. Some linguists, like Bloomfield, argued for the psychological validity of the descriptions they were writing. They held that what they wrote about was not only a description of language but it was also a description of what people had learned. Such theorists regarded themselves as dealing with a psychological product, human learning. Others, however, such as Twaddell, rejected such a goal for linguistics. They considered the description of language, not the psychological aspects of people, to be their goal. Further, theoretical entities like the phoneme were regarded simply as convenient fictions, useful for the notational purposes of description but nothing else. They denied that speakers learned or used such notions. Still other linguists, perhaps a majority, simply avoided the dispute altogether and kept on doing whatever it was that they were doing (making descriptions of various aspects of language) and leaving it to others to worry about the ultimate psychological nature of their formulations.

In the 1960s Chomsky came down heavily on the side of psychological linguistics. His thesis, that linguistics is a branch of cognitive psychology, has become so widely held that few linguists today oppose such a view. Even many of Chomsky's staunchest linguistic critics are in accord on the goal of linguistics as involving the description of knowledge that people have about language.

5.2   Chomsky's competence and performance distinction

In addition to using the term 'grammar' to indicate a certain kind of language knowledge, Chomsky uses the term *competence* with this same sense. Competence is the knowledge that people have of the grammar of their language and, as such, it is the goal of linguistics to describe this competence. A linguist will be successful to the extent that his or her formulations are true descriptions of the knowledge that is in people's minds.

Now, if the specification of competence is the primary goal of linguistics, what then should be the goal of psycholinguistics? In Chomsky's view, psycholinguistics has two major goals: (1) to specify how people use competence so that they are able to produce and understand sentences; and (2) to specify how people acquire competence (grammatical knowledge). It is the first of these goals, the use of a grammar for the production and understanding of sentences, that will be of concern to us here. The second is considered in other chapters of this book.

For Chomsky, the activities involved in producing and understanding sentences are *performance* processes. Competence (mental grammar) is just one part, albeit an essential part, of these two crucial performance functions. A theory of performance should explain sentence production, i.e. how speakers take ideas and make them into sentences which are rendered into speech sounds. A theory of performance also should explain sentence comprehension, i.e. how speakers, on receiving speech sounds, recover ideas from those sounds. In both of these performance processes, according to Chomsky, one grammar, i.e. competence, is used.

The relationship of competence to performance for Chomsky, therefore, is that of part to whole, with *competence* being a part or component of the whole, which is, *performance*. Competence is the knowledge that persons have of their grammar while performance involves knowledge for using competence so that the processes of sentence production and understanding can be realized.

5.3   Chomsky's grammatical conceptions

Before continuing with a discussion of mental grammar and performance, which will be presented in the next chapter, it is first necessary to consider various conceptions of mental grammar. In this regard, consideration of the ideas of Chomsky, who is the world's foremost grammatical theorist, is of the highest priority.

In 1957 Chomsky came out with his book, *Syntactic Structures* – a remarkable book that revolutionized linguistics and influenced a number of the social sciences, especially psychology and anthropology. With his notion of a *system of rules*, phenomena which hitherto could not be explained could now be dealt with. In particular, Chomsky demonstrated how such a system could be used to explain how speakers can, in principle, produce and understand an infinite number of grammatical sentences. (The first chapter of my 1982 psycholinguistics book provides a description of Chomsky's brilliant and powerful ideas.)

Since the advent of Chomsky, linguistics (and psycholinguistics) has never been the same. Over 35 years later, we find Chomsky still leading the field. With the help of able supporters he continues to solidify his revolution with new and challenging ideas. On the average, Chomsky shakes up his followers once per decade. Following Syntactic Structures' grammar in the 1950s, there was the Aspects' (Standard Theory) grammar in the 1960s. Then there was the Extended Standard Theory grammar in the 1970s followed by the Government/Binding grammar in the 1980s. Now, in the 1990s, once again we hear rumblings, with Chomsky proposing to abandon D-structure, that deep level of structure the name of which has become familiar even to many outside of linguistics.

Still, despite far-reaching changes in the details of his grammars, Chomsky has continued to maintain one fundamental notion, which is that the syntax of the grammar is primary, with meaning (and sound) being secondary. (Abandonment of D-structure, as Chomsky now suggests, in no way implies that syntax would not continue to be primary.) This is to say that the meaning of a sentence is specified as a function of its syntactic form, and not vice versa. This relationship, which Chomsky claims to be innate and universal, is shown in Figure 5.1. This idea of how a grammar is to be organized, however, has the effect, as shall be argued later in this and the following chapter, of rendering Chomsky's essential grammatical theorizing as psychologically invalid. By his own criterion, the linguist's grammar must be psychologically valid.

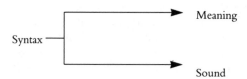

Figure 5.1   Relationship of syntax, meaning and sound

5.3.1   The Standard Theory

It was in 1965 that Chomsky proposed, in his *Aspects of the Theory of Syntax*, the theory of grammar that became known as the Standard Theory (ST). While this version has been greatly revised by later formulations resulting in his Government/Binding (GB) theory, it is useful to get some understanding of the Standard Theory before dealing with GB.

The ST grammar essentially consists of various sets of

rules: syntactic, semantic and phonological. Each set of rules is systematically integrated and serves to provide, for every sentence, a linguistic description or representation at four different levels. There is a sound level (Phonetic Interpretation) where the phonetic sound pattern of a sentence is represented; there is a meaning level (Semantic Interpretation) where the meaning and logical relations in a sentence are represented; and, there are two syntactic levels (Deep Structure and Surface Structure) where various syntactic aspects of a sentence are represented. Deep Structure represents the underlying syntactic form of the sentence while Surface Structure represents its more overt form.

A schema of the Standard Theory grammar is shown in Figure 5.2. This grammar, while incorporating ideas from his earlier Syntactic Structures' grammar, is much more complex and comprehensive. In the schema we see that the grammar consists of various components – the syntactic, semantic and phonological – and a lexicon or vocabulary repository which consists of morphemes and idioms. The syntactic component consists of two types of syntactic rules, Phrase Structure rules (also known as Base rules) and Transformational rules. Each of these sets of syntactic rules is responsible for an output: the Phrase Structure rules provide Deep Structure while the Transformational rules, operating on Deep Structure, provide Surface Structure. The phonological component consists of Phonological rules which operate on the Surface Structure to provide the Phonetic Interpretation of a sentence. The semantic component consists of Semantic rules which operate on the same Surface Structure to provide the Semantic Interpretation of a sentence.

Let us now look at the contents of the various components of the grammar and see how they function to generate representations.

Phrase Structure rules, Lexicon and Deep Structure

The Phrase Structure (PS) rules provide the basic constituent structure of a sentence. Essentially, they provide an analysis of a sentence into its underlying phrases which are further analysed into words and word parts. These words and word parts (morphemes) and idioms are stored in the

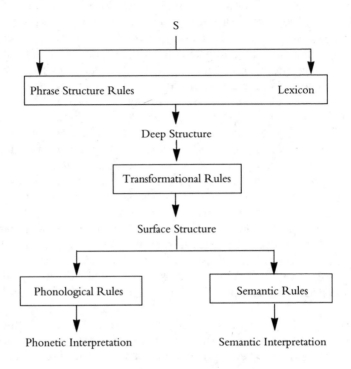

Figure 5.2 Chomsky's standard theory grammar

Lexicon. Such entries provide the vocabulary for the Deep and Surface Structures.

Consider, for example, the sentence 'The boy bought candy at the store'. This sentence is composed of the basic PS rule of S → NP + VP, where NP (the boy) and VP (bought candy at the store) are composed of the rules NP → D + N (D is a determiner such as 'the' and 'this') and VP → V + NP + PrepP, and where the prepositional phrase (PrepP) is composed of a preposition and a NP, PrepP → Prep + NP (at the store). The words 'the', 'boy', 'bought', 'candy', 'at', 'the' and 'store' are provided by the Lexicon. The Deep Structure of the sentence thus consists of certain specified PS rules along with certain words. Figure 5.3

RULE FORM

Given: S

S ⟶ NP + VP

NP ⟶ D + N

VP ⟶ V + NP + Prep P

NP ⟶ N

Prep P ⟶ Prep + NP

NP ⟶ D + N

Lexical Insertion

TREE FORM

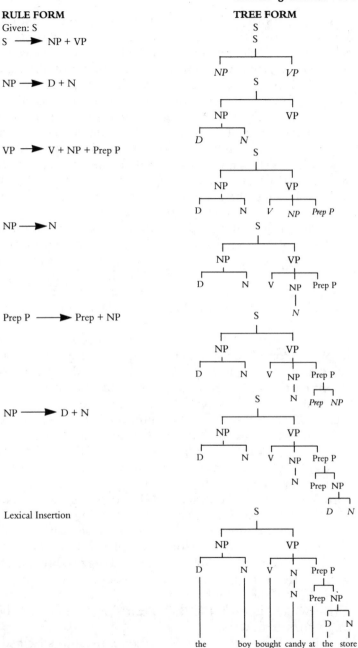

Figure 5.3 Derivation of the Deep Structure of 'The boy bought candy at the store'

shows the PS rules in terms of their successive application. Equivalent tree structure forms are shown alongside. The final structure, the one in which the lexical items have been inserted, is Deep Structure and it is shown at the end.

Thus the Deep Structure of the sentence 'The boy bought candy at the store' is generated through the application of the rules. S is the given starting point since it is from this letter (it is vacuous and has no content) that the appropriate first rule of S → NP + VP is determined. The various rules shown in Figure 5.3 define the phrase structure of that particular sentence. With the insertion of lexical items following the application of these PS rules, the Deep Structure is defined as the result.

The history of a sentence, from the elemental S and S → NP + VP structures through various intermediate structures to the final Deep Structure, is called a derivation. This, however, is only part of the derivation of a sentence. A complete derivation will be obtained only after relevant Transformational, Phonological and Semantic rules have been applied, as well.

The PS rules which have presented above are but parts of more complex rules. Thus, for example, in order to account for the subject NP in a sentence like '**The girl who dropped the spoon** laughed', where the sentential clause of 'who dropped the spoon' modifies the NP 'the girl', a structure like NP → NP + S is proposed. All of the various NP realizations that have been heretofore mentioned may be summarized in the formulations: NP → NP + (S) and NP → (D) + N, where parentheses indicate that the enclosed item is optional, i.e. it may or may not occur. These formulations describe different NP structures such as N, D + N and NP + S.

It is important to note that rules may be reapplied. This allows for the generation of a complex NP structure like that (emboldened) in the sentence, '**Dogs which attack girls who sell flowers** like cookies', where the NP consisting of the N 'dogs' is modified by the S 'which attack girls', which, in turn, the NP of 'girls' is modified by the S of 'who sell flowers.'

The VP rule, too, like the NP rule, must be specified so as to account for all VP structures which appear in sentences. Consequently, VP structures in sentences like

'John **ran**' (V), 'John **ate the hamburger**' (V + NP), 'John **went to school**' (V + PrepP), 'John **was happy**' (V + Adj) and 'John **believes the world is round**' (V + S), along with many others, must be incorporated into the rule.

Because rules may be reapplied (the important 'recursive' property of Chomsky's system), the Phrase Structure rules together with the Lexicon can generate an infinite number of Deep Structures which are not limited in length. That some of these may be so long or complex that they would never be realized in actual speech is beside the point. The main consideration is that the system has an infinite potential, just as speakers have an infinite potential, even though that potential is never realized.

Transformational rules and Surface Structure

In Chomsky's system, Deep Structure is but one of two levels of syntactic representation of a sentence. There is a second structure, Surface Structure, and this one is the *outcome* of Transformational rules operating on the Deep Structure. Consider a sentence like 'Open the door.' On the surface, this sentence consists of a single VP. Here VP → V + NP, then NP → D + N, where V → 'open', D → 'the' and N → 'door'. However, underlying that Surface Structure of VP is the Deep Structure of S → NP + VP, where there *is* a subject NP. That NP consists of N, and N → 'you' (the understood addressee). Figure 5.4 shows the Deep and Surface Structures for the sentence 'Open the door'.

From the point of view of the PS rules, the Surface Structure of a simple VP for a sentence like 'Open the door' is malformed. For, there is no PS rule where S → VP. On the other hand, the original Deep Structure of that sentence *is* well formed, conforming as it does to the S → NP + VP rule. In Chomsky's Standard Theory grammar only Deep Structures need conform to PS rules. (In the current GB framework, under 'Projection Principle', surface S-structures as well as deep D-structures must conform to requirements imposed by the PS rules.)

How, then, do these Surface Structures come about? Well, they are the result of the application of Transformation rules – rules which delete, add and move material – and

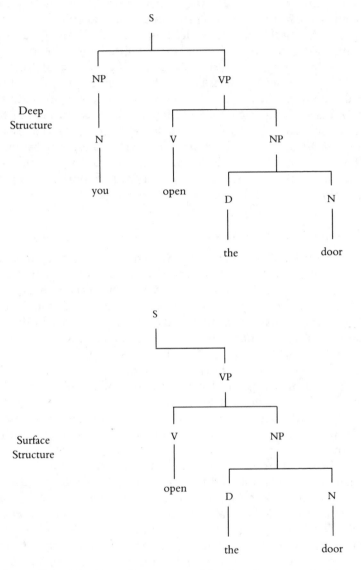

Figure 5.4 The Deep Structure and Surface Structure for 'Open the door'

which have been applied to the Deep Structure. Deep Structures are transformed into Surface Structures by means of Transformation (T) rules. Consider in this regard a sentence like 'John bought a coat at the store and so did Mary'. Here we have two sentences in a conjoined structure, S_1 + CONJ + S_2, where the S_1 of 'John bought a coat at the store' conforms to PS rules, but the S_2 of 'so did Mary' does not. The Surface Structure of S_2 ('so did Mary') is quite different from its underlying Deep Structure, which would be 'Mary bought a coat at the store'. Virtually that same Deep Structure can also be said to underlie such sentences as 'John bought a coat at the store and Mary bought a coat at the store, too' and 'John bought a coat at the store and Mary did, too'. Thus, T rules, when applied to Deep Structures, can provide different Surface Structure outcomes. (In Chomsky's later theorizing, T rules are said to leave some 'trace' or marker in the S-structure after application so as to ensure that the proper meaning can be recovered.)

Phonological rules and Phonetic Interpretation

Given the Surface Structure that has been generated, it is then up to the rules of the phonological component to interpret that structure so that it is rendered into a sequence of sound symbols; that product is called the Phonetic Interpretation of the sentence.

The Surface Structure, it should be noted, contains lexical items which are specified in something like the features of phonemes. Thus, although the words of sentences in the text above and in the figures have been written in conventional orthography, as in 'Open the door', that was done only for convenience. They really should have been written in their underlying phonological forms, forms which, along with the syntactic information in the Surface Structure, allow for conversion to phonetic symbols.

Consider a sentence like 'Mares eat oats'. In that structure, lexical items are presented in phonological form, i.e. /merz/, /it/ and /ots/. It is the function of the Phonological rules to change the Surface Structure into a Phonetic Interpretation, which is a sequence of wholly phonetic symbols that, in effect, represents the pronunciation of the sentence. Thus, when spoken at a natural speed, 'Mares eat oats' would sound like [merziydowts]. By the

Phonological rule, the /i/ gets a 'y' glide, the /o/ gets a 'w' glide, the /t/ of 'eat' changes to /d/ because there is a tendency in English for an unvoiced consonant like /t/ to become voiced (/t/ changes to /d/) when it occurs between two vowels (/t/ is preceded by the vowel /i/ of 'eat' and followed by the vowel /o/ of 'oats').

Also, based on the syntactic aspects of the sentence, the sentence would be assigned a stress pattern. For a declarative such as 'Mares eat oats', the primary stress would fall on [mer], with the next degree of stress falling on the [dow]. The weakest stress would fall on [ziy]. The tendency to form syllables of the Consonant + Vowel form is what sets a phonological rule to take the final consonant /z/ (of /merz/) and place it in front of the /i/ (of /it/) to form /zi/. The syllable /do/ is formed in the same way, with the /d/ (the /t/ at the end of /it/ is voiced) being placed in front of /o/ (of /ots/). Thus, the (almost) complete Phonetic Interpretation would be [mer^{1}ziy^{3}dow^{2}ts], where the numbers indicate the degree of stress on the preceding syllable.

Pitch, too, plays a role in the intonation pattern of a sentence. A question would get a different pattern than would a declarative or an imperative. This is also something the phonological component must deal with in converting Surface Structures to their appropriate Phonetic Interpretations.

Semantic rules and Semantic Interpretation

Given the Surface Structure that has been generated, then it is up to the rules of the Semantic Component to interpret that structure into meaning elements and logical relations.

Consider a sentence like 'The shoe hurts'. The Surface Structure for this sentence is relatively simple, as is the Deep Structure which is virtually the same: there is the subject NP ('the shoe') and the VP consisting of a V ('hurts'). While syntactically simple, such a sentence is quite complex semantically. What we understand is that something about the shoe is causing pain to someone. There is an implied cause–effect relationship here between two semantic propositions – Proposition 1: the shoe is in some predicate condition (unspecified), e.g. the shoe may be tight; and Proposition 2: Some living creature (unspecified) is in pain. A simple proposition is composed of a predicate and one or more arguments. For example, 'The boy ran' (with one predicate 'run' and with one argument 'boy') and 'The girl hit the ball' (with one predicate 'hit' and with two arguments 'girl' and 'ball'). Two propositions, however, may be brought together with a predicate ('cause' in this case) to form a more complex proposition. In our example, the two simpler propositions are brought together in a cause–effect relationship, where the first proposition is the cause while the second proposition is the effect. Figure 5.5 outlines the semantic propositional structure of the example sentence.

In language, arguments (representing entities, objects) tend to be realized as nouns and NPs, while logical predicates (representing states, conditions, relations) tend to be realized as verbs and adjectives. The argument and the predicate serve as the elemental constituents of a proposition or complete thought.

Returning to Chomsky's ST grammar, it is the Semantic rules which take a Surface Structure as input, so as to provide the Semantic Interpretation of a sentence in something like its propositional form. In this regard, it is important to note that Deep Structure, despite its somewhat misleading 'Deep' name, does *not* represent the meaning of a sentence. It is Semantic Interpretation that provides that specification. Deep Structure is a syntactic representation.

5.3.2 The Government/Binding (GB) theory of grammar

GB theory was first synthesized in Chomsky's *Lectures on Government and Binding* in 1981 and then developed in more detail in other publications in the 1980s. Figure 5.6 presents a schema of that grammar. Although much more complex and extensive than his previous grammars and although the terminology has changed to signal certain modifications (D-structure for Deep Structure, S-structure for Surface Structure, Logical Form for Semantic Interpretation or Representation, and, Phonetic Form for Phonetic Interpretation or Representation) the underlying relationship of

Deep and Surface Structure

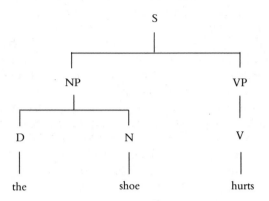

Semantic Interpretation

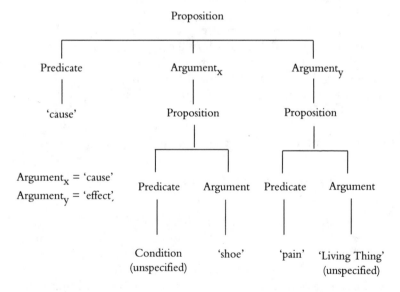

Figure 5.5 Semantic propositional structure of 'The shoe hurts'

syntax, meaning and sound remains the same: only syntax is generative. This is the case even though GB grammar involves a continuous interaction among components and sub-theories embodying different principles and parameters. D-structure requires a description of the Phrase Structure and this is achieved by the X-bar syntax, an elaboration of earlier Phrase Structure syntax. This syntax also integrates the Lexicon with syntax being concerned, as it is, with the characteristics of lexical categories (Noun, Verb, Preposition, etc.) and the properties of the lexical items of which it is composed; this, for example, specifies that the verb 'want' must be followed by an object NP but 'elapse' does not.

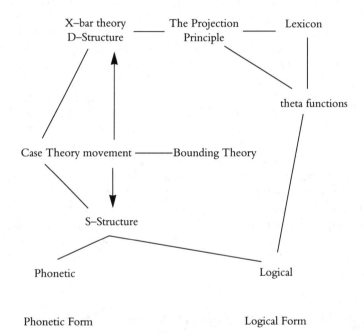

Figure 5.6 A schema of Chomsky's GB grammar

The Projection Principle, which projects the characteristics of lexical entries onto the syntax, connects D-structure to S-structure and connects the Lexicon to Logical Form (LF) by specifying the possible contexts in which a particular lexical item can occur.

The functional relationship between the parts of a sentence is specified in GB through theta roles (similar to Fillmore's semantic cases). Thus, in a sentence such as 'The boy gave the teacher an apple', there are three theta roles:

'the boy' refers to the initiator or agent of the action; 'an apple' refers to that thing that is affected by the action; and 'the teacher' refers to the entity receiving the thing. Theta roles, which involve semantic relations, are distinguished from cases which are structural, e.g. in 'He drives a jeep', 'he' is in the Nominative case. One principal function of government, in Chomsky's theory, is to ensure that a word is assigned the proper case. Thus, in the sentence 'The dog bit him', the verb governs the NP which follows it so that 'him' rather than 'he' is selected. How the nouns in such a sentence are related to each other and whether they refer to the same entities or other expressions is the function of Binding Theory. Thus, while in the sentence 'him' does not relate to the antecedent pronoun, a word like 'himself' ('The dog bit himself') would.

The relationship between D-structure and S-structure is restricted in terms of what can be moved, where it can be moved from, where it can be moved to, and how far it can be moved (the distance is limited by Bounding Theory). One great problem that Chomsky had with his earlier transformationally oriented syntax was that there were insufficient restrictions on the positing of transformations. Transformations had become so powerful and readily available for the writing that their explanatory value was seriously reduced. GB theory has attempted to remedy such a deficiency by specifying parameters and restricting movement.

5.4 Linguistic challenges to Chomsky's grammar

Challenges to Chomsky's grammar have mainly stemmed from two sources: (1) disagreement with the organization of his grammar where syntax is given a primary role over semantics; and (2) disagreement with the adequacy of his structural characterization of such basic syntactic relations and constituents, particularly Subject, Direct Object, Indirect Object and Verb Phrase. The first source has given rise to such grammars as Generative Semantics Grammar (George Lakoff, Ross, McCawley) Semantic Case Grammar (Fillmore), Cognitive Grammar (Langacker) and Montague Grammar (Montague, Partee, Peters) while the second has led to grammars such as Relational Grammar (Perlmutter, Postal, Johnson) and Lexical Functional Grammar (Bresnan). Given space limitations, I will deal only with the first of these source categories. Besides, I believe this category holds the most promise for psycholinguistics.

5.4.1 Meaning-based grammars

In his description of grammar, you will recall, Chomsky begins neither with the meaning of the sentence nor with its sound pattern. Rather, he begins with the specification of syntax, a syntax which functions independently ('autonomously') with the meaning and sound forms of the sentence being the output of that syntax. In Chomsky's terms, only syntax is 'generative'. Semantics and phonetics play secondary roles, functioning only to interpret the syntactic structure which is provided as input.

Chomsky's notion of an autonomous syntax was strongly attacked in the 1970s by a group of linguists calling themselves Generative Semanticists. They regarded meaning or semantics as the basis for grammatical theorizing. It was the logical semantic representation of a sentence (like Chomky's Semantic Interpretation and Logical Form) that was to serve as the conceptual starting point for their grammars. Syntax was given a secondary role. The role of syntax (and the Lexicon) was to provide the proper Surface Structure (like Chomsky's S-structure but without traces) of a sentence. This was accomplished through the use of one type of syntactic rule, the Transformation rule. When the Surface Structure had been formed by these rules, then Phonological rules would be applied to provide the Phonetic Representation (like Chomsky's Phonetic Interpretation or Form). A schema of this conception of grammar is shown in Figure 5.7.

This schema differs in a number of important characteristics from Chomsky's conception of grammar. Firstly, semantics is given the primary role. Syntax is given only a secondary role, which is to provide a realization of the semantic representation. Then there is only one type of syntactic rule, the Transformational; there are no Phrase Structure rules. Accordingly, there is only one level of

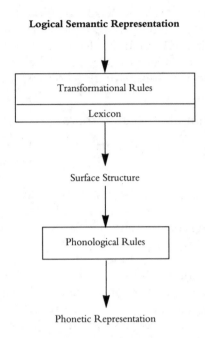

Logical Semantic Representation

Transformational Rules

Lexicon

Surface Structure

Phonological Rules

Phonetic Representation

Figure 5.7 Generative semantics grammar

syntactic representation, Surface Structure; there is no Deep or D-structure.

Thus, for example, given the Logical Semantic Representation of the sentence 'The shoe hurts' with its complex propositional structure of arguments and predicates, Transformation rules with the Lexicon would apply to provide the Surface syntactic form of NP ('the shoe') + V ('hurts'). A Transformation rule places the NP of 'the shoe' in the subject position and another Transformation rule selects 'hurt' from the Lexicon based on the underlying meaning of 'cause pain'. Phonological rules would then convert the Surface Structure to the appropriate Phonetic Representation.

Such a derivational process captured the imagination of many linguists and psycholinguistics in the 1970s. For linguists, meaning was given its rightful predominant position. For psycholinguists, here was the outline of a true psychological process, that of production, where from meaning one proceeds to sound. In contradistinction to

Chomsky's peculiar arrangement, here the components of meaning, sound and syntax were arranged in a psychologically advantageous fashion.

By 1980, however, most of the original proponents of Generative Semantics grammar had abandoned the theory. Why this happened is not so much due perhaps to shortcomings of the theory itself as it was to a lack of perseverance on the part of its proponents in developing it to meet ever-arising problems. Certainly, Chomsky's peculiar grammatical framework was less promising. Yet, Chomsky has prevailed. One factor contributing to Chomsky's success has been the tenacity with which he holds to his principles. He continually works at dealing with problems within his own framework so that his grammatical theory is always evolving. Thus, when, for example, semantics was recognized as lacking in his Syntactic Structures' theory, Chomsky did not hesitate to incorporate Katz' semantic ideas into the semantic component for his Standard Theory. Nor did he refuse Fillmore's ideas of semantic case grammar for his theta conceptions in GB theory. It is unfortunate that Generative Semanticists did not make a comparable effort to deal with problems within their paradigm. (See Newmeyer, 1986, for a readable discussion of other Generative Semantics problems.)

In any case, Generative Semantics has disappeared from the linguistic scene. However, in the 1980s two new meaning-based grammars rose from its ashes, Cognitive Grammar (Langacker, George Lakoff) and Functional Grammar (Dik, Connolly), both of which are creative developments derived from the Generative Semantics model. The future may well lie with such meaning-based grammars. For, as Langacker (1991, p. 275) puts it,

. . . it is ultimately as pointless to analyze grammatical units without reference to their semantic value [as in Chomsky's 'autonomous syntax'] as to write a dictionary which omits the meanings of lexical items.

5.5 Discussion questions

1. What is a mental grammar?
2. Why is a mental grammar important for psycholinguistics?

3. What is competence, according to Chomsky? Is it Universal Grammar?
4. What is performance, according to Chomsky?
5. Suggest Deep Structures in tree structure form for the following sentences:
    (a) Bob chased the man.
    (b) The man who discovered the robbers called the police.
    (c) The police arrested the man who stole the car at the theatre.
    (d) Be honest.
    (e) Gene sang then danced.
    (f) For sentence (c) give a second Deep Structure. (In one interpretation of the sentence, the police did the arresting at the theatre. In the other interpretation, the car was stolen at the theatre.)
6. Give a phonetic representation of the sentence: Lambs eat ivy.
7. Suggest semantic representations for:
    (a) The collar pinches.
    (b) The dog frightened John. (*Hint:* The verb 'frighten' can be analysed as 'cause to be afraid'.)
8. In what way do Phrase Structure rules differ from Transformation rules or movement?
9. What does 'autonomous syntax' mean?
10. In what ways does a meaning-based grammar like Generative Semantics grammar differ from Chomsky's grammar?
11. Why have many linguists and psycholinguists found meaning-based grammar more appealing psychologically than Chomsky's syntax-based grammar?

Suggested readings

Aissen, J. L. (1991) Relational grammar. In Droste and Joseph (1991), pp. 63–102.

Bresnan, J. (1978) A realistic transformational grammar. In M. Halle and J. Bresnan (eds), *Linguistic Theory and Psychological Reality*. Cambridge, Mass.: MIT Press, pp. 1–59.

Chomsky, N. (1981) *Lectures on Government and Binding*. Dordrecht, Holland: Foris Publications.

Chomsky, N. (1986) *Knowledge of Language: Its Nature, Origin and Use*. New York: Praeger.

Cook, Vivian James (1988) *Chomsky's Universal Grammar: An Introduction*. Oxford: Basil Blackwell.

Dik, S. C. (1991) In Droste and Joseph (1991), pp. 247–74.

Droste, F. G. and Joseph, J. E. (eds) (1991) *Linguistic Theory and Grammatical Description*. Amsterdam: John Benjamins.

Fillmore, C. (1977) The case for case reopened. In P. Cole and J. Saddock (eds), *Syntax and Semantics: Grammatical Relations*. New York: Academic Press, pp. 59–81.

Horrocks, G. (1987) *Generative Grammar*. London: Longman.

Lakoff, G. (1971) On generative semantics. In D. D. Steinberg and L. A. Jakobovits (eds), *Semantics: An Interdisciplinary Reader in Philosophy, Linguistics and Psychology*. New York: Cambridge University Press, pp. 232–96.

Langacker, R. (1987) *Foundations of Cognitive Grammar*. Stanford, CA: Stanford University Press.

Newmeyer, F. J. (1986) *Linguistic Theory in America* (2nd edn). New York: Academic Press.

CHAPTER 6

Sentence processing and psychological reality

6.1 Meaning, sound and syntax relations in Chomsky's grammar

While over the past decades, Chomsky's theory of grammar has developed into one of increasing complexity and abstractness, at the same time certain essentials have not changed. The fundamental conception, as to how the three basic components of the grammar – meaning, sound, and syntax – are related to one another, remains the same. A schema of this relationship, as was discussed in the previous chapter, is shown in Figure 6.1.

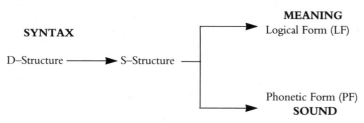

Figure 6.1 Chomsky's sound, meaning and syntax relations

Chomsky claims that the organization of his grammar is designed so as to account for the relationship of sound to meaning through the medium of syntax. What is striking here, though, is the way Chomsky relates sound and meaning. Chomsky does not begin with the meaning of the sentence nor the sound pattern of the sentence; he begins with the syntax of the sentence. In fact, he starts with the letter S, which, although one might be tempted to interpret it as meaning 'sentence', actually has no significance in Chomsky's scheme. The structures that represent the sound or Phonetic Form (PF) and the meaning or Logical Form (LF) of a sentence are first generated from the syntax, which is activated by the vacuous S. ('Generate' is used here by Chomsky in an idiosyncratic way to mean 'define' and not 'produce'.) The meaning of the sentence does not determine syntax nor does the sound pattern of the sentence determine syntax. Rather, syntax functions independently ('autonomously') of meaning and sound. The meaning and sound pattern of a sentence is defined by the function of syntax. In this conception, only syntax is 'generative'. (An outline of Chomsky's grammar can be found in Chapter 5.)

6.2 Why Chomsky's grammar is not a performance model

Given how meaning, sound and syntax are related in Chomsky's grammar, it will become clear why that grammar could not possibly be a model of speaker performance either for the production or for the understanding of sentences. Let us first consider what the true process of speaker *production* must involve. Such a process must begin with the ideas of what a person wants to express, and, it must end with speech sounds. A speaker has some ideas he or she wishes to express and then uses speech sounds to try to communicate those ideas. In Chomsky's terminology, this process would begin with something like Logical Form (LF) and end with the Phonetic Form (PF).

For speaker *understanding* the true process would involve a reverse ordering. First we hear the speech sounds that someone utters and from those sounds we recover the meaning they represent. In Chomsky's terminology, the process would begin with the PF and end with the LF.

The essence of the production and understanding performance processes are as shown below. (The question mark (?) along with syntax is merely to indicate that other, unspecified, components are included.) The order in Chomsky's grammar is also presented for comparison purposes.

Sentence production performance order
Meaning (LF) → [**Syntax** + **?**] → **Sound** (PF)

Sentence understanding performance order
Sound (PF) → [**Syntax** + **?**] → **Meaning** (LF)

Chomsky grammar order

Syntax $\begin{array}{l} \rightarrow \textbf{Sound} \ (\text{PF}) \\ \rightarrow \textbf{Meaning} \ (\text{LF}) \end{array}$

From this, it is clear that Chomsky's grammar could not be used directly as either a model of production or of understanding. Chomsky is aware of this and has long cautioned readers not to interpret his grammar as a kind of performance process. As Chomsky (1967; pp. 435–6) says:

It would be tempting but quite absurd, to regard it [the grammar] as a model of performance as well. Thus, we might propose that to produce a sentence, the speaker goes through the successive steps of constructing a base-derivation [D-structure] line by line from the initial symbol S, then inserting lexical items and applying transformations to form a surface structure, and finally applying the phonological rules in their given order. . . . There is not the slightest justification for any such assumption. In fact, in implying that the speaker selects the general properties of sentence structure before selecting lexical items (before deciding what he is going to talk about), such a proposal seems not only without justification but entirely counter to whatever vague intuitions one may have about the processes that underlie production.

Neither meaning nor sound is a starting point. Rather, meaning and sound are the products of syntax; they are not related to one another in any direct way.

Now, if Chomsky's grammar is not itself a performance process, then in what sense is it relevant to the production and understanding of sentences? Obviously Chomsky considers it relevant, otherwise he would not claim, as he does, that a mental grammar exists in people's minds. He is quite emphatic in this regard, having stated:

Hence, in the technical sense, linguistic theory is mentalistic, since it is concerned with discovering a mental reality underlying actual behavior.

(Chomsky, 1965, p. 4)

The linguist's grammar is a scientific theory, correct insofar as it corresponds to the internally represented grammar.

(Chomsky, 1980, p. 220)

Obviously every speaker of a language has mastered and internalized a generative grammar that expresses his knowledge of his language.

(Chomsky, 1965, p. 8)

In order to support his claim that his grammar is psychologically real, even though it is neither a model of production nor of understanding, Chomsky has made it an essential part of the performance process. He asserts that his grammar will be used in both the processes of sentence production and understanding. In this regard, the speaker must develop some sort of use rules, heuristics, or strategies so that the grammar can be used for such performance processes. The sort of model that Chomsky has in mind is discussed in the following section.

6.3 Types of performance models

Essentially, two basic performance conceptions are possible. The first conception takes what I call a *Resource Grammar* approach. (Formerly I have referred to this as a 'componential' model.) Here, the grammar is used as a sort of resource in order that a speaker may engage in the process of producing or understanding sentences. So that the knowledge embodied in the grammar can be tapped, certain strategies or heuristics are necessary. This approach is the one that Chomsky advocates.

The second conception takes, what I call, a *Process Grammar* approach. Here, a grammar (or grammars) is itself a process in the production or understanding of sentences. For example, since semantic-based grammars like Functional Grammar and Generative Semantics Grammar follow the Performance Production Order (shown above), such grammars could themselves be regarded as a performance model of sentence production. Grammar is itself a process.

6.3.1 Chomsky's resource grammar performance model

To understand Chomsky's conception, an analogy might be helpful here. Consider the solving of arithmetic problems such as multiplication and division. Essential to the solving of such problems is the multiplication table, a table which includes all products and combinations, e.g. a 10×10 table, where $1 \times 1 = 1$, $1 \times 2 = 2$, and so on to $10 \times 10 = 100$.

Such a table by itself, however, will not solve a problem like 468 × 32 = _ _?_ _.

In order to solve this problem (by hand or mentally), we must know what digits are to be multiplied together and in what order, and we must know what numbers to record and which to hold in storage. Thus, we start with 2 × 8 (the rightmost digits of each of the two numbers) and follow this with 2 × 6 (moving one digit leftward on the longest number). How much is 2 × 8 and 2 × 6? Well, for these answers we dip into our memorized multiplication table where we find that 2 × 8 = 16, and 2 × 6 = 12. For the product of 16, we record the 6 and hold the 1 in storage. We use storage when the product consists of more than one digit. And so the process continues. We use resource knowledge, the multiplication table, and we use rules that enable us to access that knowledge. Thus, we may say that two types of knowledge are involved here, the multiplication table and a set of rules that uses that table for the purpose of solving multiplication problems.

The multiplication table is also an indispensable resource that we use when we want to do division, as in a problem like 483/9. Here, we must apply a different set of *use* rules than those we apply for multiplication. For example, in solving this division problem (according to one method), we first take the leftmost digit of the number to be divided (4), and see if it is equal to or less than the number we are dividing by (9). Since 4 is less than 9, then we go on to the next digit to the right (8). We then divide 48 by 9. In order to carry out this division, however, we must use the multiplication table. There we search for a product where 9 times something is either equal to or less than 48, and select 9 × 5 = 45 (we reject 9 × 6 = 54 because it is more than 48). We record the 5, subtract 45 from 48, and continue on with the application of various rules until we arrive at an answer.

A model of arithmetic performance based on this discussion is shown in Figure 6.2. There we see that the multiplication table is used as a resource for the solving of multiplication and division problems. There is one set of Use rules for performance process of multiplication and another set for the performance process of division.

Chomsky's view of the role of a grammar with respect

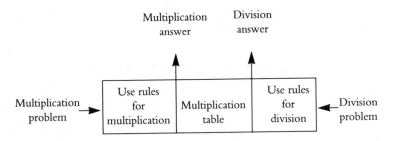

Figure 6.2 A resource model of arithmetic performance

to the production and understanding of sentences is like that of the multiplication table. One grammar serves as a resource for performance. Since there are two performance processes to be explained, two sets of Use rules are required: one set for production, the other for understanding. The schema shown in Figure 6.3 represents Chomsky's conception of a language performance model.

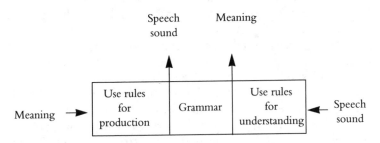

Figure 6.3 Chomsky's resource grammar performance model

Essentially, production performance involves meaning or ideas as input, and speech as output, while understanding involves speech as input and meaning as output. When given input, one of the sets of Use rules will interact with the grammar to provide an output.

Just what these Use rules might be has not been Chomsky's concern. That burden is one that he has assigned psycholinguists, an assignment based on a division of labour that he himself established. According to that division, it is for the linguist to describe grammar while it is for the psycholinguist to describe how that grammar is to be used in performance. Many psycholinguists, particularly in the early revolutionary days of Chomsky's grammatical theorizing, have willingly accepted their given assignment.

6.3.2 A process grammar performance model

In contrast to Chomsky's resource grammar conception of performance, there are process type of grammars that are part of the process itself – for example, some of the grammars discussed in the previous chapter, such as the semantic-based grammars (Functional Grammar, mainly derived from Generative Semantics Grammar) and psychological process grammars (Cognitive Grammar). The semantic-based grammars could serve directly as models of sentence production since they take the meaning of the sentence as input and provide the sound pattern of the sentence as output. However, to suppose that a speaker would actually go step by step through such a grammar to produce a sentence is doubtful. This would be too time consuming a process. A speaker would take short-cuts by processing different levelsat the same time. (See Section 6.4 below for further discussion on this point.)

That the production and comprehension processes are in some way interrelated must surely be the case. Both must share the same lexicon, for example, although how each process gains access to and uses the lexicon undoubtedly will be different. The same could be said for syntactic principles. Surely there must be a relationship, for example, between the knowledge needed to construct an interrogative form and the knowledge needed for identifying the same form. Such considerations, incidentally, would not lead to a grammar like Chomsky's because Chomsky's competence is not written with such problems in mind.

Any complete model of speaker performance, moreover, must take into account more than simple meaning. The sentences we utter are uttered for a purpose, to flatter, to insult, to praise, etc. Then, too, politeness, along with other interpersonal variables, also serves to determine the form and content of a sentence. ('Open the window' and 'Would you please be so kind as to open the window?' may have the same purpose but they differ greatly in politeness level.) Such pragmatic aspects of language are clearly essential to any model of speaker performance. As Leech (1983) persuasively argues, these are best conceived of as a set of variables which operate to determine the form of the initial semantic structure and are not included in the grammar itself.

6.3.3 No workable performance model yet with Chomsky's grammar

Although it has been more than 25 years since Chomsky first proposed his competence–performance distinction and the model of performance it entails, as yet no workable performance model using his grammar has been formulated. Even some of Chomsky's most ardent and brilliant psycholinguistic supporters, e.g. McNeill, Bever, Mehler and Garrett, have not succeeded in the task. One cannot help but wonder, therefore, why this is the case. Two distinct possibilities come to my mind. Either psycholinguists are not smart enough to create a workable model, or, there is something wrong with Chomsky's conception of grammar such that a performance model cannot be devised. I believe the latter to be the case, not only because I am a psycholinguist looking for a face-saving device but because there are strong reasons for doubting the psychological validity of Chomsky's grammatical theorizing. Before dealing with this issue (Section 6.5 below), I would first like to consider in more detail the performance processes of production and understanding.

6.4 Some features of sentence production and understanding

6.4.1 Explaining the speed of conversations

Have you ever wondered how it is that we are so quick at producing and understanding sentences in a conversation? It is truly amazing how many sentences are dealt with in a short amount of time. How this is done needs explaining. In this regard, many psycholinguists, including myself, believe that such speed is made possible by a speaker or hearer having knowledge and strategies that often enable one to jump directly from meaning to sound and vice versa without the mediation of syntax in the process of understanding and producing sentences.

A strict sequencing among the semantic, syntactic and phonetic levels need not be observed. It would not be necessary to wait until an entire level of structure of the sentence is formed (the entire Surface Structure, for example) before proceeding to the next level of structure. Rather, one could be doing different things with different parts of the sentence. In production, for example, while a part of surface structure is already being converted to Phonetic Form, other parts of Surface Structure could be just in the process of being formed from the semantic structure. Then, too, because the production of a sentence involves the output of words in a linear order, i.e. words must be uttered in a proper sequence, some portions of the sentence could be uttered in speech even while other portions are still in the process of formation.

In this respect, familiar phrases and sentences are especially useful. Items like 'the little boy', 'bread and butter', 'Where is it?' and, for linguists, a host of items from linguistic arguments such as Chomsky's 'John is eager to please', 'John is easy to please' and 'Colourless green ideas sleep furiously'. Undoubtedly these phrases and sentences are stored in memory in their entirety, in terms of their meaning, sound and syntactic properties, just as are single words like 'dog' or 'eclipse'. Such items would not need to be created or analysed in a way that novel phrases and sentences must be. When one wishes to express or to understand the meaning of some of these stock items, they could be treated as wholes and grammatical principles need not be applied. The more frequently a word, phrase or sentence occurs, the more accessible it will become for speedy use.

6.4.2 Some features of sentence production

The aim of the production process is to provide a set of sounds for the thought that the speaker wishes to convey. The essentials of that process are shown in Figure 6.4.

The following are some brief remarks on the components and their operations in the process.

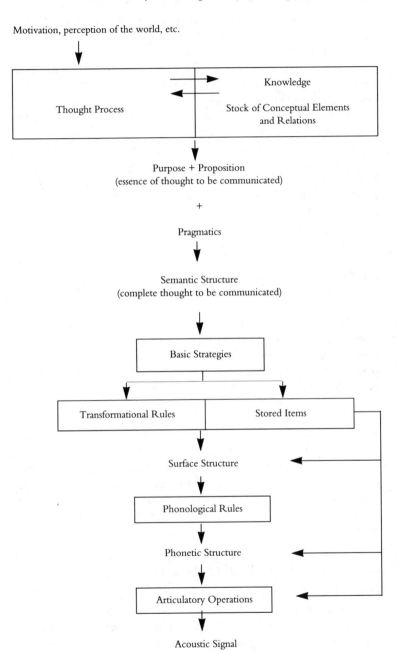

Figure 6.4 Sentence production process

Thought Process This universal process uses knowledge and a stock of concepts to create thoughts. It is stimulated by various mental and environmental influences.

Purpose + Proposition This is the essential thought which a person wishes to communicate to someone. It is conceptual and non-linguistic in nature. Communication of this thought may be realized through linguistic or behavioural means. The purpose of a thought involves such intentions as questioning, asserting, denying and warning with respect to a proposition. The proposition consists of two basic types of concepts: arguments (usually realized as nouns in language) and predicates (usually realized as verbs and adjectives).

Pragmatics and Semantic Structure Politeness, persuasion and other pragmatic factors will influence what the final meaning of the sentence (Semantic Structure) will be. It is this Semantic Structure that will get realized in speech. Parts of this structure can be phoneticized directly or through the syntax and phonological rules.

Basic strategies This component identifies certain properties of the Semantic Structure and assigns searches to be done of the Stored Items and Transformational rules. Immediate recovery of aspects of the Phonetic Structure is possible without conversion to the syntactic Surface Structure.

Phonetic Structure and acoustic signal The Phonetic Structure is a psychological (non-physical) level which represents the pronunciation of the sentence. It consists of discrete speech sounds and prosodic features (pitch, stress, etc.). On the basis of the Phonetic Structure, the movements of the articulators of speech (tongue, lips, vocal chords, etc.) are controlled so as to provide physical speech, which appears in the environment as the acoustic signal.

6.4.3 Some features of sentence understanding

Given speech sounds as input, the problem is to explain how we recover the ideas that are represented by those sounds. The discussion which I shall present here does *not* regard such a process as being principally oriented to recovering syntactic structures within a Chomskyan framework. This has been attempted by Bever, Garrett, Jerry

Fodor, Foss and Hakes with little success. Such Chomskyan theorists see the immediate goal of the sentence-understanding process as the determination of syntactic D-structure, after which the Logical Form will be recovered by means of S-structure.

For example, Fodor, Bever and Garrett have postulated that a string of incoming words are first identified in terms of their grammatical class (noun, verb, etc.) so that for English a syntactic strategy like

A FUNDAMENTAL SYNTACTIC STRATEGY
NP + V + NP → Subject + Verb + Direct Object

can apply. This means that the first NP is identified as the Subject, while the NP that follows the V is identified as the Direct Object. This would fit a large number of English sentences such as 'Mary pushed Sally' and 'The cat chased the mouse'. After the syntactic D-structure consisting of Subject + Verb + Object is recovered, then other syntactic and then semantic rules from the grammar are applied to determine the semantic structure (LF) of the sentence.

In my estimation, and that of others like Schlesinger and Wanner, such a view of the process of sentence understanding is mistaken in the extreme. A more parsimonious and relevant approach is one that is geared to the immediate recovery of the meaning aspects of a sentence. Basic strategies, therefore, are better specified in terms of semantic aspects. Thus, rather than the strategy of NP + V + NP → Subject, etc., the strategy would be a semantic strategy, something like

A FUNDAMENTAL SEMANTIC STRATEGY
Living Thing + Action + Thing → Agent + Action + Action's Object

Here, with the identification of the individual concepts of 'Living Thing', 'Action' and 'Thing', the semantic roles of 'Agent' and 'Action's Object' are assigned (to 'Living Thing' and 'Thing', respectively) with respect to 'Action'. Thus, given a sentence like 'Mary pushed Sally', the first word of 'Mary' (assuming for convenience a single word-by-word analysis) will be immediately identified in the

Stored Items (Lexicon) as the name of a person, person being an item that includes the meaning of living thing. The strategy would tentatively assign 'Mary' the role of Agent (the cause of an action). The strategy is then primed to expect some sort of action to appear next. When the word 'pushed' is heard, this expectation is confirmed. The strategy then expects the occurrence of some sort of thing, which will be assigned the role of Action's Object (the semantic rather than the syntactic object). This will be confirmed when the word 'Sally' appears, for it will be identified as the name of a person, which includes in its meaning, thing. 'Sally' will then be assigned the semantic role of Action's Object. In this way, the basic semantic structure can be recovered without having to work through syntactic rules. Of course, sometimes it will be necessary to resort to grammatical rules in order to identify structures. However, fundamental understanding strategies should all be formulated in semantic rather than syntactic terms.

6.5 The psychological unreality of Chomsky's grammar

6.5.1 The psychological contradiction in Chomsky's theorizing

Chomsky claims that the principles and rules of his grammar are psychologically real. I do not believe that this is logically possible due to an essential contradiction in Chomsky's theorizing.

When we look at the content of the principles and parameters which Chomsky writes, we find that they are necessarily based on what he conceives to be the relationship of meaning, sound and syntax. This could not be otherwise since the specific rules of a grammar cannot be written independently of the postulated relationship of syntax to meaning and sound, i.e. the directional relationship obtaining among the levels of D-structure, S-structure, Logical Form and Phonetic Form. Thus, for example, syntactic principles are written with the purpose of converting D-structures to S-structures. Phrase Structure rules are written with the purpose of converting the letter S to a D-structure.

Phonological and Semantic rules are likewise written so as to account for certain levels of structure; from S-structure to LF and PF. *The content of the rules of grammar are thus determined by the directional relationship which Chomsky postulates with respect to the levels of his grammar.*

But, what does Chomsky say about this directional relationship in his grammar? He declares, and rightly so, that it would be 'absurd' to propose that in producing a sentence a speaker would start from the initial letter S, construct a D-structure line by line, then insert lexical items and apply transformations to form a S-structure, etc. As he emphasizes in the quotation cited earlier in this chapter, '. . . such a proposal seems not only without justification but entirely counter to whatever vague intuitions one may have about the processes that underlie production.'

Thus, Chomsky asserts, the process of generating a linguistic derivation is not a process that a speaker would ever employ in producing a sentence. The same, of course, would be true for the understanding of sentences – a performance process that must begin with sound and not the letter S and a variety of syntactic principles. This being the case, it is clear that *the directional order of structure construction in Chomsky's grammar is a psychological fiction having no basis in actual speaker performance.*

Now, since the direction order in Chomsky's grammar is psychologically unreal, and since the content of his grammatical principles and parameters are determined by this directional order, we can only conclude *that Chomsky's principles and parameters are as psychologically unreal as the psychologically unreal order on which they were based.* (For more details on this argument, see Steinberg, 1976 and 1982, pp. 77–80.)

Given such a psychological self-contradiction, it is clear that Chomsky's grammatical theorizing is completely flawed psychologically. It remains the same sort of formalistic non-psychological theory of grammar that he originally proposed in the 1950s.

6.6 The anti-Mentalist skeletons in Chomsky's closet

How is it that Chomsky's theorizing has resulted in this internal psychological contradiction? A study of Chomsky's early writings provides the answer to this question. The facts show that Chomsky was not always a Mentalist and that the psychological theorizing for his grammar came some years later. For, prior to the 1960s, Chomsky did not hold that the rules of his grammar had counterparts in the minds of speakers. Nor did he hold that his grammar represented speaker knowledge. Not only that, but, as I have detailed elsewhere (Steinberg, 1982), *Chomsky in the 1950s was anti-Mentalistic, formalistic and even a Behaviourist supporter!*

Let us consider a few quotations from Chomsky.

He [mentalist philosopher Wells] offers this in criticism of Bloomfield's program of avoiding mentalistic foundations for linguistic theory. . . . I do not believe that this is relevant to Bloomfield's anti-mentalism. The fact that a certain general criterion of significance [reductionism] has been abandoned does not mean that the bars are down, and that 'ideas' and 'meanings' become proper concepts for linguistics, any more than it means that ghosts are proper concepts for physics. . . . it seems to me that *it will rule out mentalism for what were essentially Bloomfields's reasons, i.e., its obscurity and general uselessness in linguistic theory.*
(Chomsky, 1955; I, 19–20; author's *italic*)

Here we find Chomsky supporting Bloomfield, a pro-Behaviourist linguist, in his attack on Mentalism, ideas and meanings. (Ideas and meanings are attacked because such abstract entities lead to a theory of mind.)

Surprised? How about this one?

Whatever the situation may be in other sciences, I think that there is hope of developing that aspect of linguistics theory being studied here on the basis of a small number of primitives, and that *introduction of dispositions (or mentalist terms) is either irrelevant, or trivializes the theory.*
(Chomsky, 1955; I, 20–1; author's *italic*)

Is it any wonder then that Chomsky's grammatical theory in the 1950s had no meaning or semantic component? In fact, in his 1955 work, Chomsky devoted over a hundred pages to attacking the relevance of semantics to grammar! The semantic component of his grammar was only added in the 1960s, at which time Chomsky had taken up the cause of mentalism. Even so, semantics was given only a secondary role. Syntax continued to be given the primary autonomous role in the grammar, the same role that it had in Chomsky's original work in the 1950s.

It is because Chomsky continued to give syntax a primary role, while at the same time making mentalistic claims about his grammar, that Chomsky fell into psychological self-contradiction. Not even his brilliant competence–performance solution was enough to save the theory, although it did serve to detract critics from focusing psychological attention on the grammar.

6.7   Discussion questions

1. Can Chomsky's grammar serve as a model of speaker production or understanding?
2. Can a semantic-based grammar serve as a model of speaker production or understanding?
3. What is Chomsky's competence–performance distinction?
4. Why does Steinberg believe that Chomsky is obliged to postulate a resource type of performance model rather than a process type for his grammar?
5. Why does Steinberg assert that the rules of Chomsky's grammar are generally psychologically invalid?
6. How, in Steinberg's view, did the internal contradiction in Chomsky's psychologizing about grammar arise?
7. Considering the process of sentence understanding, Steinberg argues that semantic-based strategies are more essential than syntactic ones. What is his argument?

Suggested readings

Chomsky, Noam (1955) *The Logical Structure of Linguistic Theory*. Library at the MIT, Cambridge, Mass. (This is the original unedited version; the published version omits many relevant passages.)

Chomsky, Noam (1965) *Aspects of the Theory of Syntax*. Cambridge, Mass.: MIT Press.

Chomsky, Noam (1967) The formal nature of language. In E. Lenneberg, *Biological Foundations of Language*. New York : Wiley.

Chomsky, Noam (1980) *Rules and Representations*. New York: Columbia University Press.

Dechert, Hans W. and Raupach, Manfred (eds) (1987) *Psycholinguistic Models of Production*. Norwood, NJ: Ablex Publishing.

Fodor, Jerry A., Bever, Thomas G. and Garrett, Merrill F. (1974) *The Psychology of Language*. New York: McGraw-Hill.

Garman, Michael (1990) *Psycholinguistics*. Cambridge: Cambridge University Press.

Leech, Geoffrey (1983) *Principles of Pragmatics*. London: Longman.

Levelt, Willem, J. M. (1989) *Speaking: from Intention to Articulation*. Cambridge, Mass.: MIT Press (Bradford Books).

Steinberg, Danny D. (1976) Competence, performance and the psychological invalidity of Chomsky's grammar. *Synthese*, **32**, 373–86.

Steinberg, Danny D. (1982) *Psycholinguistics: Language, Mind and World*. London: Longman.

Taylor, Insup and Taylor, M. Martin (1990) *Psycholinguistics: Learning and Using Language*. Englewood Cliffs, NJ: Prentice-Hall.

CHAPTER 7

Language: from intelligence or innate ideas?

7.1 Where do language ideas come from?

7.1.1 The quest for the perfect circle

We have minds and we have ideas in our minds. We have language ideas there, and all sorts of other ideas. But where do these ideas come from? How did the ideas we have in our minds get there in the first place? To illustrate the problems involved in attempting to answer such epistemological questions, let us first look into one idea in detail – a familiar one: the perfect circle.

You look at a wheel and wonder if it is a perfect circle. Probably not, you think. But then what exactly is a 'circle', particularly a 'perfect circle'? Would you be able to identify one if you saw it? You look at the sun, a full moon, a round coin. How can you tell whether any of these circles is perfect or not?

You might think that, by measuring those objects – the coin, for example – you could find out. You say that from the centre point outward to all edges, the distance should be equal. But, how do you know exactly where the centre point is, and where exactly is the beginning of the edge? How is it possible to establish these so that the measuring can begin? Well, you might now think of another approach, drawing lines from the edge inward towards the middle of the coin. Suppose you manage to get all of your lines to meet, can you be sure that they meet exactly? Even with the most sophisticated measuring instruments, there will be some degree of error. But, measurement aside, let us consider, even more importantly, whether, physically, a perfect circle actually does exist in the world. Well, all we can say is that a perfect circle might exist but that there would be no way to determine this through measurement. It seems strange to have to say this, but, we cannot be sure that even a single perfect circle exists in this world.

Still, while we might not be clear as to whether a perfect circle exists in the world, the idea of a perfect circle seems quite clear in our minds. This being the case, how then did the idea of a perfect circle get there? Did we get it through direct sensory experience, by seeing objects that were perfect circles? Perhaps. Yet our idea of a perfect circle is very clear (perfectly clear!).

Now, if we didn't get the idea in our mind by experiencing perfect circles directly, maybe we got the idea in school. Perhaps our teachers gave it to us by telling us the definition of one, a definition that has been passed down to us by ancient thinkers, which is something like 'a circle is a figure whose closed plane curve at any point is equidistant to some fixed point (the centre)'. Well and good. But, how do we know (and we do) that this is a true or correct definition, and, that it is not the definition of something else, a triangle or a horse?

Then, too, do people really need to go to school to find out what a perfect circle is? And, what about those original ancient thinkers, mathematicians like Pythagoras and Euclid, from whom it seems we got the definition of a circle? Since they, as originators of the definition, could not themselves have learned the definition in school, does this mean that they did not know what a perfect circle was until they formulated the definition? Does it make sense to say that they therefore *invented* the idea of a perfect circle? This sounds strange. But, why? Because we know it is one thing to say that they invented the *definition* of a perfect circle but quite another to say that they invented or originated the *idea* of a perfect circle. It is odd to think that they invented the idea, because do we not intuitively think that the idea of a perfect circle must have *already* been in the minds of humans before these mathematicians came along? If so, how did that idea get there?

Thus, the question remains. How did we get the idea in our minds of perfect circle? And, how, coming back to psycholinguistics, did the ideas we have about a language, particularly its grammar – the nouns, verbs, function words and particles, syntactic structures, the component features of speech sounds, etc. – get into our minds?

7.2 Empiricist and Rationalist answers

There have been two basic answers to the question of how ideas (as knowledge) get into our minds. The Empiricist believes that ideas come through experience. The Rationalist, however, believes that basic ideas are already present in the mind at birth. The dispute then revolves around what is in our minds at birth and what role experience (of the world and of our own minds) is to have.

7.2.1 The Empiricist view: no knowledge is innate

For the Empiricist, the mind at birth does not contain any ideas that can be regarded as knowledge. This essential position allows for the possibility that, although there is no knowledge at all in the mind at birth, there is something there, although this 'something' is not knowledge. Both of these alternatives have been presented by Empiricist thinkers.

The seventeenth-century philosopher John Locke is the principal proponent of the view that, at birth, the mind is as a blank slate. All ideas, including those constituting intelligence (logic and reflective thinking), are derived from direct sensory experience. Once intelligence has been acquired, then new types of ideas, including those of an abstract nature, can be derived from thinking about sensory experiences.

However, as far back as Aristotle and up to the present, there have been theorists who have held that we must be born with something in the mind and that not everything can be derived from sensory experience. Notable twentieth-century thinkers like the psychologist Piaget and the philosopher Putnam have taken this view. Piaget held that at birth there are 'undifferentiated schemas' in the mind and that with experience, and behaviour regarding those experiences, intelligence develops out of these schemas. It is then with intelligence that such elaborate knowledge as that of the grammar of a language develops. Language is thus a product of intelligence.

Putnam, too, holds that language is the product of intelligence but for him intelligence is innate and begins to operate with the life experiences of the child. Such being the case, intelligence, therefore, is not something that we have to acquire as Piaget would have it. Putnam maintains that we are born with 'General Multi-Purpose Learning Strategies' (GMPLS), a conception which is best understood as a kind of intelligence. Since intelligence, as Empiricists hold, is not knowledge itself but is a means for acquiring knowledge, and since all knowledge is to be derived from experience (after birth), Putnam thus falls squarely within the Empiricist camp. Incidentally, the English words 'empiricist' and 'empiricism' come from the Latin *empiricus* which in turn comes from the Greek *empeirikos*, which means experienced. Thus, the focus of the doctrine, as the name indicates, is on experience as the source of knowledge.

Perhaps a caution is in order here concerning the terms empiricist and empiricism. They are often used in a sense different from that of the philosophical school of thought just outlined. The other sense is: placing a high value on facts and subordinating theory and speculation strictly in accord with facts. This is a rather neutral sense and does not necessarily involve a particular school of philosophical thought. It is in this sense (and not the philosophical one) that even Behaviourists, who do not consider mind and its functions as being worthy of study, can and often do call themselves Empiricists. (We shall discuss the difference between Behaviourists and both Empiricists and Rationalists later in the chapter.)

7.2.2 The Rationalist view: basic knowledge is innate

Although Rationalists are in agreement that basic knowledge is already in the mind at birth, there are radical differences among theorists regarding what knowledge it is that is innate, and, how that knowledge is made operational or functional. The traditional view, going back to Plato in the fourth century BC and Descartes in the seventeenth century, is that while basic knowledge is innate, it is only through reason (Latin *ratio* meaning reason) and the stimulus of relevant experience that such knowledge comes alive in the mind. As such, experience does not provide knowledge but rather serves to activate the knowledge that is already there. Reason or logic is the means whereby the latent knowledge is brought to life, and made available for use.

Thus, for example, the ideas of 'justice' (Plato), 'God' and 'perfection' (Descartes), a 'triangle' (Leibnitz) and others like 'circle' and 'infinity' are regarded as innate. Through Socrates and his persistent and incisive questioning of an uneducated slave, Plato, in one of his dialogues, attempts to demonstrate that through reason the slave will discover the abstract and complex idea of justice – an idea which was already in the slave's mind. Reason brings out what is already there. (Of course, the Empiricist is quick to retort that the questions themselves caused the idea of justice to formulate itself in the slave's mind.)

Similarly, Descartes, in discussing the ideas of God and of perfection, argues that these ideas are already in the mind and are brought to awareness through the 'clear light' of reason. Leibnitz deviates somewhat from the pure reason doctrine and allows experience to activate directly the essence of a triangle, the essence already being innate in the mind. The emphasis is more on *discovery* – finding what is already there – than it is on *invention* – creating something entirely new. For the Empiricists, however, the emphasis clearly is on invention.

7.3 Chomsky's Universal Grammar

In accord with his revolutionary temperament, Chomsky has radically revised traditional rationalist doctrine. He dispenses with reason altogether and posits essentially independent sets of basic knowledge, so-called 'faculties of the mind', each of which has its own processing procedures. Chomsky suggests that there could be a logical faculty, which consists of a set of logical ideas and that there could be a moral and ethical faculty, with a set of related ideas. However, of particular interest to us is the set of ideas that he posits to serve a language function, the language faculty. These language ideas are said by Chomsky to be innate in all human beings, i.e. they are universal, and are the basis on which human grammars are constructed. (The construction principles themselves are part of the language faculty.)

Virtually an infinite number of grammars (enough to account for any human language) can be constructed from this finite set of ideas. It is this innate set of language ideas that Chomsky refers to as the Language Faculty or Universal Grammar (UG). (In the past Chomsky referred to it as the 'Language Acquisition Device' or LAD.) Language experience, of a particular human language, is necessary before UG can operate so as to provide the child with a grammar of that language. Without such experience, a person could not acquire language.

Chomsky (1988m pp. 133–4) states that UG consists of

fixed and invariant principles . . . and the parameters of variation associated with them. We can then, in effect, deduce particular languages by setting the parameters in one or another way. . . . The environment determines the way the parameters of universal grammar are set, yielding different languages.

Universal Grammar also allows for basic categories (verbs, nouns, adjective and adpositions (prepositions or postpositions)) and phrases that are associated with these categories (verb phrase, noun phrase and adpositional phrases). Only occasionally does Chomsky get very specific about the content of UG such as when he attributes the concept of 'climb' to it:

. . .try to define a word like 'table' or 'book' or whatever, and you'll find it's extremely difficult. . . . A recent issue of a linguistics journal . . . has a long detailed article trying to give the meaning of the word 'climb'. And it is very complicated, but every child learns it perfect right away. Now that can only mean one thing. Namely, human nature [innate ideas] give us the concept 'climb' for free. That is, the concept 'climb' is just part of the way in which we are able to interpret experience to use before we even have the experience. This is probably true for most concepts that have words for them in language. This is the way we learn language. *We simply learn the label that goes with the preexisting concept.* So in other words, it is as if the child, prior to any experience, has a long list of concepts like 'climb', and then the child is looking at the world to figure out which sound goes with the concept.

(op. cit., pp. 190–1 author's italic)

Chomsky views the acquisition of any particular language as occurring independently of intelligence, logic or reason. The faculties of the mind thus are conceived of as generally operating relatively independently of one another; Universal Grammar and not intelligence (or logic or reason) is what will provide for language acquisition. Mathematics, it might be noted for future reference, was earlier regarded by Chomsky as being associated with logic and not at all related to Universal Grammar. He revised this position in the 1980s, however, due to a telling argument by Putnam in the 1970s (to be discussed later). Chomsky now argues that mathematics itself is derived from Universal Grammar. Thus, UG is said to account not only for language but for mathematics as well.

7.4 Arguments re intelligence and Universal Grammar

Until Chomsky came along in the 1960s with his Rationalist ideas, western philosophy and psychology tended to be dominated by such doctrines as Behaviourism and Logical Positivism, ones that are antipathetic to the study of mind. Chomsky not only succeeded in bringing down Behaviourism but he succeeded in making his own particular brand of Rationalism respectable. By brilliant strikes against Behaviourism on two fronts, through persuasive linguistic and psycholinguistic argumentation (see Steinberg, 1982, Chapter 1, for one summary) and through advocacy of Rationalist notions, Chomsky thoroughly discredited Behaviourism. However, once mentalism became respectable, the door was opened too for unwelcome mentalist guests, the Empiricists. These thinkers have since become Chomsky's main theoretical philosophical and psychological opponents, with Putnam and Piaget among the most prominent in this group. The result has been that Chomsky's arguments favouring Rationalism are no longer accorded the uncritical acceptance they once enjoyed.

I would like to present here some of the main arguments that Chomsky has offered in support of innate language ideas. At the same time I shall present counter-arguments that opposition theorists have raised in objection to those arguments.

7.4.1 Chomsky's ease and speed of child acquisition argument

According to Chomsky, 'A young child is able to gain perfect mastery of a language with incomparably greater ease' [than an adult] and 'Mere exposure to the language, for a remarkably short period' seems to be all that a child needs to develop the competence of the native speaker. Since the child's remarkable accomplishment in acquiring the grammar could not have been through the lengthy accumulation of language learning that the child would have had to experience if one were postulating an Empiricist-based acquisition process, then, Chomsky argues, this could only have occurred with the assistance of the innate language faculty (also called Universal Grammar). It is through the help of innate language ideas that the acquisition of language is made so easy and rapid. The Empiricist cannot account for such ease and speed of acquisition.

7.4.2 Objections to ease and speed of child acquisition argument

Putnam (1967) has countered Chomsky's argument by comparing the number of hours spent by a child in learning language with that of an adult learning a language. He contends that a child of 4 or 5 years who has learned the essentials of the language spends much more time in the process than would an adult, and that this time is not a short time at all.

To better understand Putnam's argument, let us create our own concrete example. First let us estimate the number of hours of exposure to the language that an ordinary 4-year-old child gets. We could assume that the number of hours per day that the child is exposed to language is about 10. Of course, when the child was younger, the child would have slept more, been awake less, etc. But, let us take 10 hours as a round figure. (A few hours here or there won't make much difference, as you will see.) Now, since there are 365 days in a year, that gives us 3650 hours per year. Over a period of four years, that is 14,400 hours (3650 × 4).

Is 14,400 hours a large number of hours or not? Well, let us compare it with the number of hours that, say, a student is exposed to in one language course at school over the period of a semester. If the student has 5 class hours per week and studies for 2 hours after each class hour (too idealistic? but let's give Chomsky the benefit of the doubt) that makes 15 hours per week. If one semester lasts 18 weeks, then that would be a total of 15 × 18 = 270 hours for the semester. Let us say the student studies all the year round by taking three semesters of the language; that would make 270 × 3 = 810 hours. Now, if the student had as many exposure hours as the child, then the student would have to study a language at school for (14,400/810), the equivalent of 17.8 years! Is 17 years long enough for an adult to learn the essential grammar of a language? Putnam thinks so, and so would most people. If the adult could trim some years from that 17 in order to accomplish the task (a not unlikely possibility) the adult (contrary to Chomsky's presupposition) would then be an even faster learner than the child.

The number of hours that a child spends in learning its native language is not small (which implies not so easy), when compared to that of an adult learning a second language. That being the case, there is no need to create something special to assist the child in language learning. Language acquisition can be accounted for by step-by-step learning along Empiricist lines. There is no need to posit the existence of innate language ideas, maintains Putnam.

Another problem, one that I would like to offer, concerns an implied premise for Chomsky's argument. Because Chomsky states that children learn faster than adults, and that this superior speed is the result of the child having Universal Grammar to help out, the implication is that adults do *not* have the benefit of innate language ideas. Why should this be so? If adults are denied the benefit of Universal Grammar, then Universal Grammar either weakens or dries up altogether with age. Yet, this could not be so because adults *are* able learn foreign languages. If Chomsky wishes to argue here that adults would, with the weakening or loss of Universal Grammar, have to learn language in some step-by-step Empiricist way (rather than by the flash of Rationalism) then he would have to argue that such learning is not possible. Otherwise he would be contradicting one of his other major arguments for the existence of Universal Grammar: the argument that every language has certain essential principles or functions that could not possibly be acquired through experience. (See the last Chomsky argument presented in this section.) Yet, it is a fact that, given enough time and proper language and environmental input, adult language learners can learn a foreign grammar rather well – pronunciation problems aside.

Everything considered, it would seem to Chomsky's advantage to drop this argument in favour of Universal Grammar in its entirety. The argument suffers irremediably from both empirical and internal theoretical flaws.

7.4.3 Chomsky's inadequate language data argument

Chomsky argues that children's acquisition of a well-formed grammar of the language, despite their being exposed to inadequate language data, is evidence of the assistance of innate language ideas. The language data, Chomsky (1967, p. 6) insists, are 'meager in scope', and 'degenerate in quality'. They consist, '*in large measure*, of sentences that deviate in form from the idealized structures defined by the grammar that he [the child] develops' (emphasis added). Such imperfect language data alone could not provide the basis for a perfect grammar.

Furthermore, these data are a 'minute sample of the linguistic material that has been thoroughly mastered'. Here Chomsky stresses that even structures and principles that do not appear in the language data are nevertheless acquired. Empiricist principles, depending as they do on the experience of relevant data, are therefore unable to explain how a well-formed grammar could be acquired given such imperfect and insufficient language data. Such inadequate data would necessarily result in an inadequate grammar if one took the Empiricist point of view. As Chomsky (1986, p. 12) puts it,

It seems there is little hope in accounting for our knowledge [of language] in terms of such [Empiricist] ideas as analogy, induction, association, reliable procedures, good reasons, and justification in any generally useful sense, or in terms of 'generalized learning mechanisms' (if such exist).

This latter reference, the reader might now recognize, is a dig at Putnam and his theory of General Multi-Purpose Learning Strategies.

7.4.4 Objections to the inadequate language data argument

Imperfect language data as input

Empirical research by Labov, Newport and others have convincingly demonstrated that, as Labov (1970, p. 42) neatly phrases it,

The ungrammaticality of every-day speech appears to be a myth with no basis in actual fact. In the various empirical studies which we have conducted . . . the proportion of truly ungrammatical an ill-formed sentences falls to less than two percent.

Newport, in a long-term study with 15 mothers, reports an incidence of only 1 ungrammatical utterance in 1500. (See Cromer, 1980, for a review of such studies.)

While Chomsky could, on the basis of these findings, have dropped his 'degenerate' argument without much loss to his overall theory, he chose not to. He presents the following counter-counter-argument (Chomsky, 1975, fn. 6), obviously with Labov's the 2 per cent finding in mind.

. . . suppose that a scientist were presented with data, 2 per cent of which are wrong (but he doesn't know which 2 per cent). Then, he faces some serious difficulties. . . . The fact that these difficulties do not seem to arise for the language learner, who is, of course, faced with degenerate data of experience, requires explanation.

Instead of proposing a complex theory of innate language ideas to try to deal with the 2 per cent ungrammatical sentences (which can be due to a speaker being interrupted in mid sentence, a change of mind, etc.), would it not be much simpler to suppose that the child simply disregards those sentences he or she cannot analyse? To think that the child would attempt to construct a whole grammar to account for these few ungrammatical sentences is unreasonable. Is it not more likely that the child will focus on the 98 per cent that are grammatical and simply discard the sentences which present particularly difficult problems? True, a meticulous scientist might spend a great amount of time puzzling over the 2 per cent. There is no good reason, though, to think that a child would do the same, especially since, once spoken, the physical data disappear and the child's attention is drawn to other things. Neither does the child write down data for future reference. Such problem data, therefore, can easily be disregarded by the child.

Minute sample as input

As to Chomsky's claim that only a 'minute sample' of language is experienced, I am aware of no empirical evidence which he presents to support that claim. It could well be that the sentences which the child experiences (finite though their number may be) does contain in them an adequate representation of the syntactic structures which the child has learned. The multitude of child language studies that have been done seem to bear this out. Researchers do not report that children have learned of structures without ever having been exposed to sentences bearing those structures.

7.4.5 Chomsky's poverty of stimulus argument

This argument is similar to the one just discussed except that it focuses on special linguistics problems, particularly complex structure-dependent rules. Chomsky claims that certain structures are acquired by children despite the input data being 'impoverished' or limited. In support of his view, Chomsky presents a number of examples. A typical example, one he presents in detail, concerns the formation of simple questions. Let us consider that example.

The following are declarative-question pairs given by Chomsky (in Piattelli-Palmarini, 1980, p. 39):

(1) (a) The man is here. – Is the man here?

(b) The man will leave. – Will the man leave?

Chomsky asks the reader to consider two possible hypotheses (H) to account for these pairs. For both (a) and (b), the declarative is first analysed and then, on the basis of this analysis, the interrogative is formed.

Chomsky first offers H1.

H1: process the declarative from beginning to end {left to right}, word by word, until reaching the first occurrence of the words *is*, *will*, etc.; transpose this occurrence to the beginning {left}, forming the associated interrogative.

Thus, for the sentence 'The man is here', one would proceed from 'The' to 'man' to 'is' and when one gets to 'is' one takes 'is' and places it in front of all of the preceding words, in this case 'The man'. Thus, the result will be 'Is + the man here', which is the proper interrogative.

Chomsky then offers H2.

H2: same as H1, but select the first occurrence of *is*, *will*, etc., following the first noun phrase of the declarative.

Thus, as in H1, one processes the sentence from the beginning. However, unlike H1, one looks for a noun phrase. When the identification of a noun phrase, in this case 'The man', has been made, and when the word 'is' which immediately follows is also identified, only then is the word 'is' placed at the beginning of the sentence. (This transposition is the same as in H1.) The result is, as with H1, the proper interrogative of 'Is the man here?'.

Thus, we see that while both hypotheses will yield the proper interrogative, one hypothesis, H2, is much more complex than the other, H1. H1 only requires an analysis of a sequence of words, whereas H2 requires not only an analysis of a sequence of words but also into an abstract phrase, the 'noun phrase'. As Chomsky rightly says, 'The phrases are "abstract" in that their boundaries and labeling are not in general physically marked in any way; rather, they are mental constructions'. In other words, our grouping of words into a noun phrase like 'the man' or of more complex ones like 'the happy man' and 'the man who is here' is not something that we can observe in the physical world. Only the individual words appear in the world. The grouping and labelling are done in our minds.

Chomsky then introduces new data to complete the basis of his argument.

(2) (a) The man who is here is tall. – Is the man who is here tall?

(b) The man who is tall will leave. – Will the man who is tall leave?

Chomsky then states, correctly, that the data in (2) are predicted by H2 but that they refute H1. For, since H2 involves a noun phrase in its operation, and since 'the man who **is** tall' is the first principal noun phrase, then the 'is' which is in that noun phrase (heavy type) will not be shifted to the front of the sentence. Rather the proper 'is' the one that serves as the main verb (relating 'man' and 'tall') will be shifted.

On the other hand, H1 would wrongly generate the interrogatives shown in (3). (These sentences are also provided by Chomsky.)

(3) (a) Is the man who here is tall?

(b) Is the man who tall will leave?

These ungrammatical sentences would occur since, in (3) (a), the wrong 'is' (the one that is in the relative clause of 'who is here') is selected because H1, you will recall, simply specifies that the first 'is' is to be selected for placement. In (3) (b) the incorrect 'is' and not the correct 'will' has been selected because, according to H1, the *first* instance of either 'is' or 'will' is selected.

On the basis of these data, Chomsky then makes his argument. First, he states as follows,

A scientist observing English speakers, given such data as (1) ['The man is here', etc.], would naturally select hypothesis H1 over the far more complex hypothesis H2, which postulates abstract mental processing of a non-trivial sort beyond H1. Similarly, given such data as (1) it is reasonable to assume that an 'unstructured' child would assume that H1 is valid. In fact, as we know, it is not, and H2 is (more nearly) correct. [Chomsky properly cautions 'more nearly' because other modals (can, may) and other phenomena such as the auxiliary (have) have also to be accounted for by the rule.]

Then, he goes on for the conclusion,

. . . how does a child know that H2 is correct (nearly), while H1 is false? It is surely not the case that he hits on H1 (as a neutral scientist would) and then is forced to reject it on the basis of data such as (2). No child is taught the relevant facts. Children make many errors in language learning, but none such as (3), prior to appropriate training or evidence. . . . [the child] will unerringly employ H2, never H1, on the first relevant occasion (assuming that he can handle the structures at all). . . . The child need not consider H1; it is ruled out by properties of his initial mental state [Universal Grammar].

Thus, Chomsky argues, because there is insufficient language data in the environment, a 'poverty of the stimulus', there is no way that the child could have acquired H2 by any Empiricist means. The relevant data is simply not there to be experienced. That being the case, the only reasonable thing is to assume that the child was assisted by innate language ideas, Universal Grammar.

7.4.6 Objections to Chomsky's poverty of stimulus argument

To begin with, Chomsky is undoubtedly correct in holding that a child would not develop H1 so that errors like those in (3) would result. However, does it then follow that these empirical findings require the use of a genetic Universal Grammar, a Universal Grammar which would 'rule out' H1 and thereby allow the child to focus on H2? I believe not. I would like to offer a simpler explanation for why the child would formulate H2 – one that does *not* require the postulation of innate language ideas.

Let us consider the child's learning of language. Before attempting to deal with questions, the child deals with declaratives first. This is also a general finding in child language studies. (By implication Chomsky is in agreement since both his H1 and H2 hypotheses derive the question from the declarative.) Now, in the mastering of declaratives the child must and does acquire the phrase structure of sentences. Otherwise the child would not be able to understand the meaning of declarative sentences. That being the case, it is clear that the child has knowledge of phrase structures, even *before* he or she attempts to deal with the more complex-question structures. Incidentally, acquiring phrase structures for the comprehension of declaratives, Chomsky would likely admit, is not so formidable a task that a Universal Grammar need be posited for its explanation.

Now, since the child knows and understands phrase structures, which are essential to comprehending the meaning of declarative sentences, then, when the child hears questions that are spoken by others, the child will naturally attempt to understand the meaning of those questions by means of those same phrase structures. The child cannot help but formulate a hypothesis which will incorporate phrase structure in dealing with interrogative sentences, for it is only through using phrase structure that the child will be able to understand the meaning of those sentences. The child is thus obliged to search for such structures.

It is worth noting that since parents would not utter such malformed sentences as those in (3), then the interrogative sentences which the child hears will generally be well formed, like those in (1) and (2). As a result, the presentation of such proper and relevant input on the part of parents will serve to assist the child in developing the correct hypothesis for dealing with questions. Stimulus input, thus, is quite adequate and not at all 'impoverished' as Chomsky claims.

Let me put the main objection another way. Since, in the child's acquisition of language, speech understanding necessarily precedes speech production (see Chapter 2 for a discussion of this fundamental principle), the child will learn to understand the meaning of question structures (through the use of phrase structure) before he or she is able to produce such structures. That being the case, when the child attempts to produce a question on his or her own, the child will automatically use the same structural knowledge that was already acquired during the process of understanding the question structures. The child will not consider anything like H1 because H2 will simply pop out on the basis of prior learning.

One further issue I would like to raise is this. Just who is that 'neutral scientist' that Chomsky is always talking about? This same scientist, you will recall, also assisted Chomsky in formulating his argument against Labov. One cannot help but wonder how objective this scientist really is. Could it be that he or she is secretly in Chomsky's employ?

7.4.7 Chomsky's irrelevance of intelligence argument

Chomsky holds that language acquisition is essentially independent of intelligence. In support of this thesis he argues that grammar is so peculiar, so different from any other kind of knowledge that it cannot be a function of rational operating intelligence. It is because animals are born only with intelligence and not with innate language ideas that they cannot learn language to any significant degree. An animal that is otherwise intelligent in so many realms of life (like Washoe and Koko in Chapter 3), is unable to learn more than the simplest of language structures. This is evidence for Universal Grammar in humans, a species-specific innate language structure that does not appear in animals.

Chomsky has also argued that, concerning humans, '. . . vast differences in intelligence have only a small effect on resulting competence [knowledge of a particular grammar]' (Chomsky, 1967, p. 3). By this he implies that if intelligence is relevant to language acquisition, then more intelligent people should acquire a greater competence. But, more intelligent persons do not acquire a greater competence than do less intelligent persons, he says. That being the case, he then concludes that different degrees of intelligence do not affect language acquisition, and, intelligence itself is irrelevant to the acquisition of language. Since the uniformity of competence regarding all linguistic essentials observed among speakers of a language is not due to intelligence, it must be due to something else. That something else must be Universal Grammar, according to Chomsky.

7.4.8 Objections to the irrelevance of intelligence argument

Animals and high–low intelligence

Chomsky's argument concerning the inability of otherwise intelligent animals to acquire language need not be attributed to their lack of Universal Grammar. They may just as well be limited in their intelligence. Animals may lack the necessary analytical skills and abstract reasoning that would enable them to learn language. This is how Putnam essentially counters Chomsky (even though Putnam is more impressed with the ability of animals to learn language than are most people, including myself). This would also serve to explain why Ai, the Japanese chimp mentioned in Chapter 2 (p. 45), could not learn to count beyond number 6. (Chomsky has a different explanation for number ability, as shall be described later in this section.)

Let us now consider Chomsky's high–low intelligence argument. Here Chomsky supposes that increases in intelligence beyond that of low intelligence should result in greater or improved competence, from a supposed Empiricist point of view. I would counter by saying that there is no basis for assuming that a grammar needs high intelligence for its acquisition. It could well be that low intelligence is sufficient for the acquisition of a grammar. After all, people of both high and low intelligence (but not defective), learn to drive cars, play cards and do many other things. There do not seem to be significant differences between these groups. Thus, it may well be that although intelligence *is* relevant for those tasks, and for language too, only a low degree of intelligence is necessary for their mastery; a high degree being superfluous. That being so, Chomsky's argument is insupportable.

Mathematics and intelligence

In 1975, Putnam provided a particularly strong argument against Chomsky on the issue of intelligence. This was at a conference in France where he, Chomsky, Piaget and other notable thinkers were present (Piattelli-Palmarini, 1980), Putnam challenged Chomsky with the following argument.

The concepts of mathematics could not have developed genetically through evolution because humans have only been using such concepts for a few thousand years. The use of mathematics did not come into existence 'until after the evolution of the race was complete (some 100,000-odd years ago)' (Putnam in Piattelli-Palmarini, 1980, pp. 296-7). Since such a complex system of thought as mathematics could not be the result of genetic inheritance (evolution being completed), it must, therefore, be an invention of the intelligence of the mind. If such an intelligence can invent mathematics, it surely should have no trouble inventing grammar as well. Thus, there is no need to postulate the existence of innate language ideas.

It seems that Chomsky was unprepared for such an argument. The best he could do at that conference was to assert that considering 'fairly deep properties of the number system, I suppose that this ability is genetically determined for humans. . . . [and that] These skills may well have risen as a concomitant of structural properties of the brain that developed for other reasons' (op. cit., p. 321). Such an argument in response to Putnam's challenge must have struck Chomsky himself as weak, for, what we find in Chomsky's later writings is the formulation (a complete reversal of his 1960s position) that mathematics is not independent of language but is one of the outcomes of Universal Grammar.

We find Chomsky (1988) saying that: 'At this point we can only speculate, but it is possible that the number faculty developed as a by-product of the language faculty' (p. 169). He goes on to say,

. . . there couldn't be a mathematical capacity without a language capacity. . . . If you think about the history of mathematics, say from Euclid to fairly recently, there are really two basic ideas. One idea is numbers; the other is the structure of three-dimensional space, which is based on the concept of continuity. . . . we can have the relevant thoughts about geometrical space because we have language. . . . The other notion, of number, probably comes from our language capacity directly.

(op. cit., pp. 184–5)

Chomsky further states that our language ability and our number ability have certain features in common, most notably the notion of 'discrete infinity' (to be distinguished from an innumerable mass). A child, for example, can be taught to count from one to infinity (in theory) without which concept the child would not be able to perform most mathematical operations. Language, too, has the property of discrete infinity in that while any particular sentence has a finite number of words, in principle, the sentence can be expanded in length to infinity (theoretically) by the addition of modifying and conjoined clauses, and the like.

Thus, according to Chomsky's latest formulation (one that he probably would never have made had he not been goaded by Putnam), mathematics is a product, directly and indirectly, of Universal Grammar. However, one cannot but wonder whether by expanding the scope of Universal Grammar in order to take in problem areas (areas that challenge the very existence of UG) like mathematics, UG has become too powerful a theory, one that could possibly encompass any complex abstract field of human endeavour. That being the case, unless Chomsky is able to specify in more detail the contents of UG, UG seems to simply serve as a filing cabinet for problems which are filed away for later consideration and then forgotten.

7.4.9 Conclusion

Neither the Rationalist nor Empiricist side can be said to have presented definitive arguments for their positions. Such a state of affairs should not be surprising since the controversy deals with such highly abstract, complex and often vague entities such as ideas, knowledge, rules, principles and intelligence. Explaining the source of such ideas as God, infinity, truth and grammatical structures is not easy to do.

For the Empiricist it is not easy to explain how, for example, the concept of infinity is derived from experience only with the finite. How could perfection in anything come from environmental experience which is by its very nature limited to finite and often imperfect individual physical objects? How could intelligence (Putnam's GMPLS) or the essence from which intelligence is formed (Piaget's schemas) have developed genetically so that it will yield abstract knowledge when exposed to experience?

Nor is it at all easy for the Rationalist to explain how ideas become innate in the first place. Could this have been through experience initially, genetic mutation or some as yet undiscovered mechanism? Certainly Descartes' simple answer that it was God who put ideas (including the idea of God itself) into the minds of humans is no longer scientifically acceptable.

It would not be surprising, then, if a neutral observer were to remain unconvinced one way or another on this

Rationalist–Empiricist grand debate. This debate, which has gone unresolved for thousands of years, may well continue for thousands more.

7.5 Mentalism and Behaviourism contrasted

7.5.1 Self-test: are you a Behaviourist or a Mentalist?

Before the test, how about a little warm-up?

You are playing tennis. Your opponent is standing on the left towards the front of the court so you place a shot to the back on the right. A simple enough event but not so simple when we ask how your action, the placing of the shot, is to be explained? More particularly, did your mind have anything to do with creating this action? Did your mind in any way influence the movements of your arm and hand?

Or, to take an example involving language, you ask a friend if you could borrow a videotape. How is your speech, the spoken request for the videotape, to be explained? Did your mind have anything to do with creating this speech? Did your mind in any way influence the creating of the sentences and their pronunciation through the organs of speech (vocal chords, mouth, tongue, lips, etc.)?

The general question this raises is: How is human behaviour, including the psycholinguistic problems concerning the production and understanding of speech, to be explained? Is mind needed for the explanation? Is mind essential to the understanding of these language processes?

So much for the warm-up. Now, for the test.

Instructions: This is not an essay test. Simply answer 'Yes' or 'No' to the following questions.

1. *Do humans have minds?*
   (A mind is said to have, for example, consciousness, feelings and ideas.)
2. *If humans have minds, do their minds influence the behaviour of their bodies?*

(The tennis shot and the talking about a videotape are cases in point here.)

3. *Should the subject matter of psychology and linguistics include the study of mind?*
(You could agree with Questions 1 and 2 but disagree with this one.)

Scoring: A 'No' to any one of the above, makes you a Behaviourist. A 'Yes' to all three makes you a Mentalist.

Mentalists like Locke, Descartes, Piaget, Putnam and Chomsky would answer all three questions in the affirmative. Anti-Mentalists, like the Behaviourists, would give one or more negatives. For example, John B. Watson, the founder of the doctrine of Behaviourism, would have given a resounding 'No' to the first question had he taken the test. Naturally, he would have followed with negative answers to the other two questions.

Watson regarded mind and consciousness as religious superstitions, and, as such, irrelevant to the study of psychology. He stated that

. . . belief in the existence of consciousness goes back to the ancient days of superstition and magic. . . . These concepts – these heritages of a timid savage past – have made the emergence and growth of scientific psychology extremely difficult. . . . No one has ever touched a soul or seen one in a test tube or has in any way come into relationship with it as he has with other objects of his daily existence.

(Watson, 1924, pp. 2–3)

Watson's view that the mind does not exist was too radical for most Behaviourists. Most Behaviourists will allow that the mind exists (a 'Yes' to Question 1) and they may even allow that mind plays a role in determining behaviour (a 'Yes' to Question 2). However, no Behaviourist agrees that mind is a proper object for scientific study.

Skinner was a Behaviourist who agreed that the mind exists. He said, 'The fact of privacy (non-objective subject events) cannot, of course, be questioned [a great departure from Watson's view]' (Skinner, 1964, p. 2). However, he vehemently denied that it had any role in the determination of behaviour. For him, the mind exists but only as a reflection of bodily processes. (This has been traditionally called an 'epiphenomenal' view, and is shared by others such as the Behaviourist philosopher, Ryle.) The contents of the mind or states of mind are said not to influence behaviour. One may feel pain as the result of being stuck with a pin; however, that feeling in the mind will have nothing to do with any behaviour that follows. Thus, Skinner (1971) maintained that 'It [Behaviourism] rejects explanations of human behavior in terms of feelings, states of mind and mental processes . . .' (p. 35). In an address to the American Psychological Association just prior to his death, Skinner (1990), an anti-Mentalist to the very end, stated that '. . . cognitive science is the creationism of psychology' (p. 6).

Chomsky, as was noted at the beginning of the chapter, played a significant role in the downfall of Behaviourism. His review of Skinner's 1957 book *Verbal Behavior* (Chomsky, 1959) was devastating to Behaviourist explanations of language learning and processing. But this alone is insufficient to explain Chomsky's success, since, ever since its inception, other cogent criticisms of Behaviourism had been offered. It was Chomsky's brilliant alternative for accounting for language – a generative system of rules in the mind – that was the principal cause of Chomsky's success. (See Steinberg, 1982, pp. 1–47, for a description of Chomsky's ideas.) Psychology, linguistics, philosophy and a variety of other fields, including anthropology and music theory, have not been the same since.

7.6 Discussion questions

1. What is the dispute between Empiricists and Rationalists all about?
2. In what way does Chomsky differ from traditional Rationalists like Descartes?
3. In what essential ways do the Empiricists, Locke, Piaget and Putnam, differ from one another?
4. According to Chomsky, are humans born with the grammar of some language?
5. The ability of animals to learn language and to learn to count is very low. How would an Empiricist like Putnam explain this? How would a Rationalist like Chomsky explain this?

6. Chomsky asserts that the concept of climb is innate (p.138). How can such a claim be supported? Denied?
7. In claiming that the concept of climb is innate, Chomsky is making claims about ideas outside of the realm of language. How far do you think he might develop his theory in this non-language area?
8. Chomsky argues that the basis for question formation must be innate. Are you convinced by his argument?
9. How does Putnam's mathematics' argument relate to Chomsky's theory of Universal Grammar?
10. Can a theory like Universal Grammar be true even though arguments produced in its favour are weak or invalid?
11. Are you a Behaviourist? Explain your answers on the self-test.
12. How do you think you got the concept of a perfect circle?

Suggested readings

Botha, Rudolph P. (1989) *Challenging Chomsky*. Oxford: Basil Blackwell.

Chomsky, Noam (1959) Review of Skinner's *Verbal Behavior*. *Language*, **35**, 26–58.

Chomsky, Noam (1967) Recent contributions to the theory of innate ideas. *Synthese*, **17**, 2–11.

Chomsky, Noam (1975) Conditions on rules of grammar. Article based on lectures presented at the Linguistic Institute, University of South Florida.

Chomsky, Noam (1986) *Knowledge of Language: Its Nature, Origin and Use*. New York: Praeger.

Chomsky, Noam (1988) *Language and Problems of Knowledge*. Cambridge, Mass.: MIT Press.

Cromer, R. F. (1980) Empirical evidence in support of non-empiricist theories of mind. *The Behavioral and Brain Sciences*, **3**, 16–18.

Labov, William (1970) The study of language in its social context. *Studium Generale*, **23**, 1–43.

Piatelli-Palmarini, Massimo (ed.) (1980) *Language and Learning: The Debate between Jean Piaget and Noam Chomsky*. Cambridge, Mass.: Harvard University Press.

Putnam, Hilary (1967) The 'innateness hypothesis' and explanatory models in linguistics. *Synthese*, **17**, 12–22.

Skinner, B. F. (1964) Behaviorism at fifty. In T. W. Wann (ed.), *Behaviorism and Phenomenology*. Chicago: University of Chicago Press.

Skinner, B. F. (1971) Humanistic behaviorism. *The Humanist*, May–June, 35.

Skinner, B. F. (1990) *The American Psychological Association (APA) Monitor*, **21**, 10, 1, 6.

Steinberg, Danny D. (1982) *Psycholinguistics: Language, Mind and World*. London: Longman.

Watson, John B. (1924) *Behaviorism*. New York: Norton.

CHAPTER 8

Language, thought and culture

8.1 The arrest of the Sunday School teacher

Probably no topic is more central to psycholinguistics than that which concerns the relationship of language, thought and culture. Does language influence thought? Does it create thought? Can we think without language? Does language affect our perception of nature and society? Before attempting to answer these questions, I would like to begin in a rather indirect way by first telling you a story, a true story. It concerns a Sunday School teacher in the US and a 10-year-old boy who was his student. The teacher was arrested by the police. His crime? Well . . .

In May of 1920, in Hamilton County, Nebraska, a rural area of the United States, a teacher, Mr Robert Meyer, was arrested for violating state law. Meyer had been teaching Bible stories in German at Zion Parochial school to a 10-year-old boy. Nebraska law forbade the teaching of a second language to children under the age of 13. Not only Nebraska but 21 other states as well prohibited the teaching of foreign languages, except 'dead' languages such as Latin and Greek. According to Nebraska's 1919 Siman Act,

No person . . . shall teach any subject to any person in any language other than the English language. Languages other than English may be taught only after a pupil shall have . . . passed the eighth grade. . . . Any person who violates any of the provisions of this act shall be deemed guilty of a misdemeanor and, upon conviction, shall be subject to a fine of not less than twenty-five dollars ($25), nor more than one hundred dollars ($100) or be confined in the county jail for any period not exceeding thirty days for each offense.

If found guilty, Meyer could have been fined or even sent to jail.

The states had passed these laws essentially with the German language as the target. America had just finished a war with Germany and there was a hatred of Germany and things German, particularly its military values, ideals and political institutions. The law reflected the widespread belief that the German language was the embodiment of all that was evil in German culture and that to teach such a language to young Americans would be immoral and corrupting.

Meyer decided to appeal his case to the Supreme Court of the State of Nebraska. Ironically, lawyers for the state of Nebraska took essentially the position presented in the German language by the German philosopher, Wilhelm von Humboldt, in 1836. That is, a language by its very nature represents the spirit and national character of a people. If this were true, then, by teaching them the grammar, structure and vocabulary of the German language, Meyer could indeed have been harming American children by making them into German militarists right there on the plains of Nebraska.

The Nebraska Supreme Court denied Meyer's appeal, but Meyer did not submit. He then took his case to the highest court in the country, the United States Supreme Court, where he won his case. That court overturned his conviction and declared unconstitutional all laws in the United States which forbade the teaching of a foreign language. In its 1922 ruling the court stated as one basis for its decision, 'Mere knowledge of the German language cannot reasonably be regarded as harmful.'

We see in this story that a seemingly purely theoretical issue can have very practical consequences in everyday life. In making a legal decision on the matter, the court also made a psycholinguistic decision, on the relationship of language, thought and culture. Was the court correct? It is this question that we shall now consider.

8.2 Speech as the basis of thought

Over the years, a number of ideas have been presented which are widespread and have received scholarly support. One of these ideas is that thought comes from speech. Accordingly, thought is not something different from speech, but is actually a kind of speech that is not spoken aloud. It is speech that controls what and how we think; thought does not control what we say. Typically it is Behaviourists who have expressed this view.

The founder of Behaviourism, John B. Watson, said in 1924, for example, that thought is 'nothing but talking to ourselves' and that this talking to ourselves originates from speaking aloud. Following Watson, the linguist Bloomfield and the philosopher Ryle proposed similar views on both the nature of thought (a kind of speaking to ourselves) and the origin of thought (from speaking aloud). For Bloomfield, thinking was a system of movements that had been reduced from actual speech to the point where they were no longer visible. For Ryle, much ordinary thinking was an internal monologue where, in order for us to talk to ourselves (to think), 'We should have previously learned to talk intelligently aloud and have heard and understood other people doing so.' The psychologist Skinner, too, emphasized that thought 'is not some mysterious process responsible for behavior but the very behavior itself'.

8.3 Arguments against this idea

8.3.1 In speech, understanding precedes production

Normal children learning a language understand speech before they are able to meaningfully produce it. A 1-year-old child, for example, may be able to understand a sentence like 'Put the banana on the table' or 'Put the cup under the chair', yet still only be able to say single isolated words, or even no words at all. Researchers studying children have found that children's understanding of speech is well in advance of their ability to produce it. For example, in one study children who could say only single words such as 'ball', 'truck', 'kiss' and 'smell' could understand entirely new structures composed of more than one word, e.g. 'Kiss ball' and 'Smell truck'. We know the children understood what was said to them because they did what they were told to do – unusual acts of kissing a ball and smelling a truck, things they had never done before.

Then there is the case of a normal child (my son) who

from 1 to 2 years of age was taught to read and understand a number of written words, phrases and sentences even before he had actually developed the ability to say them. He could respond correctly to written sentences like 'Shut the door', 'Push the button' and 'Hit the ball', even though he couldn't say any of them. The fact that children with little or no speech can understand speech or read what is written surely demonstrates that these children have formulated concepts and ideas – in short, are thinking. Since they have thought and since this thought did not originate in their being able to speak, one must conclude that speech production is not the basis of thought.

8.3.2 Speech understanding by people with speech disabilities

Those born without the ability to speak, but who are otherwise intellectually normal, can learn to understand speech even though they cannot produce any. There is, for example, the case of a 3-year-old Japanese girl who was mute from birth but could hear and was normal in all other respects. The fact that she could respond correctly to a variety of complex commands proved that she could understand what was being said to her. If someone said, 'Rie, put the red paper under the table', or 'Bring me a banana from the cupboard', she could do it. Furthermore, she was even taught (at 3 years of age) to read complex Japanese characters (*kanji*), which she demonstrated by putting written cards on objects or by responding appropriately to written commands. The fact that she could understand speech and could read a little is clear evidence that she had ideas and was a thinking person. The very existence of her thought shows that thought could not have come from her ability to speak – because she had no such ability!

Not long ago the case of author Christopher Nolan came to the world's attention. Nolan's 1987 book *Under the Eye of the Clock* has been compared to the writings of Yeats and Joyce. Yet since birth Nolan has had but little control over his body, even having difficulty in swallowing food. He must be strapped to his wheelchair because he cannot support himself. With only slight muscle control at his disposal, he was able to 'type' his manuscript using a pointer attached to his head to point to letters. Yet while he has never had the ability to produce speech, he obviously is not only able to think but even to think more creatively than a large majority of the speaking population.

8.3.3 Thinking while paralysed by a drug

In 1947 one group of researchers (Smith, Brown, Tomas and Goodman) wondered what would happen to a person's thought if the body were almost completely paralysed. Their wondering led to Smith having himself injected with a curare-like drug which induces complete paralysis of the voluntary muscles of the body. Since only smooth muscle systems such as the heart and digestive system continue to function under the drug, Smith even needed the assistance of an artificial respirator in order to breathe.

When the effects of the drug wore off, Smith reported that he had been able to think quite clearly and could solve the series of problems given to him. At the risk of his life, Smith had made a scientific point. Since while paralysed he could in no way speak and could make only minimal bodily responses, it is clear that thought was not dependent on body movement or movements of the organs of speech, because there were no movements, not even subliminal ones. Unless one wants to advance the interesting but unlikely notion that the heart beat or perhaps bowel movements are somehow at the basis of thinking, then it would indeed seem that speech-associated muscle movements are not necessary for thought.

8.3.4 Talking about one thing while thinking about another

Suppose you are talking to someone, say, about a movie you both have seen, and further suppose that you are thinking about something else at the same time, such as where you are going for dinner. We often speak about one thing and think about another at the same time. We might even tell a lie, saying we have enjoyed someone's company, while thinking what a terrible time we had. All of this is clear evidence that two distinct processes with different content, speech and thought, are occurring simultaneously. This would be impossible if thought were merely some kind of internalized speech, for if we were speaking aloud we would not be able to use our vocal apparatus to talk to ourselves. Therefore, according to Behaviourist doctrine, we would not be able to think because our speech organs are already in use. Obviously there is something seriously wrong with this theory – it does not fit the facts.

This might be the place to point out that just because many of us talk aloud to ourselves while thinking does not imply that we are using speech to think with. A more adequate interpretation is that the speech is simply a reflection of the thoughts we already have. We are only giving voice to our thoughts when we speak to ourselves. What we utter occurs after we have formed a thought. We often tend to speak aloud when no one else is around or when we are under stress. We are so used to putting our thoughts into speech that this process needs to be inhibited, otherwise we might place ourselves in embarrassing situations. When there is no one around we find it easier to relax these inhibitions.

8.4 Language as the basis of thought

Many people believe that the language system, with its grammatical rules and vocabulary, forms thought or is necessary for thought, and that a particular language imposes particular ideas of nature or of one's culture. This view, like that of Humboldt's cited above in the case of the Sunday School teacher, is generally referred to as the Sapir–Whorf Hypothesis or Linguistic Relativism. It is a more sophisticated theory than the previous 'Speech is the Basis of Thought' one since it involves language in general and not simply speech production. However, whether this theory will stand up under examination is something we have yet to assess.

Sapir spoke of language as a 'tyrant' that not only reflects experience, but which actually defines it, imposing upon us particulars and ideas about the world. Whorf, who was Sapir's student, also shared his views stating that 'language is not merely a reproducing instrument for voicing ideas but rather is itself the shaper of ideas . . . We dissect nature along lines laid down by our native language.' Ideas, he further claimed, are not independently derived but are given by the grammar of our language. Thus Whorf asserted that the ideas of speakers of different languages would differ from slightly to greatly, depending on how different the various languages were. According to this theory, a speaker of Japanese, for example, would have very different ideas from a speaker of English because the grammars of the two languages are so very different. On the other hand, a speaker of German would automatically have more similar ideas to the speaker of English because the grammars are less different.

Whorf's research with the American Hopi Indians convinced him that their language forced them to see the world in a completely different way than do speakers of European languages. He believed that the Hopi language had few words relating to time, and that this gave them radically different concepts of space and time. In the Hopi language, Whorf claimed, for example, that you could never use spatial terms to refer to time, such as 'before noon', because the Hopis lack the concept of time seen as a continuum. Speakers of some languages – for example, English – use spatial terms for 'front' when they want to indicate the future ('to look forward to something'), presumably because they see themselves as moving forward through time.

More recently, however, other researchers have found that Whorf was wrong in claiming that the Hopi language is a 'timeless' one. Gipper, for example, who lived with a Hopi family for a period of time and studied their language, found that while Hopi does not have a formal tense, it nevertheless contains a whole series of expressions for time. Many of these expressions appear as adverbs or prepositions. (Even English uses non-tense expressions of time, such as 'I leave tomorrow', instead of 'I will leave tomorrow'.) According to Malotki, another researcher who spent years living with the Hopi, 'They [the Hopis] live with time every moment of their lives, but not like the white man' (from a 1980s American television programme on language and the mind). His detailed research has shown that the Hopis use a variety of time referents such as periods relating to harvest, the moon, the sun, and other significant events. We do much the same in English ('Let's go when it gets dark', 'I'll fix it when the weather gets warm'). Malotki very neatly concludes (again from the same television programme), 'People are not different because of their languages, but because of their experience. Deep down, we're all the same. It couldn't be otherwise.'

There are dramatic vocabulary differences from language to language. The Inuit (commonly called 'Eskimos') have a large number of words involving snow. For example: *apun* = 'snow on the ground'; *qanikca* = 'hard snow on the ground'; *utak* = 'block of snow'. However, simply focusing on single-word vocabulary can be very misleading. English speaking skiers, for example, do, in fact, create phrases such as 'powder snow', 'wet snow', 'flaky snow', to describe different snow types for which Inuit languages have single words. It is need that motivates us to create vocabulary. Phrases such as 'baby blue' or 'powder snow' serve just as well as their one-word counterparts in other languages.

Then, too, some languages have only a small number of colour words. The Dani language of New Guinea has only two colour words, one for light colours and one for dark colours. If language were the basis of thought and of the perception of nature, one would expect speakers of this language, with such a limited repertoire of colour terms, to have perceptual difficulty in distinguishing colours they have no terms for. The research of Kay and McDaniel, Heider and others, however, has shown that this is not the case. Speakers of languages which have only two, three or four colour terms are as capable of distinguishing among the many colour bands of the visible spectrum as those whose languages have more than eight basic colour terms. People can see the differences but will not give them a name unless there is a good reason to do so. The claim that you cannot see the difference in colours because you lack the words for those colours makes as much sense as saying you cannot hear the difference between two musical notes because you do not know the terms 'B-flat' and 'F-sharp'.

A very strong expression of the idea that language determines thought is offered by Korzybski, who said that the subject and predicate form of language 'leads to the humanly harmful, gross, macroscopic, brutalizing, biological, animalistic types of orientations . . . such "Führers" as different Hitlers, Mussolinis, Stalins, etc.' From this, one pictures hordes of Mongols and Huns sweeping through the centuries like millions of vicious, difficult-to-conjugate irregular verbs, good people at heart, perhaps, but helpless captives of their own bloodthirsty subject–predicate view of the universe, and, hence, forever doomed to burn and pillage!

Korzybski claimed, too, that the improper use of language causes damage to the brain and insanity, but that we could correct this situation through retraining the cell pathways in our brains by the proper use of language. A proper correspondence between language and brain, he said, would eliminate maladies such as arthritis and alcoholism. Cure the language and you cure the patient.

Just as silly, if somewhat less dramatic, is the view of the Japanese educator, Takao Suzuki, who holds that 'we recognize the fragments of the universe as objects or properties only through words . . . without words we could not even distinguish dogs from cats'. One wonders, too, if Suzuki has ever noticed that dogs and cats can tell each other apart even if they have no words for 'cat' and 'dog'. If they can do this without words, why can't humans?

8.5 Arguments against this idea

Let us now look at some special situations concerning language and thought which, I shall argue, sheds light on the true nature of the relationship between language and thought.

8.5.1 Deaf children without language can think

There are many deaf children who do not begin to acquire language until a rather late age, often after 3 or 4 years when they begin to attend special school. However, if you were to observe young deaf children playing in a playground, you would not notice much difference between them and

ordinary hearing children. They are not animalistic creatures. At play and when participating in activities around
the home, they behave just as intelligently and rationally
with respect to their environment as do hearing children.

If one holds that language is the basis for thought, one
would have to argue that these children do not think and are
either wild animals or automatons. And, if one holds that
grammar determines how we analyse nature, then it must
be argued that either the non-language deaf children cannot
analyse nature or they do so radically differently from
hearing children who do have language. But it has never
been observed that children who learn language at a late age
undergo a radical change in perception. Rather, research
points to the opposite conclusion. Furth, for example,
provides research data which show no difference in
intelligence between mature hearing and deaf persons, even
though the language knowledge of the deaf is generally far
below that of the hearing population.

The case of Helen Keller, who became deaf and blind
due to disease at the age of 18 months, is relevant and
interesting in this regard. After her illness, she was not
exposed again to language until she was 8 years old. In her
autobiography, *The Story of My Life*, Keller talks of her
teacher's 'despair' and her own 'repentance' and 'sorrow'
when she had behaved badly (a more detailed discussion of
this incident is described in Chapter 3). These were
experiences for which she had no words at the time (it is
unlikely that she would have learned such words in her
infancy) but for which she had concepts. If she could not
think, she would not have been able to remember details of
her past mental states. Her memories of her past, before she
had the language with which to express them, were more
than just a sequence of feelings and emotions. Keller had
thoughts and ideas which she had organized into a complex
conceptual framework. Clearly, such a mental construction
as this did not require language for its establishment.

8.5.2 Bilinguals are not schizoids

According to Whorf, common experience does not result in
common ideas. Simply knowing a language affects our view
of reality. Speakers of different languages are led by the

same physical evidence to the same picture of the universe only to the extent that 'their linguistic backgrounds are similar or can in some way be calibrated'. Given this view, it would be predicted that bilingual persons who knew very different languages would have two different or opposing views of reality. The existence of persons who speak two or more quite different languages but have one coherent view of the universe would contradict the Sapir–Whorfian presumption that different languages generate different realities.

The fact is that people do *not* develop multiple personalities or behavioural problems from learning two or more languages. The world is full of normal bilinguals, even trilinguals. I know of a family in America in which a child was exposed to three languages, English, Japanese and Russian, all at the same time. The father spoke only English to the boy, the mother spoke only Japanese, and the grandmother, who lived in the same household, spoke only Russian. By the age of 3, the boy spoke English with the father, Japanese with the mother, and Russian with the grandmother. When he went out to play, the child behaved no differently from his playmates, who were English monolinguals. A second boy was born into the family and he, too, became trilingual in the same way. And, just as his brother, he had no confused 'picture of the universe' or defects in thinking.

8.5.3 Creoles: new languages from old

Related to bilinguals not having split minds because of learning two languages is the case of *creole* languages. A creole language is a language that has developed through the contact of two established languages. Suppose you meet a Tibetan who does not know your language. What do you do? In order to communicate, you will both use some of the other's words and in time come to agree on some grammar. An English–Tibetan pidgin could result. This pidgin would have some of the features of the 'Me Tarzan, You Jane' kind of talk so popular in Hollywood films. As a pidgin, it would be a basic, practical means of communication consisting of a simple vocabulary and a simplified grammar; a primitive type of language.

What is of interest for our discussion, however, is what happens to pidgins over a period of time, when their speakers are in contact, marry and have children. These pidgins become fully developed languages, which are called 'creoles' by linguists. A creole has all of the aspects of a true natural language. A prime example of entirely different languages becoming a creole is Tok Pisin (Talk Pidgin), the official language of Papua New Guinea. There, English blended with native New Guinea languages to produce a new language. Research shows that many creoles develop along remarkably similar lines and, in many instances, develop rather quickly, even within the space of a few generations.

Now, if one were to take the Sapir–Whorf hypothesis seriously, such creoles would not have been able to develop because of the inherent conflict of the views of nature and of the world which the original languages supposedly embody. Languages could only blend into a creole if the original component languages represented similar perceptions and thoughts. The fact that creoles actually have developed with the English language (and other European languages, as well) and other languages in Melanesia, Africa and elsewhere is evidence that basic perception and basic thought are shared in some non-linguistic form by humans everywhere.

8.6   Where language does affect thought

Although I have argued for the view that language is not the basis of thought, by this I do not wish to imply that never language affects the content or direction of particular thoughts. Thus, while language is neither the basis of thought nor is necessary for the functioning of thought, language can affect thought once thought is established. For example, language may be used to provide us with *new ideas*. If you read the sentence, 'Ludwig van Beethoven was a good football player, when he was sober', that is probably a sentence you have never been exposed to before, yet you can understand it. It is important to realize though that novel (new) sentences such as this do not involve novel words or grammatical rules. What is novel is their arrangement. Thus, such sentences are created and understood on the basis of what the speaker already knows about the language in terms of its grammar and vocabulary. If new words are introduced, they can be explained in terms of vocabulary which is already known.

Language is also used to bring about a *change in beliefs or values*. People who have undergone religious or political conversion are often said to think differently. What has really become different, however, is not their basic logical processing or conceptual categories, but the truth and attractiveness values which they attach to certain ideas. For example, people become convinced, through the medium of language, that the world is round instead of flat (despite their perception to the contrary). Or, people are swayed to and away from capitalism or communism by attaching, through the medium of language, new emotions and values to these ideological systems. People may be persuaded to change, and though we might say that they are 'thinking differently', what has really changed are their values and goals. What they previously regarded as bad or false, they may now think of as good or true, or vice versa.

8.7 Thought as the basis of language

8.7.1 The non-linguistic origin of meaning

Except for the minor case of onomatopoeia, the relationship between the sound of a word and its meaning is conventional. The meaning that is to be associated with a sequence of speech sounds does not come with it; it must be acquired.

Meaning for words is acquired in four main ways: (1) a sound form is associated with an object, situation or event in the world, e.g. the sound 'dog' with the object 'dog'; (2) a sound form is associated with an idea or experience in the mind, e.g. the sound 'pain' with the feeling of 'pain'; (3) an analysis of known component morphemes may suggest a meaning, e.g. the meaning of *unprimitive* can be gained through knowledge of *un* and *primitive*; (4) by a linguistic description (definition) or by linguistic context (guessing based on the meanings of other words). With respect to these four ways of acquiring word meaning, only the latter two involve linguistic sources. Yet, even these had their origins in the first two. Thus, the ultimate source of meaning is based on experiences of the world and mind, experiences which are of a non-linguistic nature. It must therefore be the case that thought, with its ideas and concepts, is created in the mind by a process that is independent of language.

8.7.2 The true relationship between language and thought

Thus, after due consideration, the most plausible version of the relationship between language and thought is that the thought system in the mind has its origins in sources that are distinct from language. Only when thought is sufficiently developed through the child's experience of objects, events and situations in the world can language begin to be learned. Then, over a period of time, the complete language system is formed but through this medium of thought.

The philosopher, John Locke, some centuries ago proposed precisely this view: that the relationship between language and thought is such that thought is independent of language, with language deriving from thought. Given such a relationship, language can thereby fulfil its primary role, which is as an instrument for the expression or communication of thought. I find no good reason to challenge this view.

8.8 Discussion questions

1. What significance is there in the fact that it is possible to hum a melody or sing the words of a song and think of something else at the same time? How would this relate to the speech as the basis of thought notion?
2. 'I know what I want to say, but I can't find the word.' What implications does this phenomenon have for the language and thought controversy?

3. 'That which we call a rose by any other name would smell as sweet.' If we changed the name of the flower to 'bigstink', would it still smell as sweet or was Shakespeare wrong? What would an advertising agent say?

4. Some advocates of non-sexist language claim that language 'reinforces' habits of thought. In this regard consider that Japanese men and women are all addressed in the same way, with a *san* ending, Tanaka-san, Suzuki-san. (There is no differentiation as there is in English with Mr and Ms (Miss, Mrs).) Should one argue, therefore, that the Japanese language reinforces the notion of equality for men and women?

5. I do not believe that sexist language ('All men are created equal') affects our values. Yet, I do believe that such language can give offence. Am I being consistent?

6. Consider a monolingual English-speaking family in America. The mother and father are both Christian and Republicans. Their son and daughter, though, are atheists and Democrats. How does this situation of same language but different world views relate to the claim that a language has a world view inherent in it?

7. Many countries having widely different languages may share similar political, social and religious views. For example, China, North Korea and Cuba share Communist ideology, an ideology that was mainly formulated by German speakers. How does this situation of different languages (the Chinese, Korean and Spanish languages are all vastly different from one another) but similar world views relate to the claim that each language has a world view inherent in it?

8. Since the establishment of the communist government in 1949, the culture of China has changed greatly in political, social, economic, educational and religious terms. Yet, the Chinese language has changed relatively little in terms of its basic syntax and phonology although some vocabulary changes such as in forms of address, e.g. comrade, have occurred. How does this fact (that the world view of a people has changed radically but the language has changed little) relate to the claim that knowing and using a particular language shapes one's world view?

Suggested readings

Carroll, John B. (ed.) (1956) *Language, Thought and Reality: Selected Writing of Benjamin Lee Whorf.* Cambridge, Mass.: MIT Press.

Furth, H. G. (1971) Linguistic deficiency and thinking: research with deaf subjects, 1964–1969. *Psychological Bulletin*, **76**, 58–72.

Humboldt, Wilhelm von (1836/1971) *Linguistic Variability and Intellectual Development.* Coral Gables, FL: University of Miami Press.

Kay, P. and McDaniel, C. K. (1978) The linguistic significance of the meanings of basic color terms. *Language*, **54**, 610–46.

Korzybski, A. (1933) *Science and Sanity: An Introduction to Non-Aristotelian Systems and General Semantics* (4th edn, 1958), Lakeville, CN: The International Non-Aristotelian Publishing Co.

Liu, L. G. (1985) Reasoning counterfactuality in Chinese: Are there any obstacles? *Cognition*, **21**, 239–70.

Malotki, E. (1983) *Hopi Time: A Linguistic Analysis of the Temporal Concepts in the Hopi Language.* New York: Mouton.

Malotki, E. (*c.* 1985) Television programme: *The Mind's Language.* Station WNET New York.

McNeill, David (1987) *Psycholinguistics: A New Approach.* New York: Harper & Row.

Nolan, Christopher (1987) *Under the Eye of the Clock.* London: Pan Books.

Steinberg, Danny D. and Chen, Shing-ren (1980) A three year old mute-hearing child learns to read: the illustration of fundamental reading principles. *Working Papers in Linguistics* (University of Hawaii), **12**, 2, 77–91. Also in *Dokusyo Kagaku* (Science of Reading), **24**, 4, 134–41 (in Japanese).

US Supreme Court Reports (1922) October Term, Meyer v. Nebraska, pp. 392–403.

CHAPTER 9

Language and the brain

9.1 Brain structure and function

If you are left-handed, you have probably been discriminated against at one time or another: most school desks are built to be written on by right-handers, scissors work much better if you are right-handed, and in some cultures you are not permitted to eat or even touch food with your left hand. The Devil, too, is said to be left-handed, and many words such as 'sinister' and 'gauche' come from words meaning 'left'. 'Dexterity' comes from the Latin word for 'right'. Being 'right' in the moral sense of the word also derives from the use of the right hand.

Nature, too, seems to discriminate against left-handers, for they are more likely to suffer from a variety of language disorders and learning disabilities than do right-handers. It may also be that left-handers die younger (Halpern and Coren, 1991 *New England Journal of Medicine, vol.* 325). Observed differences in mortality (adjusting for sex differences) though may simply reflect the widespread effort of parents and teachers earlier in the century to convert left-handed children to right-handedness. Thus there may be no true difference between the proportion of older and younger *natural* left-handers in the general population (Salive, Guralnik and Glynn, Feb. 1993 *American Journal of Public Health*).

Interestingly, there is a higher proportion of natural left-handedness for males than females and this seems to occur everywhere in the world. Some estimates in the U.S. indicate about 10% for males and 4% for females. The effect of sexual hormones released in the brain during the development of the foetus may be the cause of this phenomenon.

Left-handers need not throw up their hands in despair, however, because among them there is a greater proportion of artists, musicians and writers than is found among right-handers. And, if you use both hands equally well, i.e. are ambidextrous, you can take heart, for you are in the company of such people as Leonardo da Vinci, although you might not like the word 'ambidextrous' since it comes from Latin, meaning to have two right hands!

Handedness is directly related to the structure and development of the brain. The brain and the spinal cord, together, make up the central nervous system. From the top of the spine upwards are the *medulla oblongata*, the *pons Varolii*, the *cerebellum* and the *cerebral cortex* (cerebrum) in that order. These four major parts of the brain form an integrated whole by means of connective tissue. The first three are concerned with essentially physical functions, including breathing, heartbeat, transmission and coordination of movement, involuntary reflexes, digestion, emotional arousal, etc. In comparing the brains of lower vertebrates with those of higher vertebrates and primates, such as man and the apes, the most noticeable difference is in the part of the brain which developed last in the course of evolution, the cerebral cortex. While in fish, for example, the cerebral cortex is barely visible and is one of the smallest parts of the brain, in humans it has increased in size and complexity to become the largest part of the brain. The cerebral cortex, itself, is a layer of grooved, wrinkled and winding tissue. In time, due to dense growth in the number and complexity of brain cells, the cerebral cortex takes on a pinkish-grey appearance, giving us the common term 'grey matter' for referring to this part of the brain or our intelligence.

The cerebral cortex is characterized by a division into halves, termed *hemispheres*, which are connected by tissue called the *corpus callosum*. The corpus callosum, it should be noted, is not only a connector for the hemispheres, but is the principle integrator of the mental processes carried out in the two hemispheres. The general appearance of the cerebral hemispheres as a whole is that of a walnut with the two adjoined parts, mirror images of one another. Each cerebral hemisphere is divided into four sections: the frontal, parietal, temporal and occipital lobes. This is a convenient division of the brain into parts, loosely based on physical features. Functions such as cognition (to some

Overhead View

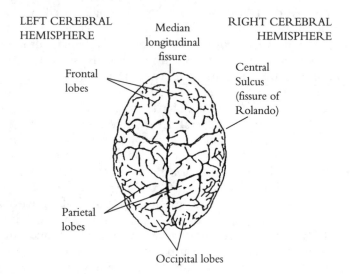

Side View

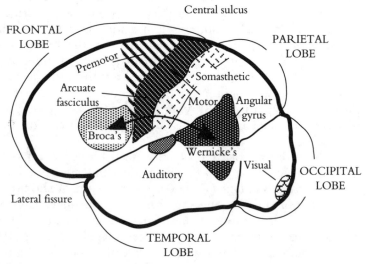

The left hemisphere of the human cerebral cortex (side view). It shows the language areas — Broca's and Wernicke's connected by the arcuate fasciculus, and the angular gyrus; four lobes — frontal, parietal, occipital, and temporal; and the lateral fissure and the central sulcus.

Figure 9.1 The brain: overhead and side views

degree) occur in the frontal lobe, general somasthetic sensing (in the arms, legs, face, etc.) in the parietal lobe, hearing in the temporal lobe and vision in the occipital lobe. As we shall see later, some of these areas are also involved in the structure and function of language.

As far as our linguistic abilities are concerned, however, it is not evident exactly how important the actual size and weight of the brain are. Whales and elephants have bigger brains, including more cortex, but they also have bigger bodies, so perhaps the ratio of brain to body size and weight which is important. However, the brain of the average 13-year-old human weighs 1.35 kg (3 lb) and the proportion to a body weight of 45 kg (99 lb) is 0.03 (1 : 34) and this is the same ratio as in a 3-year-old chimp. Thus, while brain size is almost certainly related to general intelligence in a very broad sense as one moves up the evolutionary ladder from species to species, size alone is not the crucial factor which would explain human language and non-human lack of language. Structural differences must exist which account for intelligence, language and other highly cognitive functioning.

9.2 Hemispheric dominance and lateralization

The brain controls the body by a division of labour, so to speak. The left hemisphere controls the right side of the body, including the right hand, the right arm and the right side of the face, while the right hemisphere controls the left side of the body. Those who have suffered a stroke (cerebral haemorrhage) provide clear examples of how this kind of cross-over control operates. A stroke in the right hemisphere of the brain will leave victims affected on the left side of the body. Thus, they can lose control over the muscles in the left hand, left leg and the left side of the face (including that side of the tongue and mouth), with the result that their ability to move the left arm and leg and to speak clearly will be affected.

However, a stroke would not affect vision and hearing in exactly the same way. A stroke in the relevant areas in one side of the brain would not automatically render useless the eye and ear on the opposite side of the body, because there is a criss-cross control when it comes to our organs of sight and hearing. For sight, there is what is termed 'fields of vision', in which the connections from each eye are separated, sending the left half (left field) of what it sees to one hemisphere and the right half (right field) to the other. The left and right fields are then integrated as a whole in the brain. Hearing works in a somewhat similar fashion with fibres of the acoustic nerve in each ear distributing the incoming signal to both hemispheres. More fibres from the left ear cross over and connect directly to the right hemisphere than the number of fibres connected directly to the left hemisphere. Conversely, more fibres from the right ear cross to the left hemisphere than the number of fibres connected to the right hemisphere.

Now, even though the hemispheres of the brain divide the labours of the body, they do not do so evenly. In a sense, we might say that the body cannot serve two masters; one side must take charge. Perhaps, to have the two hemispheres competing over which hand should be used first to fight off an attacker or to hunt with would not be advantageous for the survival of the species. This phenomenon, where one hemisphere is the major or controlling one, is called *dominance*.

For right-handed persons, the left hemisphere generally dominates the right hemisphere, with the result that those people tend to prefer their right hands. Counter to expectations, only about 40 per cent of left-handers have right-brain dominance. The majority have left-brain dominance but their dominance is much less marked than in naturally right-handed persons. This lack of strong dominance for left-handers is believed to be a factor contributing to speaking problems and to various reading and writing dysfunctions, such as reversal of letters and words when reading and writing. (Forcing naturally left-handers to be right-handers does not remedy such problems but only serves to worsen them and create others.)

Also, some studies suggest that there are differences between the brains of males and females. In one experiment, Marion Diamond at the University of California at Berkeley, has shown that injecting sex hormones into young rats can affect the development of the thickness and size of the hemispheres of their brains. While females normally have a thicker left hemisphere (one specialization of which involves general sensory functions) and males have a thicker right hemisphere (one specialization of which involves visual-spacial functions), her injection of hormones had brought about a reversal of hemisphere thickness in the sexes by the time the rats became young adults. A related study with human children (aged 2 to 8 years), who had high levels of androgen (a predominantly male hormone) due to a genetic glandular disorder, was recently published in a 1992 issue of the journal *Psychological Sciences*. The researchers found that the girls with this condition (of being exposed to the male hormone as foetuses), when given two sets of toys that children traditionally show preference for by sex, played twice as long with so-called boys' toys (blocks, trucks, cars) than girls who had not had such an exposure.

The brain assigns, as it were, certain structures and functions to certain hemispheres of the brain. Language, logical and analytical operations, and higher mathematics, for example, generally occur in the left hemisphere of the brain, while the right hemisphere is superior at recognizing emotions, recognizing faces and taking in the structures of things globally without analysis. This separation of structure and function in the hemispheres is technically referred to as *lateralization*: incoming experiences are received by the left or right hemisphere depending on the nature of those experiences, be they speech, faces or sensations of touch.

Associated with lateralization is what might be termed 'earedness', where right-handed persons with lateralization for language in the left hemisphere will perceive more readily *speech* sounds through the right ear than the left. For, when speech sounds are presented simultaneously to both ears (dichotic) in listening experiments, those to the right ear are preferred. For example, a person with normal hearing who is simultaneously presented with 'ba' through an earphone on the left ear and 'da' through an earphone on the right ear, will perceive 'da' more strongly or dominantly. This is probably because 'da' passes directly to the language-processing centres in the left hemisphere while the 'ba' speech sound coming in the left ear must travel a longer route; the 'ba' will automatically go to the right hemisphere first, but then be rerouted to the language areas in the left hemisphere through the corpus callosum connection. (As noted above, incoming sound mainly crosses over to the opposite hemisphere.) Because of the longer path the speech sound presented to the left ear must travel, that sound would arrive at the language centre *after* that of the sound presented to the right ear. Arriving later may well be what weakens its effect. This situation does not hold for all types of sound, however. Music and non-linguistic sounds, noises and animals sounds, for example, are perceived more strongly in the left ear, since they are processed in the right (non-language) hemisphere.

For our purposes, we are concerned with the lateralization of language – that is, the areas of the brain which are involved in the use of language. Research has clearly shown that language centres predominate in the left hemisphere in right-handed people and sometimes in the right hemisphere for left-handed people. The main language centres in the left hemispheres are *Broca's area*, in the front part of the brain, *Wernicke's area*, towards the back, and the *angular gyrus*, which is even further back. Broca's area and Wernicke's area are connected by tissue (the *arcuate fasciculus*). These areas are not found in the right hemisphere.

While the two hemispheres superficially appear to be identical mirror images of one another, research has demonstrated that this is not the case, neither structurally nor functionally. Wada has shown that infants at birth have a bulge in the left hemisphere, where language is typically located, but not in the corresponding area of the right hemisphere. Also, in a group of 100 normal humans, Geschwind and Levitsky have demonstrated that Wernicke's area is generally larger than the corresponding area in the right hemisphere. Moreover, such asymmetry of the brain is even present in the foetus, appearing by the 31st week. Certain aspects of lateralization have been dramatically confirmed by the work of Sperry, who separated the hemispheres of the brain by severing the connecting tissue, the corpus callosum, of a number of patients. (The purpose of the procedure was to treat extreme cases of epilepsy.) With the corpus callosum no longer intact, information no longer flowed from hemisphere to hemisphere as it does in normal persons. The functions of the complete brain were no longer integrated. By experimentally allowing information to reach only one hemisphere or the other, e.g.

showing written words to the right visual field only, researchers were thus able to test the abilities of the separate hemispheres. It was found that 'split-brain' persons still could use speech and writing in the disconnected left hemisphere but that their right hemisphere had little such capacity. In normal persons, the right hemisphere has more capability.

When tactile (touch) information passed to the left hemisphere, split-brain patients were completely capable of verbally describing objects and talking about things they had just touched, for example. If, however, patients experienced things only with the right hemisphere, they could not talk about the experience at all, since the information could not be passed through the severed corpus callosum to the left hemisphere for expression in speech. The right hemisphere, in general, was also incapable of imagining the sound of a word, even a familiar one, and patients failed simple rhyming tests, such as determining by reading, which word, 'pie' or 'key', rhymes with 'bee', while the right hemisphere was better at spatial tasks such as matching things from their appearance, e.g. being able to correctly reassemble halves of photographs. Generally, these tests showed that only the left hemisphere is used for speaking and writing.

9.3 Language areas and functioning

The model most researchers use today in describing how we comprehend language is still one largely based on that proposed by Wernicke over a century ago. Wernicke observed that Broca's area was near that part of the brain which involves the muscles which control speech while the area which he identified, later called Wernicke's area, was near the part of the brain which receives auditory stimuli. Based on these observations, Wernicke hypothesized that the two areas must in some way be connected. Later research showed that they are indeed connected, being connected by the arcuate fasciculus.

Thus, according to Wernicke, on hearing a word, the sound of the word goes from the ear to the auditory area of the temporal lobe and then to Wernicke's area. If a heard

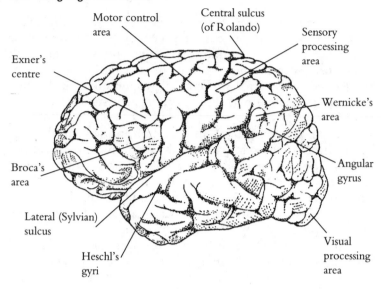

Exner's centre

Motor control area

Central sulcus (of Rolando)

Sensory processing area

Wernicke's area

Angular gyrus

Broca's area

Lateral (Sylvian) sulcus

Heschl's gyri

Visual processing area

Language areas

The areas which have been proposed for the processing of speaking, listening, reading, writing, and singing are mainly located at or around the Sylvian and Rolando fissures (p. 258). Several specific areas have been identified.

• The front part of the parietal lobe, along the fissure of Rolando, is primarily involved in the processing of sensation, and may be connected with the speech and auditory areas at a deeper level.

• The area in front of the fissure of Rolando is mainly involved in motor functioning, and is thus relevant to the study of speaking and writing.
• An area in the upper back part of the temporal lobe, extend-ing upwards into the parietal lobe, plays a major part in the comprehension of speech. This is 'Wernicke's area'.
• In the upper part of the temporal lobe is the main area involved in auditory reception, known as 'Heschl's gyri', after the Austrian pathologist R. L Heschl (1824–81).
• The lower back part of the frontal lobe is

primarily involved in the encoding of speech. This is 'Brocha's area'.
• Another area towards the back of the frontal lobe may be involved in the motor control of writing. It is known as 'Exner's centre', after the German neurologist Sigmund Exner (1846–1926).
• Part of the left parietal region, close to Wernicke's area, is involved with the control of manual singing.
• The area at the back of the occipital lobe is used mainly for the processing of visual input.

Figure 9.2 Language areas of the brain

word is then to be repeated aloud, the sound must pass to Broca's area (by way of the arcuate fasciculus). Here, a programme for the vocalization of speech would then be activated.

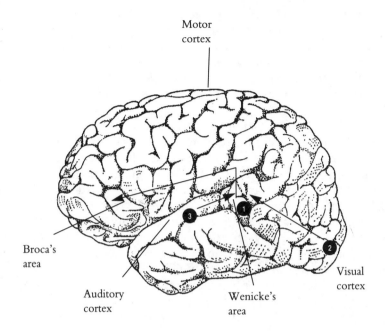

Some of the neural pathways that are considered to be involved in the processing of spoken language.

1. *Speech production* The basic structure of the utterance is thought to be generated in Wernicke's area and is sent to Broca's area for encoding. The motor programme is then passed on to the adjacent motor area, which governs the articulatory organs.

2. *Reading aloud* The written form is first received by the visual cortex, then transmitted via the angular gyrus to Wernicke"s area, where it is thought to be associated with the auditory representation. The utterance structure is then sent on to Broca's area, as in (1).

3. Speech comprehension The signals arrive in the auditory cortex from the ear, and are transferred to the adjacent Wernicke's area, where they are interpreted.

Figure 9.3 Some speech and reading processes

Broca's area is adjacent to the region of the motor cortex which controls the movement of the muscles of the tongue, the lips, the jaw, the soft palate and the vocal chords. When a word is read, according to Wernicke, the information goes from the eyes to the visual area of the cortex, and then to the angular gyrus which causes the auditory form of the word to be activated in Wernicke's area. Recent research in brain-scan imaging, however, shows that the latter part of the reading process, where

Wernicke's area is said to be activated, does not occur in many instances thereby indicating that the auditory aspect of the theory is in radical need of modification. In other words, one can directly recover the meaning of written words without having to access their sound. (Further discussion on this particular problem is presented later in this chapter.)

Although most language processes occur in Broca's area, Wernicke's area and the angular gyrus, some language functioning does occur elsewhere in the left hemisphere, and some even occurs in the right 'non-language' hemisphere. The ability to attach and understand intonation, such as the rising tone of a question, the ability to interpret emotional intentions, such as anger or sarcasm from inflections in the voice, and the ability to appreciate social meanings from something such as whispering, may very well be located outside of what have been traditionally regarded as the main language areas of the brain. Such secondary components of language are not only more spread out than previously thought but may vary in location from person to person.

9.4 Brain maturation and critical age for learning language

Much speculation has been devoted to whether there is a critical age in first-language learning and in second-language learning. By 'critical age' is meant here an age beyond which language learning will be difficult or even impossible. (Discussion of a critical age for first-language learning is presented in Chapter 3 while discussion of a critical age for second-language learning is presented in Chapter 10.)

There is evidence that damage to language areas in the left hemisphere of very young children are compensated for, with the right hemisphere taking over the reacquisition of language functions. Language then becomes located in the right hemisphere for these individuals. (This sometimes happens with adults.) Lennenberg, who based on his work with aphasic children, set puberty as the age or time in a child's life beyond which this kind of recovery would no longer occur. Other researchers, such as Krashen, have since found that the age limit of recovery (the right hemisphere taking over damaged left hemisphere functions) is much lower, approximately age 5 years.

Some theorists have interpreted studies such as these as indicating that there is an age beyond which normal children would no longer be able to learn a first or any language. According to them, a child who had been deprived of language until after the 'critical age' had passed, would no longer be able to learn language, or only learn a little with great difficulty. However, it is my view that evidence regarding the recovery of lateralization in brain-damaged children is irrelevant to the issue of a critical age for first-language learning in normal children, for it is not known how an *undamaged* left hemisphere, normal in every other respect except for never having been exposed to language, would react when it is exposed to language for the first time. As a result, the age limit of potential language learning in an undamaged left hemisphere might well be beyond the 5-year limit proposed by Krashen on the basis of damaged brains.

The findings of research with language-deprived children (Chapter 3) is relevant here. These children *were* able to learn significant portions of their first language well after the age of 5 years. Although it is possible that there was some acquisition prior to their deprivation and that this acquisition had assisted their later learning of their first language, this could not have helped much. In the case of Helen Keller, only a little of first language could have been learned before the age of 18 months at which time she was deprived of language by disease. Most of her first language had to have been acquired after the age of 8 years. Similarly, Genie, who had been cut off from language since she was 20 months, learned most of her first language after the age of 13 years.

Of course, with regard to a critical age for second-language learning, 5 years could *not* be a critical age because it is a commonplace observation that children learn a second language easily until about 12 years of age and that almost everyone can learn some or most of a second language after that age. All we can say for sure is that children are generally better than adults at acquiring native-speaker *pronunciation* in a second language (see Chapter 10 for further discussion). Since pronunciation is a motor skill where speech articulators such as the vocal chords, tongue and mouth are controlled by muscles, an adult's difficulty in acquiring native-speaker pronunciation in a second language is probably part of the overall decline in motor skills which occurs around puberty. Clearly, one will make a better gymnast or pianist if one starts at age 7 than if one starts at age 27. Undoubtedly, the decline in motor skills is related to the maturation of the brain, although just what that development might be has yet to be determined. Similarly, it is likely that the rote memory ability (simple association) which declines with age (see Chapter 10) is also related to the maturation of the brain. Since other aspects of second language learning do not decline with age (the learning of the abstract rules and principles of a grammar seem unaffected), it may be that, as far as language is concerned, only motor skills and rote memory decline as the result of brain maturation.

9.5 Language disorders

Language disorders, known as aphasias, are presumed to have as their cause some form of damage to some specific site in the hemisphere where language is located. Such damage causes characteristic problems in spontaneous speech, as well as in the understanding of speech and writing. An extensive study, using radioisotope scanning, in 1967 by Benson served to support the traditional distinction that aphasias are generally classifiable into two groups, Broca's aphasias and Wernicke's aphasias, by finding abnormalities in the two areas. (In most persons, Broca's area is located in the frontal lobe of the left hemisphere and Wernicke's area is in the temporal lobe of that same hemisphere.) In addition to these two basic groups, other dysfunctions were found.

9.5.1 Broca's aphasia

The traditional view of Broca's area is that it coordinates speech movements. It was in 1861 that the Frenchman, Paul Broca, published the first in a series of studies on language and brain. This was the beginning of the true scientific study of cases of aphasia, a term which describes a very broad range of language disorders which is commonly caused by tissue damage or destruction in the brain. Car accidents, war injuries and strokes are frequent causes of such injuries. Broca was one of the first researchers to discover that damage to certain portions of the brain, but not to others, will result in speech disorders. The portion of the brain which he identified as involving the coordination of speech movements continues to bear his name.

One particular condition, now called 'Broca's aphasia', is characterized by meaningful but shortened speech and also occurs in writing. Grammatical inflections are often lacking, such as the third person present tense '-s' ('Mary want candy' for 'Mary wants candy') and the auxiliary 'be' ('Joe coming' for 'Joe is coming'), as are articles, prepositions and other so-called function words. In a way, the speech is similar to that of children at the 'telegraphic' stage of speech production (Chapter 1).

Although the feature of Broca's aphasia most noted is the fragmentary nature of speech *production*, it has only been recently discovered that speech *comprehension* is also affected. In one experiment, a patient with Broca's aphasia, when presented with the sentence, 'The apple that the boy is eating is red', could understand the sentence, particularly with regard to who is doing the eating (the boy is doing the eating). However, when presented with the sentence 'The girl that the boy is looking at is tall', the same patient could not figure out who was doing the looking (the boy is looking at the girl). In the first sentence, one can guess the meaning from knowing the vocabulary items *'apple'*, *'boy'* and *'eat'*, and from knowing what usually happens in the world (boys eat apples and not vice versa). But you cannot guess the meaning of the second sentence simply from the vocabulary, because boys look at girls and girls look at boys. To understand such a sentence, one must be able to analyse its syntactic relations. Thus, there is a loss of syntactic knowledge in both speech production and understanding for those with Broca's aphasia. Interestingly, people with Broca's aphasia can often sing very well, even using the same words and structures which they are unable to utter in conversation. This shows that Broca's aphasia is not simply a breakdown in the muscular control of speech movements, since those with this disorder *can* pronounce words to some extent. The loss, therefore, must extend to something of a deeper nature, probably involving intention and control.

9.5.2 Wernicke's aphasia

This condition is characterized by speech which often resembles what is called nonsense speech or double-talk. It sounds right and is grammatical but it is meaningless. It can seem so normal that the listener thinks that he or she has, as is often the case in ordinary conversation, somehow misheard what was said and therefore did not understand it. A patient with Wernicke's aphasia may say, 'Before I was in the one here, I was over in the other one. My sister had the department in the other one', 'My wires don't hire right' or 'I'm supposed to take everything from the top so that we do four flashes of four volumes before we get down low'.

Patients with Wernicke's aphasia also commonly provide substitute words for the proper ones on the basis of similar sounds, associations or other features. The word 'chair', for example, elicited the following in some patients: 'shair' (similar sound), 'table' (association), 'throne' (related meaning), 'wheelbase' (uncategorizable) and 'You sit on it. It's a . . . (word loss). As with Broca's aphasia, Wernicke's aphasia can also cause a severe loss of speech understanding, although the hearing of non-verbal sounds and music may be unimpaired.

9.5.3 Other speech-related aphasias

In addition to the kinds of aphasias which can occur from damage to the two main language centres of the brain, Broca's area and Wernicke's area, there are other aphasias which occur due to damage at sites near or between those areas and at other sites in the brain as yet undetermined. Damage to the area which leads into Wernicke's area from the auditory cortex may result in *pure word deafness*, where one cannot recognize the sounds of words as speech but can hear other types of sounds. For example, a person might be able to hear music quite clearly and even sing a melody which he or she has just heard, but be unable to recognize the lyrics of that song as words.

A condition known as *conduction aphasia* is characterized by a poor ability to repeat words despite relatively good comprehension. Persons with this aphasia might substitute a closely related sound for the one they actually hear, e.g. for 'teethe' they say 'teeth' and for 'bubble' they say 'bupple' (here inventing a new word but one that fits the way sounds are combined to make English words). Some may also have the ability to repeat strings of four or five digits, e.g. 4-5-9-2, 3-8-4-2-7, yet be unable to repeat a simple three-syllable sentence accurately, e.g. 'Joe is here', 'Betty sang'.

Anomic aphasia involves problems in finding the proper words for spontaneous speech, even though language comprehension and repetition are good. Typically, such a person has difficulty finding the correct names for objects. This is a phenomenon which we all experience on a much reduced non-pathological level at times, e.g. 'Hand me that . . . uh . . . uh . . . uh . . . thing over there.'

There are also reported cases of patients being unable, in response to a verbal command, to perform skilled motor movements with their hands, even though they understand the command and their spontaneous hand movements are perfectly normal. Thus, while a person might spontaneously be able to pick up a pen, he or she may not be able to perform the same task when asked to do so. This inability to respond appropriately to verbal commands is called *apraxia*.

There is also *global aphasia*, a terrible condition in which many or all aspects of language are severely affected, presumably due to massive damage at numerous sites in the left hemisphere or to critical connections between language areas. Such patients demonstrate little speech comprehension and display, at best, some stereotypic and automatic sequences of speech sounds. One woman who had suffered a massive stroke could say nothing but four nonsense syllables, 'ga dak la doh', every time she tried to speak.

In trying to determine what kind of aphasia will be produced by what kind of damage, there are a number of variables that must be taken into consideration. It is not just the location of damage to the brain which matters, it is also important to know what the nature of the damage or the lesion is. Was tissue completely destroyed or was the damage slight? Did the damage occur suddenly or gradually over time? Since childhood lesions may leave a mild deficit that can be difficult to detect, and since the same lesions in an adult would be much more noticeable, it is necessary to know the age at which the damage occurred.

9.5.4 Reading and writing aphasias: dyslexias

The type of aphasia which involves disorders in reading and writing is called *dyslexia*. There are many sorts of dyslexia, one category of which is due to damage to the brain after reading and writing have been acquired. With children, dyslexias may be observed in the process of their acquiring reading and writing skills. Problems of hemispheric dominance, defects in visual perception or the effect of using a poor teaching method, are all believed to play a role in causing some persons to read or write backwards (*deer* as *reed*), confuse the orientation of letters (*b* and *d*, *p* and *q*), (*u* and *n*, *m* and *w*) and to engage in other anomalies.

Dyslexia may be subdivided into two basic categories: *alexia*, which involves disorders in reading, and *agraphia*, which involves disorders in writing. One may be afflicted by both conditions at the same time, in which case the person is unable to both read or write. In 'pure agraphia' there is a total loss of the ability to write, although the hand can be used skilfully for other purposes. Thus, for example, a person who has had a left hemisphere stroke or damage due to other causes may be able to read the simple sentence 'How are you?', and yet be unable to write it when it is dictated verbally. Also, some may be unable to read a phrase yet be quite able to write it as dictation. That condition is termed *alexia without agraphia*. (They will not even be able to read what they themselves have just written!) It is, in a way, the written equivalent to certain aphasias mentioned earlier, where individuals may be able to say what they want, yet, when their speech is auditorily recorded and the tape played back to them, they are unable to understand what they have just said.

Studies involving languages with unusual writing systems provide interesting findings. Japanese aphasics display quite unusual characteristics due to the nature of their writing system, which involves both a syllabic system (in which symbols represent syllables) and Chinese type characters (in which symbols represent meanings). Imura at the Nihon University College of Medicine studied a patient with Broca's aphasia who was able to write the correct character for dictated words but was unable to write the same words in the syllabic system, something that any normal Japanese can do. Then there was a patient with Wernicke's aphasia who was able to write characters quite fluently, but, as is the case with much of the speech of those with Wernicke's aphasia, what was written was nonsensical: the characters were malformed or made up of invented sets of strokes.

Besides writing problems, reading by Japanese can also be affected in strange ways in terms of the syllabic (*kana*) and character (*kanji*) systems. The noted researcher Sasanuma has found that while some patients may have their reading of kana words impaired, their reading of kanji words (familiar ones) may not be much impaired, or vice versa, even when the kana and kanji words are familiar. These are right-handers who have had damage, due to strokes (cerebral haemorrhages) and automobile accidents, in the temporal or parietal regions of their left hemisphere. In some cases, the loss is undoubtedly due to damage of storage areas in the brain for kana and kanji words. However, as Sasanuma points out, there may also be damage to some processing or retrieval areas in the brain that yield these results and other strange outcomes. Incidentally, it might be worth pointing out a common fallacy concerning Chinese characters and kanji. These are not located in the right hemisphere (in ordinary right-handed persons), even though these symbols are historically derived from pictures (as is the case for all writing systems). They are located in the left hemisphere, as are all writing systems.

9.5.5 Localism and holism

Much of the discussion in this chapter has been aimed at showing in a very broad way how the production and understanding of language is related to certain areas of the brain and their interconnections. This particular model of looking at the structure and function of language by relating specific aspects of language to certain localized areas of the brain is called the *localist* model. Although it is true that certain areas of the brain are involved in language, it is also necessary to take into account holistic or global brain phenomena in order to understand the effect on language of broader psychological factors, such as attention span, motivation, alertness, the rate at which auditory and visual memory traces dissipate, etc. A *holistic* type of model does just this. For example, you start to say something and suddenly you are distracted and break off, or you forget what you wanted to say. It would not be justifiable to conclude that you suffered a momentary breakdown in speech production due to some damage to your Broca's area. Or, when a friend says something but you do not catch the words and you respond with a 'What?'; this is not an indication that your Wernicke's area is breaking down. Some sort of holistic multi-dimensional explanation is required here.

Also, there are cases of aphasia which have been examined clinically that do not correspond to the localist model. Some patients with aphasia have turned out to have areas of their brains affected or unaffected in ways that do not correspond to the view that a certain behavioural dysfunction must always be the result of damage to one particular area of the brain. The localist model has been successful in explaining roughly 85 per cent of aphasias, but the other 15 per cent are anomalous and baffling. They represent people who have language disorders but do not have damage in the expected language areas, or, conversely, certain damage has not resulted in the predicted symptoms. This cannot but make us reflect on the more global aspects of language in the brain. Furthermore, it is possible that, as some studies now suggest, the failure to produce grammatical sentences in some aphasias may not be a loss of actual knowledge, but rather a breakdown in the process of constructing sentences; that is, aphasics still 'know' grammar, but they no longer know how to use it.

While there is an impressive accumulation of scientific knowledge on the brain to date, it is well to keep in mind the fact that even such linguistic concepts as simple as that of the noun or a verb has yet to be localized. Science is still a long way from providing the detailed knowledge of the correspondence between language and the brain's structure and function that we would like to have.

9.5.6 Sign language aphasia

There is a striking parallel between speech and sign language that is especially interesting since it confirms what research has found about language and the hemispheres of the brain. Readers will recall that it is the left hemisphere that is the site of the major language areas of the brain, and this includes Broca's and Wernicke's areas. The right hemisphere, on the other hand, has been shown to be superior at spatial tasks such as facial recognition and visuoconstructive tasks such as copying designs and patterns. Following this division of the hemispheres as 'left for language' and 'right for spatial', it might seem that the right hemisphere would be the one to be more involved with the production and comprehension of sign language, since signing is a space-related phenomenon. Strong evidence, however, from the study of sign language aphasics shows that this is not the case.

Native signers of American Sign Language who have suffered trauma such as a stroke (cerebral infarction) to the left hemisphere will produce sign language equivalents of Broca's aphasia or Wernicke's aphasia. The signed language of a Broca's aphasic consists largely of uninflected forms with little ability to use the signing space as a grammatical framework to mark verbs or persons, aspect or morphological changes. It is as awkward and as halting as is Broca's aphasia in spoken language. Patients may be accurate in making a single sign in response to a request to name an object or they may make a sign successfully when it has a simple uninflected meaning but be unable to produce a similar movement to indicate grammatical function such as the direct object. One patient was able to make the proper path movement towards the body to sign 'accept', but not a similar movement for 'blame-me'. The implication is that the inability to produce correct signs is not due to a motor dysfunction but rather a defect in the ability to access the grammar properly.

Similarly, the sign equivalent of Wernicke's aphasia will, in general, be grammatical in nature. A patient will produce fluent strings of signs, taking advantage of three-dimensional space for morphology, aspect, pronoun reference, etc. However, because of frequent 'slips of the hand', with substitutions made in terms of the three characteristics of signs (configuration, location and movement), the result is the production of many meaningless individual signs or of signs which have meaning but are nonsensical in sentences. And, just as in Wernicke's aphasia for speech, much substitution occurs within the same lexical category: nouns for nouns, verbs for verbs, etc. Furthermore, substitution occurs, too, along semantically related lines, such as 'daughter' for 'son' or 'bed' for 'chair', producing similarly bizarre results. One signing patient displayed Wernicke's aphasia symptoms in his writing as well as sign language, leading researchers to conclude that there is a general linguistic dysfunction at work and not just a motor dysfunction impairing the ability to sign.

Signers who have suffered damage to the right hemisphere generally do not display aphasia symptoms in the production of signs. Their sign production seems to remain grammatical and unimpeded. However, these same persons are likely to suffer some impairment in their comprehension of signs. Why it should be the case that their ability to understand signs is disturbed but their ability to produce signs is not, as yet remains unexplained.

In any case, the same general patterns of aphasia emerge in sign as with speech. Patients with left-hemisphere damage suffer the same aphasias whether their language is a spoken one or a signed one. Thus, even though the right hemisphere is disposed to process spatial tasks, when the task involved is a linguistic one and spatial syntax is involved, the left hemisphere asserts dominance. Clearly this shows that it is the left hemisphere that is specially equipped to handle language, whether the modality of the language be that of speech or sign.

9.6 Methods of investigating brain and language

9.6.1 Established methods: post-mortem, injured people, electrical stimulation

The comparatively little understanding we have of the neurological basis of language in the brain is the result of the application of a relatively small number of methods. The oldest method, that used by Broca himself, is the post-mortem examination of the brains of patients who had displayed language disorders while they were alive. The abnormalities he found in certain areas of their brains in post-mortems correlated with the language symptoms they displayed while alive. Another method involves observing the language of patients who have had brain operations. A person might require – because of an accident or a tumour for example – the removal of a lobe of the brain (lobectomy) or even of an entire hemisphere (hemispherectomy). Then, too, the study of the language of living patients with severe brain damage caused by accidents or war-time injuries was and still is a fruitful method of investigation.

A more recent method, pioneered by Penfield in the 1950s, involves the electrical stimulation of the cerebral cortex in patients who are conscious during brain surgery (electroencephalography). On being stimulated, patients would report, for example, that they remember childhood events or old songs. (How to verify what the patient says about the past is a problem.) The use of this procedure has been very limited since it is restricted to the open brain areas of persons who are undergoing surgery without the use of anaesthesia.

9.5.7 New high-tech methods: CAT and PET

In recent years, revolutionary new methods have been developed which lend themselves nicely to the study of language and the brain. These involve powerful new techniques in radiological imaging. CT (best known as CAT, Computerized Axial Tomography) and PET (Positron Emission Tomography) are the most widely used in this regard. Both of these techniques use the brain as it is, without surgery or any other radical procedure. As such they may be used with normal persons as well as those with brain problems.

A CAT scan involves using an X-ray source so as to make numerous slice scans, the images of which are integrated by computer to construct an image of the whole brain or portion of it. Curious scientists recently used CAT to examine a section of the brain of Broca's original patient,

Leborgne, who is better known in scientific literature as 'Tau'. (He was nicknamed this because that sound was the only one that he could utter.) The brain has been preserved for over a 100 years in a medical museum in Paris! Modern researchers were able to re-examine, as it were, the patient, to determine just which areas of the brain had been affected. Tomography has shown that Broca was essentially correct in concluding that the language deficits of the patient had indeed involved trauma to the area of the brain which bears his name.

Fascinating though the CAT method may be, undoubtedly the most exciting one to come along to date (in 1972) is PET, Positron Emission Tomography. Unlike CAT, which images slices of the brain and integrates them into a whole by computer, PET allows for the direct observation of the brain as a whole. Like CAT, it also allows for the study of language in both the normal or damaged brain. The PET procedure involves injecting a mildly radioactive substance into the blood and then tracing the blood flow patterns within the brain by means of special detectors surrounding the person's head. These detectors then provide a colour image. With PET, areas of the brain light up in different colours when there is an increase in blood flow (an indication of increased brain activity). As subjects perform various linguistic tasks given to them by researchers, it becomes possible to map the areas which underlie language use in the brain in a way that was never possible before.

In reading, for example, the PET scan shows that light signals from the eyes (as we look at the printed word) are sent to the visual area of the cortex (in the occipital lobe) then forward to the visual association areas. When speech is heard, on the other hand, the acoustic signals from the ear go to the auditory cortex (in the temporal lobe). PET scans are able to determine how closely models of speech production and understanding and models of reading and writing conform to reality.

PET has already provided evidence that counters one view of reading which holds that the printed word must always be sounded out in order to be understood. It showed that visual forms of words may be sent directly to the semantic areas in the frontal lobe for comprehension. Access to the stored auditory form in the angular gyrus for mentally sounding out words is not necessary in the recovery of meaning. This direct semantic connection occurs mainly with common, familiar words. However, even when people have learned to read by a method of sounding out letters, like Phonics, after repeated exposure to the written words, the sounding-out activity will be bypassed and the semantic areas will be directly activated. Only when a special task is presented, such as trying to determine whether 'blue' or 'go' rhymes with 'shoe' (the words are presented in written form), will a portion of the brain near the auditory cortex light up, indicating that internal sounding out is taking place.

New discoveries by using PET are of such widespread interest nowadays that they are being reported frequently in the newspapers and magazines. In October 1991 I read where researchers, investigating the recall of a word, discovered that both the frontal and visual lobes of the *right* hemisphere are activated. Such functions of the right hemisphere were previously unknown. Then, on 17 February 1992, the New York Times News Service reported that, by means of PET:

1. The brain distributes language processing over a few or many cerebral areas. According to researcher George Ojemann, many additional areas of the brain, besides Broca's and Wernicke's areas, are involved in language.
2. Second languages are rather loosely organized in the brain. A second language can even be localized in the right hemisphere. The case of Carla, 22, is cited. She grew up speaking both her native Italian and English. When she began training to become a simultaneous translator, her language abilities in both Italian and English were localized in the left hemisphere. After translation training, however, English shifted to the right hemisphere although Italian remained on the left! Such findings, if replicated, will somehow have to be incorporated into general theory.

9.7 Mind and brain

What is the relationship between mind and brain? Certainly,

without brain, there would be no mind. But does this necessarily imply that the mind is under the complete control of the brain? These questions take us back to Chapter 7 where the relationship between mind and body was discussed. What was said for body, of course, applies to brain since brain is a part of body.

The issue is this: *Is there a perfect correlation between a person's experiences and the events which take place in the brain?* While there is strong evidence of a general dependence of mental occurrences on the functioning of the brain, it has never been shown that the correspondence is so exact that from observation of a person's brain one could arrive at a knowledge of the person's experiences in every detail. Many theorists believe that consciousness plays a role in determining events in the mind and, hence, in the brain; and that, if it were not for conscious control, we would find ourselves in a continual dream-like state where events would occur and be experienced in the mind but where we would have no power to act in order to control such events.

We have now arrived at another philosophical problem: the issue of free will and determinism. Are events in the mind wholly determined by other events? These can be events which had occurred in the brain or events which had occurred in mind. The determinism of events can be physical (from the brain and other parts of the central nervous system) or it can be mental (from the operations of the mind), or both, depending on whether one takes a dualist or monist view of the universe. According to dualists, there are two kinds of stuff in the universe, the physical and the mental. For monists, there is just one kind, with the physical usually being preferred. Other recent approaches, such as Functionalism, have tried to avoid such distinctions altogether by offering pragmatic analyses. These, however, have not been successful. Even the principal founder of Functionalism, Jerry Fodor, has found it necessary to abandon that philosophy.

Although the free will versus determinism issue has engaged thinkers for over thousands of years and many solutions have been proposed concerning its resolution, it has yet to be solved to the satisfaction of any but the most zealous. Whether future enquiry into the functioning of the brain can provide a resolution to the issue, remains to be seen.

9.8   Discussion questions

1. Are you right-handed or left-handed? Are you a mixture of both? Why might you have the hand preference that you have?
2. Does the size or weight of the brain or the cerebral cortex have anything to do with language in humans?
3. What functions are typically handled by the left hemisphere? By the right hemisphere?
4. What is dominance and how does it differ from lateralization?
5. Why might left-handed people have reading and writing problems?
6. What happens to people's functioning when the connection between the hemispheres is cut? Also, how does this relate to lateralization?
7. If a person produces fluent but nonsensical sentences like 'We down and to the other' or substitutes words for the correct word, such as 'pool' or 'wet' for 'water', what kind of aphasia might this person have?
8. What aphasia is characterized by speech such as 'Go store milk'?
9. Why might right-handed people generally prefer listening to speech with their right ear?
10. If a friend of yours was in a car accident and his or her brain was damaged, how would you test for the following language functions: (a) speech production; (b) speech understanding; (c) reading; (d) writing?
11. Do you think there is a critical age for first- or second-language learning?
12. Why is it necessary for a comprehensive theory of brain structure and function to include localization and holistic approaches?
13. What advantages does PET have over traditional methods of brain investigation?
14. Is brain different from mind? Can a complete understanding of brain provide a complete understanding of mind?

Suggested readings

Blumstein, Sheila (1988) Neurolinguistics: an overview of language-brain relations in aphasia. In Newmeyer (1988).

Caplan, D. (1987) *Neurolinguistics and Linguistic Aphasiology: An Introduction*. New York: Cambridge University Press.

Lenneberg, Eric (1967) *Biological Foundations of Language*. New York: Wiley.

Newmeyer, F. (ed.) (1988) *Linguistics: The Cambridge Survey, vol. III, Language: Psychological and Biological Aspects*.

Poizner, H., Klima, E. and Bellugi, U. (1987) *What the Hands Reveal About the Brain*. Cambridge, Mass.: MIT Press.

Sasanuma, S. (1985) Surface dyslexia and dysgraphia: how are they manifested in Japanese? In K. E. Patterson, J. C. Marshall and M. Coltheart (eds), *Deep Dyslexia*. London: Routledge & Kegan Paul.

Sperry, R. W. (1982) Some effects of disconnecting the cerebral hemispheres. *Science*, **217**, 1223–6.

Journals

Brain and Cognition
Brain and Language
Neurolinguistics
Studies in Neurolinguistics

PART 3

Second language

CHAPTER 10

Children vs adults in second-language acquisition

10.1 A common belief

Most people believe that children are better than adults when attempting to learn a second language. That seems to be backed up by common observation, since young second-language learners do seem to pick up another language rather quickly, just by being exposed to it. Whether this belief is justified is the focus of this chapter. As we shall see, all of our psycholinguistic knowledge (and then some) will be needed in order to approach a reasonable answer to this problem.

Factors involved in second-language acquisition can be divided into two kinds, the psychological and the social. Under 'psychological' we shall consider *intellectual processing*, which is involved in the determination of grammatical structures and rules, *memory*, which is essential for learning to occur, and *motor skills*, which involve the use of the articulators of speech (tongue, lips, vocal chords, etc.) for the production of the sounds of a second language. Under 'social' we shall consider the *types* of situations, settings and interactions which affect our ability to learn a second language, in particular the *natural* and *classroom* situations.

10.2 Psychological factors affecting second-language learning

10.2.1 Intellectual processing

There are only two ways to learn the structures and rules of a second language: someone can explain them to you or you can figure them out for yourself. The first way may be termed 'explication', the second 'induction'.

Explication

Explication is the process whereby the rules and structures of a second language are explained to the learner in his or her native language. The person is then expected to understand, learn and apply them in the second language. No second language, however, can be learned entirely by such means. Although many second-language teachers assume that the rules of a language have all been discovered and written down, and that all they have to do is read enough to find them, this is not so. One cannot go to a bookstore and buy a book or any number of books which come close to explaining completely the grammar of any language. Even for a language such as English, the most studied of all languages, one still finds linguistic journals discussing the concepts involved in such commonplace features of English as the article and tense.

Explaining is rarely done by parents or others when children acquire a native language, yet children by the age of 4 or 5 understand and speak most of their native language quite well. Parents do not even attempt to explain a relatively simple morpheme rule, like that of the plural. You don't hear them saying: 'Now, Mary, to make the plural of "dog" you add a "z" sound to the end of the word, while with "duck" you add an "s". You do this, Mary, because the last sound of "dog" has a voiced consonant and the last sound of "duck" has an unvoiced one.' Even if parents were able to formulate the explanation, which most cannot, they know that their children would not be able to understand it. Similarly, parents do not tell their children that there is a Subject + Verb + Object ordering in their language, or that, in order to negate a sentence like 'John wanted some chocolate ice-cream', *do* must be inserted, the tense on the verb must be shifted onto the *do*, the negative marker *not* must be inserted after *do*, and *some* must change to *any*, so that the sentence 'John did not want any chocolate ice-cream' will be the result. It is only with a high degree of intellectual maturity that a person can understand such explicit explanations.

However, while some syntactic rules may be so complex and abstract that few people other than students of linguistics can comprehend them (let alone remember them so as to use them correctly!), there *are* simple rules which can be taught by explication to adults and older children without much difficulty. For example, a mature Korean speaker studying English could be told that there is a Subject + Verb + Object order of constituents or that English requires count nouns to have a plural marker added when more than one object is involved. On the basis of these descriptions, a learner can learn relevant usable rules. In such cases, explication may even be a faster means of learning than induction, since induction requires that a learner be repeatedly exposed to words, phrases and sentences along with relevant situations that give some indication as to their meaning.

Induction

Learning rules by self-discovery is the essence of the process of induction. The child who is exposed to second-language speech and remembers what he or she has heard will be able to analyse and discover the generalization or rule that underlies that speech. Actually, not only must the learner devise, consciously or unconsciously, the rule based on the speech that has been heard, but he or she must also figure out how those rules are to be applied in other cases. For example, given the sentences 'John danced then John sang' and 'John danced and then he sang', spoken in a relevant situation, the learner can determine that the two sentences are related, with *he* being a replacement for *John*. The learner must also figure out that while *he* can replace *John* in the second of the conjoined sentences, it cannot do so in the first (e.g. in 'He danced then John sang') since in that case the pronoun *he* must refer to someone other than John. With such a rule, the learner is on the way to being able to use and understand increasingly complicated structures involving pronominalization. Such phenomena as pronominalization, negation and the plural are learned by induction and become part of a young native speaker's language knowledge quite early, long before the child enters school.

10.2.2 Memory

Memory is crucial to learning. It is inconceivable that a person with a severe memory impairment could ever learn his or her native language, much less a second language. The learning of the simplest word requires memory. A child learning the word 'dog', for example, must retain a connection between the hearing of 'dog' and the experience of seeing or touching a dog. More than one occurrence of such a situation may be necessary so that it becomes part of the person's permanent memory.

Memory is similarly crucial for the learning of grammatical structures and rules. For example, in order to determine the type of questions that require *do* (as in 'Do you want some candy?' but not in 'Is the dog barking?'), how to negate sentences, how to use politeness structures ('Please close the door', 'Would you please close the door?', 'Would you mind closing the door?'), etc., memory is essential. It is only through memory that a child can accumulate the vast amount of speech and relevant situational data which serve as the basis for analysing structures and formulating rules, processes which constitute induction. Thus, for example, to devise the rule for the use of *do* when making negative sentences, the child must remember particular negative sentences, e.g. (1) 'John doesn't want to play with you, today', (2) 'John cannot play with you, today', (3) 'Mary isn't happy', and contrast them with previously remembered affirmative sentences which have corresponding relevant structures: (1') 'John wants to play with you, today', (2') 'John can play with you, today' and (3') 'Mary is happy'. In this way, the child can determine when *do* is and is not inserted for negation. (For a specification of the negation rule, see Chapter 1 on the acquisition of negation.)

Actually, it is unlikely that the child would experience the exact negative counterparts of prior learned affirmative sentences. Sentences having different vocabulary and somewhat different structures are more likely to have been learned. What is perhaps even more remarkable about this learning phenomenon is that all of the relevant negative sentences are not likely to have been experienced by the child at one time. It may be minutes, hours or even days before a second and third relevant negative sentence is heard and noted by the child. Yet the child does remember the negative instances and is able to bring them up for analysis later.

The kind of simple memorization where words, phrases and sentences are remembered just as they are, is called 'rote' memorization by psychologists. Items are stored as they are, without any analysis or processing. The rote memory ability of very young children seems to be excellent in that they easily absorb a phenomenal amount of data. (Many parents tell of the experience of reading a lengthy familiar bedtime story to their young child and, when the parent began nodding off to sleep, of being sharply corrected by the child as to exactly which words had been skipped.) While children at age 5 or 6 still display a phenomenal ability at rote memorization, it seems that older children do not, with some decline beginning around 8 years of age and with more of a decline from about 12 years of age. In this regard, it seems that children's ages can be usefully divided into two categories, under 7 years and 7 to 12 years.

Given that memory is essential for language learning, and that at some age it begins to decline, we may well ask what the reason for the decline might be. Everyone probably knows some elderly person who has an excellent memory, yet it may be that they stand out because they are exceptions to the general phenomenon of memory decline. This may be due to changes in brain development since there are noteworthy differences between brain development at age 20 and age 50 and, again, at age 70. By 50, for example, there appears to be a decrease of about 20 per cent in the number of brain cells in the cortex; by 75 years of age that loss will have reached approximately 40 per cent. This is apparently a normal loss in all humans and has nothing to do with pathological processes such as Alzheimer's disease. Exactly why memory loss occurs is not known, but it does occur along with subtle chemical changes in the brain of older persons.

Adults develop strategies and seek more practice and exposure so as to compensate for a weakening rote memory ability. In the normally aging brain, long-term memories seem relatively unaffected; with one's knowledge of the world, built up over decades, remaining intact. On the other hand, the ability to deal successfully with material such as lists of new names and words (clearly relevant to learning vocabulary in a second language) is affected.

10.2.3 Motor skills

Good pronunciation, which is related to the ability to control the organs of speech, is clearly an essential part of learning a foreign language. Jaws, lips, tongue, vocal chords, etc., are controlled by muscles, all of which are under the general control of the brain. The organs of speech have to do the right thing at the right time if one is to speak, and especially if one is to speak a second language like a native. Evidence shows that the particular motor skill of speech pronunciation is best developed at a younger age. In areas other than language, one can observe related phenomena. Few people who start some new sport or involve themselves in such disciplines as gymnastics or violin playing at the age of 20 are able to attain the same level of proficiency as those who start 10 or so years earlier. Somewhere around the age of 10 and 12 years the ability to acquire new motor skills begins to decline.

The reason for this decline is as yet unknown, although since the decline is of such a general nature, involving all parts of the body, it seems likely to be due to some change in central functioning in the brain. This is not to deny, however, that there may not be other, secondary reasons why a foreign accent persists in a second language. One's perceptual ability to hear foreign speech sounds accurately (especially those which differ only slightly from sounds in the native language), may also contribute to incorrect pronunciation.

Children learning a second language typically learn to speak it with a pronunciation that is indistinguishable from that of a native speaker. Few adults, on the other hand, are able to achieve such a level. What is puzzling, however, is that there appear to be exceptions among adults. I am of the view that some adults (mature persons beyond the age of puberty) do learn to speak a second language with native pronunciation. (A counterviewpoint on whether there are truly exceptions is discussed in Section 10.5, 'Critical age'.) Is this simply a matter of individual differences or are some persons somehow exempt from the barrier experienced by most adults in learning the pronunciation of a second language? There is no way of answering this at our current stage of scientific knowledge. Research studies that have been done on pronunciation in second-language learning are unanimous in their findings (e.g. Oyama, 1976; Tahta *et al.*, 1981; and for a book length consideration see Scovel, 1988). Younger children in immigrant families, for example, are found to acquire perfect or near-perfect accents, while their older siblings or parents generally do not, even when these older people have mastered other aspects of the language such as its syntax and vocabulary. While there is general agreement that the ability to acquire pronunciation declines, there has been little discussion as to whether there is a decline in the ability to acquire syntax and other aspects of language. Most theorists seem to think, and I would agree, that there is little or no decline in this respect.

A summary of the various psychological factors and their functioning according to age is shown in Table 10.1. Thus, for example, children under the age of 7 years are rated 'high' on all psychological factors except 'explicative' processing, while, adults are rated 'high' on 'inductive' and 'explicative' processing but 'low' on 'memory' and 'motor skills'.

Table 10.1 Psychological and social factors affecting second-language learning for children and adults

	Psychological factors				Social factors	
	Intellectual				Situation	
	Inductive	Explicative	Memory	Motor skills	Natural	Classroom
Children						
Under 7	High	Low	High	High	High	Low
7–12	High	Medium	Med/High	Med/High	Medium	Medium
Adults						
Over 12	High	High	Low	Low	Low	High

10.3 Social situations affecting second-language learning

What are some of the social factors which might explain why children and adults seem to differ so much in their ability to acquire native speech in a foreign language? Such a discussion can be divided into two parts, learning in a 'natural' setting and learning in the 'classroom'.

10.3.1 The natural situation

A natural situation for second-language learning is one where the second language is experienced in a situation that is similar to that in which the native language is learned. That is, language is experienced in conjunction with the objects, situations and events of everyday life; it is not taught in a classroom. The paradigm case would be that of a young child going to live in another country and learning that country's language, not by any explicit teaching, but by interacting with playmates, as, for example, an English-speaking 4-year-old girl from London who goes to Beijing with her parents. Through playing with Chinese children, she soon learns Chinese.

Generally speaking, as one gets older there is a decline in the kind of social interaction which promotes language learning. Adult second-language learners will have significantly fewer good language-learning opportunities in a new culture than will children. Of course, if the adults stay at home, they will not be able to meet and talk much to native speakers. If they work, then, because of their lack of second-language ability, they will not be hired to do work that requires native speakers to linguistically interact with them. Whether their work allows them to use their native language (as business people, language teachers, etc.), or whether their work involves a minimal amount of second language (construction work, dishwashing), in either case learners will have but a limited opportunity to experience appropriate second-language data in the natural situation. Except for situations involving love or money, it is almost impossible to imagine a situation in which adults would be continually exposed to the same good quality and quantity of language that a child receives.

For adults, social interaction mainly occurs through the medium of language. Few native-speaker adults are willing to devote time to interacting with someone who does not speak the language. The adult foreigner, therefore, will have little opportunity to engage in meaningful language exchange except for picking up bits of language that are experienced in the workplace or in shopping. In contrast, the young child is often readily accepted by other children, and even adults. For young children, language is not essential to social interaction. So-called 'parallel play', for example, is common among children. They can be content just to sit in each other's company and just speak occasionally. Adults rarely find themselves in similar situations.

The older the child, however, the greater the role that language plays in social interaction and the more the person will experience difficulty in being accepted. Peer group acceptance becomes a problem, especially around the age of puberty. Even children who speak the same language but come from a different school or town have difficulty in gaining acceptance. Without such acceptance, second-language learning in a natural situation can hardly begin.

Because language is essential for social interaction and because people generally crave such interaction, foreign adults often tend to stick together in a new environment. Friendships for the adult are easier to form in the old language and even business can often be conducted at least partially in the old language. Then, too, many large cities with sizable foreign populations have radio, television and newspapers in the foreign languages. All of these things tend to reduce the amount of second-language exposure for adults in a way that does not occur for children.

10.3.2 The classroom situation

The classroom for second-language learning is a planned, or some might say, an artificially constructed, situation. As we all know, physically, there is a room which is arranged so that it is isolated from the rest of life. In the room there is a teacher and a number of students. The teacher is the one who knows the language and the students are there to learn the language. In the enclosed space of the classroom, nothing happens unless the teacher makes it happen.

Students do not act on their own but follow the directions of the teacher. All other aspects of life are suspended or subordinated to language learning. This, of course, is very different from the home or street where the learner eats at a table, walks around doing things, bathes, plays outdoor games, etc., all while hearing and using language in conjunction with these activities.

In the natural situation, language is but one aspect of life, an aspect which accompanies other life events. In the classroom, however, language itself becomes the prime aspect of life around which all else revolves. The language that is to be experienced by the students is planned. While there are degrees of planning with more or less emphasis on speech, literacy, spontaneity, etc., nonetheless, the course of events is planned and the teacher is the planner. In a physically isolated room, where only one person, the teacher, is the prime source of the new language, planning is unavoidable. This is true even for methods which attempt to simulate the natural situation (discussed in some detail in the next chapter) by attempting to reproduce in the classroom some of the natural language experiences which occur outside the classroom. Exposure to good native speech, role playing and games are some of the devices employed to allow for the natural self-discovery of language and its use. Still, it is the teacher who plans and controls such activities.

There are other characteristics of the planned classroom situation which distinguish it from the natural situation. These include social adjustment to group processes (individuals must subordinate their behaviour and follow classroom procedures for the benefit of all), the need to attend class in order to learn, the need for long periods of concentration and, when required, having to do home study. As far as language is concerned, the explicit teaching of grammatical structures and rules may be involved, depending on the method used. Using books and taking notes are often expected of the student. Students have to get used to learning language as a academic subject. Thus, when considering overall the demands of the classroom situation, it is clear that the older one is, the better one is able to adjust and function within that situation. Young children will do quite poorly in comparison to older children and adults.

Whether the classroom is in a school that is in the community where the second language is spoken is a matter of some importance, for this will determine whether students will have access to a natural situation outside of the class and thereby may supplement their classroom learning. Thus, for example, Pakistanis learning English in a classroom in London will have beneficial language experiences outside of the classroom that Pakistanis learning English in a classroom in Karachi will not. The former (learning English in Britain) is an English as a Second Language (ESL) context while the latter (learning English in Karachi) is an English as a Foreign Language (EFL) context. Because the ESL context provides more language-learning opportunities for the second-language learner through exposure to natural situations outside the classroom, such learners, unsurprisingly, will generally progress more rapidly than learners living in an EFL context. Furthermore, in comparing children and adults, we may say that, given that the natural situation benefits children more than adults, the ESL context will benefit children more than it will adults. Of course, the ESL context will benefit adults too, but to a lesser degree.

A summary of the social situational factors, natural and classroom, and their functioning according to age is shown on the right side of Table 10.1. Thus, for example, while children under the age of 7 years are rated 'high' concerning the quality and quantity of language interactions in the natural situation, they are rated 'low' on adjustment and skills in the classroom situation. The opposite is the case for the adults who rate 'low' in the natural situation but 'high' in the classroom situation.

10.4 Who is better?

Because the answer to this question depends on whether we are dealing with the natural or the classroom situation, each situation must be considered separately in relation to the psychological factors which affect the learning of language. With this approach, we shall then be able to reach some conclusions in comparing the achievements of children and adults in second-language learning. The summary data presented in Table 10.1 will serve to make it easier to draw conclusions in this regard.

10.4.1 The natural situation

In the natural situation, *younger children will do best*. First of all, the natural situation is more favourable to children because adults undergo a marked decline in the quality and quantity of the social interaction conducive to good language learning. There is no question that, in a natural situation, the social activities of children, especially young children, expose them to massive amounts of good, natural language. This does not occur for adults, and, in many cases not even for older children. In extreme cases, members of these groups may even find themselves in social conditions which are hostile – conditions which discourage second-language learning. Still, the older child will have an advantage over the adult.

Psychologically, while both children and adults have optimal powers of induction, and are able to induce the grammar of a second language more or less equally well, nonetheless, it will be easier for children to learn syntax than it will be for adults. This is because adults undergo a decline in memory, and, without remembered data, there is nothing to analyse. Adults and even older children no longer have the formidable powers of rote learning that young children do. Although adults may devise memory strategies and can seek out more practice, nevertheless, this places an additional burden on them, one that the child does not have. Therefore, children, particularly younger children, will have an advantage over adults in learning the grammar of a second language. For the same reason, older children can be expected to learn faster than adults, because of a better memory.

As we age and as our ability to acquire new motor skills declines, our ability to command our organs of speech to carry out the new movements of a second language is negatively affected. Therefore, because children possess the flexibility in motor skills which adults do not have, children will do much better in acquiring native pronunciation in a second language. Although other factors may be involved in speaking like a native, nonetheless, motor skills is undoubtedly the major contributing factor. Again, as with the problem of memory, adults can attempt to overcome this deficit, such as through practice. But again, as with memory, that adds an additional step to the process and makes learning more difficult for them.

Thus, it can be concluded that in all respects of language learning, for the natural situation, children will do better than adults, with younger children doing better than older children.

10.4.2   The classroom situation

In the classroom situation, *adults will do better than young children*, because, not only are they better in explicative processing but, simply put, they know how to be students. They have sufficient maturity to meet the rigours of a formal learning environment, where concentration, attention and even the ability to sit still for a long time, all play a role in learning.

Because the older child's memory and motor skills are better than the adult's, the advantage in explicative processing enjoyed by the adult may not be sufficient to overcome the disadvantages experienced in these areas. Thus, an older child will probably do better than an adult in the classroom situation. The best age to learn a second language in a classroom situation is probably that age where the individual retains much of the memory and motor skills of the very young, but where the individual has begun to reason and understand like an adult. That age would probably be somewhere around 12 years.

10.5   Critical age

Once before, in a different context (Chapter 3 on Wild Children), the concept of a critical age for first-language learning was discussed. Recall, if you will, that although evidence was lacking, some theorists hypothesized that there was an age (puberty, for example) beyond which it would be impossible to acquire a first language. Brain changes were suggested as a possible explanation for such a psychological barrier.

It is reasonable to ask the same question about the acquisition of a *second* language. Is there any barrier to the learning of a second language and, if so, at what age does this barrier become operational? As far as adults learning a second language is concerned, we have the common observation that a very great number of adult speakers do, in fact, learn the syntax of other languages perfectly. There are those who speak second languages so well that, on the basis of the grammar alone (not the pronunciation, which we shall deal with shortly), they would be judged native speakers. There is no evidence, for example, that a speaker of a Subject + Verb + Object language such as English cannot learn a different word ordering of sentence constituents, such as the Subject + Object + Verb ordering that occurs in Japanese. Or that negating a sentence by changing a word internally, such as is done in Turkish, presents insuperable problems to speakers who negate sentences in their native language with unattached negative markers, such as 'not'. Complicated systems of grammatical cases, such as occur in Russian and Finnish, can be learned by a normal adult Chinese (whose language, like English, has no cases) who is willing to devote the time to learning them. It is safe to affirm the view that there is no critical age in terms of acquiring the syntax of a second language.

This brings us to pronunciation. Is it possible to learn a second language so well that one truly sounds like a native speaker? One psycholinguist, Thomas Scovel, recently has claimed that *no* adult can ever be successful in that regard. 'The critical period for accentless speech simply means that adults will never learn to pass themselves off as native speakers phonologically. . . .' He describes this as 'The Joseph Conrad Syndrome', after the famous novelist and master of English prose, who, a native speaker of Polish, did not even begin to study English until he was 20. Scovel has in mind a certain category of adult second-language speakers: those who have mastered the grammatical and communicative complexities of another language but still speak with an accent. We could add former US Secretaries of State, Henry Kissinger (who left Germany and went to the US at age 14) and Zbigniew Brzezinski (who left his native Poland and went to Canada at age 10) to this class.

While I would agree with Scovel that in second-language acquisition there is not a critical age for syntax, I cannot agree that there is an absolute critical age for pronunciation. There is a critical age for most people, but not for all. Based on my own personal experience and the observations of others, I believe that there *are* persons whose pronunciation can pass as native speakers in a second language, a language which they have learned as adults. However, only if documented cases are provided can Scovel's absolute critical age notion be disproved.

10.6 Discussion questions

1. Can you think of evidence in your own life that your memory ability and your ability to acquire new motor skills are not as good as when you were a pre-teen?
2. Why is memory so important for language learning?
3. Are children better second-language learners in the natural situation?
4. Can adults be better second-language learners than younger children?
5. Do think there is a critical age for second-language acquisition? Consider the cases of both syntax and pronunciation.
6. Why, concerning the classroom situation, is an English as a Second Language (ESL) situation more advantageous to second-language learners than an English as a Foreign Language (EFL) situation?
7. Do you personally know any counter-evidence to Scovel's claim that no adult can learn the pronunciation of a second language well enough to pass as a native speaker?

Suggested readings

Dulay, H., Burt, M. and Krashen, S. (1982) *Language Two.* Oxford: Oxford University Press.
Lenneberg, Eric H. (1969) On explaining language. *Science*, **163**, 635–43.

McLaughlin, B. (1984) *Second Language Acquisition in Childhood* (2nd edn). Hillsdale, NJ: Earlbaum.

Oyama, S. (1976) A sensitive period for the acquisition of a nonnative phonological system. *Journal of Psycholinguistic Research*, **5**, 3, 261–84.

Scovel, Thomas (1988) *A Time to Speak: A Psycholinguistic Inquiry into the Critical Period for Human Speech*. Cambridge: Newbury House (Harper & Row).

Tahta, S., Wood, M. and Loewenthal, K. (1981) Foreign accents: factors relating to transfer of accent from the first language to a second language. *Language and Speech*, **24**, 265–72.

CHAPTER 11

Second-language teaching

11.1 Dimensions and methods

Second-language teaching is a field which provides an excellent meeting ground for many of the theoretical and practical aspects of psycholinguistics to come together. It is here that we have a chance to see how ideas of human language and human learning interconnect.

In my view, language-teaching methods may be conveniently characterized on the basis of five principal dimensions:

1. Language Mode: Speech–Reading
2. Meaning: Actual Object/Situation–Translation
3. Grammar: Induction–Explication
4. Psychology: Mentalist–Behaviourist
5. Linguistics: Mentalist–Structuralist

These dimensions do not involve all aspects and theories but only those which have been realized in principal second-language teaching methods.

A brief description of each of these dimensions, some aspects of which have been described elsewhere in this book, follows.

11.1.1 Language mode: speech–reading

Methods can be divided into two categories, those which approach language through the spoken aspects of language and those which approach language through literacy. The Grammar–Translation Method is virtually alone in the literacy category, for all others emphasize speech as the primary means for acquiring a second language. Although teachers using the Grammar–Translation Method will include some speech in their curriculum, and teachers using speech-based methods will include reading and writing in their curriculum, both are distinct. Generally, the proponents of the speech-based methods regard Grammar–Translation as the ultimate enemy, since, for them, speech is primary in the learning of language. Still, that does not prevent adherents of speech-based methods from attacking one another.

11.1.2 Meaning: Actual Object/Situation–Translation

In providing the meaning of second-language items, a method may use translation (in the native language), as is commonly the case with the Grammar–Translation Method. For example, English-speaking students studying Italian may be told that *libro* means 'book', and that *Come sta?* means 'How are you?'. The meanings of single vocabulary items and entire phrases and sentences may be learned in this way. This is very different, though, from acquiring meaning by being exposed to actual objects or situations which indicate the meaning of foreign words. For example, the learner can be shown a book and hear '*libro*', or see two persons meet, with one saying to the other '*Come sta?*'.

11.1.3 Grammar: Induction–Explication

Explication involves explanation, in the native language, of the grammatical rules and structures of the second language. For example, a teacher can explain to Japanese students in the Japanese language that English has a Subject + Verb + Object ordering of basic sentence constituents. (Japanese has a Subject + Object + Verb ordering.) In learning the same by induction, however, students would have to discover that order of constituents on their own. It would be necessary for them to hear sentences of the sort, 'Mary caught the ball', while experiencing a situation in which such an action (or a picture of the action) occurs.

11.1.4 Psychology: Mentalist–Behaviourist

The psychological presumptions of a method can have a great effect on how that method is formulated and used. A Behaviourist would prefer, for example, to mechanically drill students on sentences while a Mentalist would prefer to have students think about sentences and their structure and learn about them in this way. For the Behaviourist, there is nothing for a learner to think about; thinking is irrelevant for language learning. One's psychological orientation has definite implications for how and what one is to teach.

11.1.5 Linguistics: Mentalist–Structuralist

What one believes to be the concept of a sentence, and what grammatical rules and structures may underlie the sentence, will affect greatly what one teaches. A Structuralist analysis of a sentence like 'The dog jumped' is easy to make in that it is a simple order of word classes (Article + Noun + Verb), yet, as Chomsky pointed out in his original attacks on Structural Linguistics in the 1950s and 1960s, other sentences having the same observable structure such as 'John is easy to please' and 'John is eager to please' cannot be explained by a simple listing of word classes or even phrase structures since both of these sentences are identical in this regard, e.g., Noun + Verb + Adjective + Preposition + Verb. A Mentalist grammarian with a Chomskyan orientation would explain these sentences by discussing specific syntactic relations that *underlie* those sentences. Thus, a Mentalist could say that, in 'John is easy to please', 'John' is the underlying object of 'please', while in 'John is eager to please', 'John' is the underlying subject of 'please'. In practical terms, a teacher would have quite different explanations to offer students for such sentences or would organize sentences for presentation quite differently, depending on which linguistic theory he or she followed.

11.2 Traditional methods

Keeping the above five dimensions in mind, let us now look at a variety of major second-language teaching methods.

The reader may be somewhat surprised to discover that the methods of the present may not be so very different from those of the past.

11.2.1 The Grammar–Translation Method

The Grammar–Translation method is characterized by its emphasis on reading and writing. Knowledge of the grammar and vocabulary of the target language is taught through explication and translation using the native language. There is little emphasis on oral skills. Historically speaking, the translation component of the method is by far the oldest, with the grammar component developing later as knowledge of grammar increased. Translation from one language to another has been used as a teaching method itself for thousands of years everywhere where different languages have come into contact.

Grammar, on the other hand, was something that was studied and the knowledge derived from that study was applied to learning foreign languages. This happened in ancient Greece, Rome, India and China. It was in Europe, particularly in the seventeenth century, that intensive and detailed studies of various languages were done, for, with the spirit of the Renaissance, came an interest in the understanding and teaching of ordinary (non-Classical) languages. The teaching of grammar went hand-in-hand with translation for the teaching of a second language; both relied on the use of the native language to impart knowledge.

Typically, textbooks using the Grammar–Translation (GT) Method have lessons which include: a reading passage in the target language, a list of vocabulary items and their translations, and an explanation in the native language of important points of grammar contained in the text. The lesson often ends with a series of exercises, ranging from straight translation to questions on points of grammar. Translations are typically done from the target language into the native language with reverse translations (from the native language into the target language) seldom being done.

Despite the method's indifference to speech and oral communication, and, despite its being disparaged by leading language educators for what is now well over 100 years, the GT Method has enjoyed and continues to enjoy acceptance in many countries around the world. This may seem a mystery, until one looks at the advantages of the GT Method. This method is unique in that it can be applied to masses of students by teachers who lack verbal fluency in the target language both in terms of understanding and producing speech. This situation is common in Japan, for example, where such teachers are placed in a class with 30, 40 and more students.

The method also lends itself well to self-study. By using books, students can study on their own outside of the classroom. There is much that they can learn from studying and reading on their own. Of importance, too, is the fact that the method is appropriate for all levels of learners. From the introductory to the very advanced, there is an abundance of materials available for classroom use.

One of the GT Method's strongest points is its extraordinary capacity to adapt to ever-changing psychological and linguistic theories. The distinguishing features of the method, explication of grammar and the use of translation, can be adapted to any psychological or linguistic theory. As for translation, the process never changes. As for grammatical explanations, these can be couched in the linguistic theory of the day. Whether a grammatical point is to explained according to Chomsky's or Bloomfield's theory of grammar is not a matter of concern to the method. Neither is it a matter of concern whether a Behaviourist or a Mentalist psychological theory is applied. The GT Method can accommodate almost any theory. In this way, the GT Method need never become obsolete from a psychological or linguistic point of view. The fact that it thrived under Behaviouristic psychology and Structural linguistics does not prevent it from thriving under Mentalism.

The principal disadvantage of the GT Method involves the lack of emphasis on oral skills. Students who pass through many years of strict GT training generally come out unable to comprehend or utter sentences at a level that allows them to engage in even simple conversations. That the GT Method cannot be used with young children, since they cannot read or write well, or understand grammatical explanations, is a limitation of the method, or perhaps a blessing in disguise.

11.2.2 The Natural Method

The Natural Method (NM) originated in the early nineteenth century and was the outgrowth of scientific thought on the nature of language and learning which had flowered earlier in Europe. The philosophy of that era was particularly interested in the natural state of human beings. Questions concerning the natural development of humans and how their natural aspects could be maintained became of great interest.

That approach to language and learning, where 'natural is better', so to speak, led to a method of teaching that stressed the value of presenting a second language to a learner exactly as the native language had been presented. The model for the Natural Method of second-language learning was the child learning its native language. This meant adherence to the natural sequence of the child's acquiring its native language, i.e. first speech comprehension, then speech production, and, much later, reading and writing. Grammar was not taught. Rather, grammatical rules and structures were to be learned through induction by exposure to sentences in a situational context. Vocabulary meaning was to be gained through experience and exposure to objects; translation was to be avoided.

Typically, teachers would not use prepared situations or material. Learning was through *spontaneous* conversation and demonstration, all of which was done in the target language. The teacher used language appropriate to the students' level of understanding, much in the same way as parents would with a child. The method was totally oriented towards the acquisition of oral skills. Student participation in situational activities was virtually the definition of this kind of second-language teaching.

The great advantage of the Natural Method was that by exposure to natural language in a natural context, learners could acquire a speech capability both in production and understanding. However, one problem for this method is that it requires the teacher to create interesting situations so that students may be naturally exposed to language. This, and the reliance on spontaneous speech, places an extremely heavy burden on even the best of teachers. Besides possessing an undue amount of ingenuity teachers must, of course, be fluent in the target language. Such a demand cannot always be met, particularly if mass education is involved. Class size, too, could be a problem, since the number of students must be quite small, usually less than 15. Actually, the problems mentioned here are not unique to NM. Indeed, speech-based methods which stress exposure to natural speech and student participation in communicative situations have similar problems.

11.2.3 The Direct Method

In the late nineteenth and early twentieth centuries, there were efforts to combine the advantages of the Natural Method (NM) with systematic procedures based on knowledge gained from psychology and linguistics. It was thought that applying scientific knowledge from psychology and linguistics would make language acquisition more efficient with students learning faster than they would under the spontaneous and unplanned lessons of the Natural Method. This approach, which still retains the principle of natural speech in a natural context, became known as the Direct Method, with Harold Palmer perhaps its most articulate and eminent advocate.

Like the Natural Method, the Direct Method (DM) is mentalistically oriented since it presumes that the learner is a thinking being who can learn abstract language ideas. Also, like the Natural Method, the Direct Method relies on learning language by induction. However, unlike the Natural Method, language materials for teaching in the Direct Method are explicitly preselected and graded on the basis of linguistic complexity. Simple sentences, for example, precede those with relative clauses or in the passive construction. All of this is done for the purpose of making the acquisition task easier for the learner. Then, too, while there is still much spontaneous use of speech by the teacher, it is considerably less than is the case for the Natural Method.

Lessons in the Direct Method are mainly devoted to oral communication, following the acquisition order of the first language: with speech understanding preceding speech production which, in turn, precedes reading and writing. Elementary social dialogues are introduced almost immediately: 'How are you?', 'Fine, thanks', as are questions: 'Where is . . .?', 'When is . . .?', 'Who is . . .?' and commands for action: 'Stand up', 'Sit down' and 'Give the book to Mary'.

Sometimes oral pattern drills and memorization of dialogues were also included in Direct Method lessons. Such techniques were devised and applied for the purpose of giving practice in speech production. (Later, these techniques came to be used – over-used is probably more accurate – by proponents of the Audiolingual Method.) Sometimes, too, translations might be given, as might grammatical explanations. However, these were used sparingly. For the most part, the Direct Method is typified by its reliance on natural speech in context and on the students' mental powers of induction.

The structured nature of the Direct Method is such that, in the hands of a good teacher, it can be used in relatively large classes of even 40 students, with teachers getting students to speak in chorus. Still, like the Natural Method, and unlike the Grammar–Translation Method, the Direct Method requires a teacher with high fluency in the second language. Some school systems may find it difficult to find a sufficient number of such teachers.

11.2.4 The Audiolingual Method

Despite the Direct Method's rather long and widespread acceptance (in other than Grammar–Translation circles), it was overshadowed and then virtually wiped out with the advent in the late 1940s of the Audiolingual Method (AM). The phenomenal rise of AM was due, I believe, to the popularity of the American linguistic and psychological theories which it incorporated into its foundations. (The great popularity of America in the world following the Second World War is itself a factor here.) The language analyses provided by Structural linguists and the stimulus and response learning psychology provided by Behaviourists endowed the Audiolingual Method with a credence that no other method could claim.

Structural linguists regarded sentences simply as

sequences of grammatical word classes or phrases. New sentences would be created by substituting words within a word class. For example, a sequence such as Article + Adjective + Noun + Verb + Article + Noun could yield a large number of sentences such as 'The rich boy bought a car' and 'The friendly girl kissed the boy', by substituting members of the same grammatical class. Because Behaviourist psychologists, too, regarded sentences as the simple association of word classes, it was not much of a step for AM to adopt the repetition of sentence patterns as a fundamental learning principle.

Unfortunately for the theory, as Chomsky pointed out, substitution cannot prevent the creation of sequences like 'The happy dust memorized the table', or 'A poor mountain elapsed the wine', which also fit the pattern for the sentence 'The rich boy bought a car'. Nor could Structuralist theory account for a speaker's ability to generate a non-finite number of grammatical sentences which were not defined by such sentence patterns.

Behaviourist psychology, which was the dominant school of psychology in America for most of the first half of this century, regarded mind and thinking to be irrelevant for the understanding and production of speech. Repetition and mechanical drills were considered to be the essence of learning, with learners not acquiring knowledge but behavioural responses. The defects of such a view concerning language and psychology were demonstrated by Chomsky during the 1950s and served as the basis for the subsequent collapse of Structural Linguistics and the weakening of Behaviourism in the 1960s.

The Audiolingual Method incorporated into its methodology many of the same features which the Direct Method had developed, namely, planned situations, graded materials and such techniques as pattern drills and dialogue memorization. In contrast with the DM, the Audiolingual Method almost entirely dropped the use of natural situations and spontaneous speech. Speech occurrences were under the rigorous control of the teacher. There was even a tendency for some AM advocates (like Moulton) to reduce the meaningfulness of the speech that was taught – a practice which was frowned on by Charles Fries, one of the founders of the AM method. Nonetheless, AM definitely had characteristics which contrasted sharply with DM.

In its time the Audiolingual Method generated an enormous amount of enthusiasm. Teachers everywhere lined up to teach second languages according to principles which reflected the latest scientific word on how humans learn language. All the more was the sense of disappointment when AM failed to produce the fluent communicating speakers that it was aiming to. The drilling of sentence patterns and memorization of dialogues proved inadequate to prepare students for communication with speakers in the real world.

11.3 The Chomskyan revolution and contemporary methods

11.3.1 Chomsky's Mentalism and effect on methods

Chomsky's idea that 'Ordinary linguistic behavior characteristically involves innovation, formation of new sentences and patterns in accordance with rules of great abstractness and intricacy' was a truly revolutionary one. Chomsky faulted Behaviourism for its inability to account for the fact that speakers do not simply imitate but create, *by means of rules*. They make novel sentences and understand sentences they have never heard before. Such language creativity cannot be explained in the stimulus and response terms of Behaviourism or the related notions of Structural Linguistics, but only through recourse to a mental grammar, i.e. a system of abstract language rules which speakers have in their minds. Language develops on the basis of a learner's knowledge of these rules, some of which are so abstract and intricate that they could not have been taught but only acquired by learners on their own. Linguistics and psychology requires a mentalistic base, therefore, if language and language acquisition were to be explained.

While Chomsky has proposed ideas concerning first language acquisition, he has avoided speculation which is directly relevant to the teaching and learning of a second language. Nevertheless, the effects of his ideas in the field of second-language teaching have been profound. His basic ideas in linguistics and psychology have been applied by others in quite a variety of ways.

11.3.2   Contemporary methods

Since the downfall of the Audiolingual Method in the 1960s, a number of methods have arisen. However, only a small number have managed to survive, and fewer still have managed to thrive. In the thrive category, we have Communicative Language Teaching, Total Physical Response and The Natural Approach. In the struggle-to-survive category, we have Silent Way and Suggestopedia. (I believe that it is time to recognize the passing of Community Language Learning and Cognitive Code.) A description and assessment of each of these five methods now follows.

Total Physical Response

Total Physical Response (TPR) is very much a 'natural' type method: speech understanding precedes speech production, which, in turn, precedes reading and writing. Only the target language is used in the classroom and meaning is derived from actual objects and situations. Students are encouraged to induce rules on their own and speak when they are ready. Again, as with other natural type methods, things go best with a small number of students.

Asher, the founder of TPR in the 1970s, considers its unique characteristic to be the having of learners perform physical actions in response to the teacher's commands in the target language. His idea is that memory will be enhanced. with the result that language will be more easily remember and accessed. Interestingly, this idea and the other major ideas comprising TPR are to be found in the Direct Method, particularly under Gouin in the nineteenth century and Palmer in his 1925 book, *Language through Actions*. Asher, though, has emphasized physical activity much more than did Palmer. In any case, there is no doubt that TPR is a very useful method and one which deserves attention.

Initially, in a classroom of beginners in English, commands are given such as 'Stand up', 'Sit down', 'Open the door', 'Walk to the table', 'Point to the table', 'Point to the door', 'Where is the table?', 'Where is the book?', etc. Soon after, sometimes even within the same class hour, statements or questions are paired with commands, 'This is a book. Give the book to Susie', 'The book is on the table. Put the book on the chair', 'Who has the book? You? Alright. Give the book to Anne', 'Where is the ball? On the table? Alright. Tony bring me the ball'. After the proper groundwork has been laid, students are presented more complex sentences, like 'Give the book to Bob and give the pen to Jean', 'Walk to the table and then turn around', 'Take the yellow card and place it under the book', 'If you have a blue card then raise your hand', 'If you have the big card then place under the small card.'

From the beginning the student is introduced to whole sentences. The teacher demonstrates the meaning of the words and sentences by pointing to the objects and by following the commands for all to see. It is claimed that with this method a student can easily learn around 25 new lexical items in an hour, along with a variety of structures. I believe this to be true. In fact, with regard to vocabulary, the number could be much higher. For example, students of my own psycholinguistics class in Japan, who were given a TPR demonstration lesson in German from my colleague, learned to understand more than 50 to 70 different words in just a little over an hour. And this was their first experience with German. While hesitant in their actions at first, students soon gained in confidence performing their task swiftly and with assurance. Such behaviour is a direct measure of their progress in speech comprehension.

After the teacher has determined that the students are firm in what they have learned, they are asked to say what they have learned to their classmates, with their classmates performing the actions. Games can be devised to encourage speaking.

TPR has essentially the same advantages and limitations as the Direct Method. Students do learn to communicate in speech in a natural way and also relatively quickly. In order for this to happen, however, they must have fluent and creative teachers. Nowadays, perhaps the teacher need not be especially creative, since a great deal of curriculum materials have been developed and published for TPR instruction. TPR is best used for the introductory phases of second-language learning. With more advanced language knowledge, action becomes less useful and relevant to communication. Then, too, there is the problem of homework. Once out of the classroom, there is nothing a student can do to review or gain new knowledge. In this regard, adopting the Grammar–Translation Method along with TPR would be one good solution.

One problem which TPR has, relates to its special reliance on action ('Physical Response'). For social reasons, many adults, more so than children, feel embarrassed marching around a room and doing things. Probably, while the required action could be modified to lessen this problem, there is not much else a teacher can do to remedy this situation. Adults become more accepting in time, especially after they see their teacher doing the same things that they have to do.

Communicative Language Teaching

In the early 1970s, Wilkins proposed a system of dividing communicative speech into two aspects: functions and notions. 'Functions' are things like requests, denials, complaints, excuses, etc. They are expressed through whole sentences and essentially the learner is provided with a means for performing a given function. For example, learners may be told that, to make a request, they may say 'Please open the window', 'Would you mind opening the window', 'It's awfully stuffy in here, isn't it?', etc.

'Notions' are expressions of frequency, quantity, location, etc. These are typically words or phrases within a sentence. For example, students may learn 'I *often* go to the movies', 'I have *a lot of* friends' and 'He's standing *by the window*'.

Communicative Language Teaching (CLT) posits that students want to communicate and it enables them to do just that. Lessons often start with the simultaneous reading and hearing of a dialogue based on a real-life everyday situation, such as greeting a friend or buying something in a shop. Initially, there is no translation and no explanation of structure, although the method does not exclude native language aids if that is what the students feel they need for a particular point. There is total reliance on situations and the students'desire to communicate within those situations.

Since this kind of teaching stresses communication, it

has developed a flexibility which allows anything that will further the communicative competence of a student. This eclectic approach can include, as noted above, translation and grammatical explanations in the native language. If a teacher feels that an audiolingual technique such as drilling a phrase a number of times might help a student to learn, then this is done, as long as that phrase is later used as an integral part of speech in a meaningful situation. Often, these are phrases which the student has initiated, has started to create, but is having trouble with. For example, if a student would like to say in English something like 'I wish I could have gone' but can get out only 'I wish . . .' the teacher might model the whole sentence a few times, let the student repeat it a few times, and then return to the situation where the student was trying to use it and let him or her use it. Later, there might (but not necessarily) even be an explanation of the grammar involved, or even a structure drill, letting the student substitute other past participles in the sentence, thus producing a number of similar sentences: 'I wish I could have *been* there', 'I wish I could have *done* it', 'I wish I could have *seen* him'.

In comparing Communicative Language Teaching with strictly speech-oriented methods, the Natural Method, Direct Method, Total Physical Response, the Natural Approach (to follow), we can see that there are marked differences. CLT permits reading and writing almost immediately, as long as it serves the cause of communication. It also permits grammatical explanations, not relying totally on the student learning by induction. Furthermore, it permits translation. In these regards, CLT is a very eclectic method of language teaching, one which is concerned with getting people to communicate by any means available. It can, and often does, borrow as much from other methods as it deems necessary. TPR is often employed by advocates, particularly for developing oral skills in the introductory stages of communication. Thus CLT may adopt ideas from methods as divers as TPR and GT, as long as they help students to communicate.

CLT is probably the most widespread of all teaching methods today, with the exception of GT, which is common in Asian countries, particularly China and Japan. CLT is especially popular in the United Kingdom where so many of its originators and developers have been active (Widdowson, Wilkins, Alexander, Yalden).

The Natural Approach

This is the name given by Terrell and Krashen to their 'new philosophy of language teaching' developed in the early 1980s; it is to be distinguished from the Natural Method, although the Natural Approach (NA) has a number of similarities with that and other natural type methods. Yet, perhaps the Natural Approach is more an attempt to provide a theoretical description of the processes involved in second-language acquisition than it is a body of specific innovative techniques for teaching.

In agreement with the Natural Method, Direct Method and TPR, the importance of listening comprehension and delayed speech production is stressed in the Natural Approach. Production is delayed until the student is believed to be ready. The idea that you can only effectively produce speech that you already understand is in keeping with the comprehension-precedes-production aspect of native language acquisition. As for grammatical structures and rules, these are seldom explained and are expected to be acquired by receiving appropriate language input. In this respect, sentences are presented in a simple to complex grading and at a level that may be slightly higher than students can understand.

NA defines itself as a method for developing basic personal communication skills, oral and written. Goals of the method would include the ability to engage in simple conversational exchanges, to understand announcements in public places, to read newspapers, write personal letters, etc. Like most other speech-based methods, teachers of the Natural Approach make ample use of pictures, objects, charts and situations in the classroom as the source of language input.

Such personal learning factors like motivation, self-confidence and anxiety are given special consideration in NA. These constitute what Krashen calls the learner's 'Affective Filter' and play a significant role in influencing the acquisition/learning of a language. A 'low' Affective Filter is said to be most desirable, for in such a case students would be highly motivated, very confident and under little stress. Such desirable conditions can be fostered if, for example, students are allowed to communicate in situations without having to worry about any grammatical mistakes they may make. A 'high' condition of the Affective Filter would have the opposite effect. While it is probably the case that students learn better when they are motivated, not over-anxious and when they feel relaxed and receive encouragement for their efforts, to label this as an 'Affective Filter' is rather pretentious, but harmless, academic jargoneering.

The Natural Approach differentiates between *acquisition* and *learning* in a second language. *Acquisition* is said to involve a kind of inductive process similar to what occurs in the acquisition of the native language. Such a process is claimed to be unconscious. *Learning*, on the other hand, is said to be a formal process by which one learns the rules of a language, i.e. by explication. According to Krashen, language knowledge which is 'learned' never becomes unconscious or internalized as does knowledge which is 'acquired'. This distinction is based on Krashen's so-called Monitor Hypothesis. According to the hypothesis, 'learned' rules are always monitored, i.e. consciously applied in the production of sentences. No such 'monitoring' of speech production, however, is said to occur with grammar that had been 'acquired'. It is because of the monitoring process that Krashen claims that once students 'learn' grammar (instead of 'acquiring' it) they will be unable to use it unconsciously, and thus, effortlessly. Consequently, any teaching of grammar by explication is considered negatively.

The Monitor Hypothesis, however, is not able to stand up to criticism, as many theorists, such as Gregg and McLaughlin have convincingly argued. Krashen has not really answered his critics, nor has he provided evidence in support of his claim. Krashen's claim that knowledge gained from presentation of rules and explanations cannot become unconscious and automatic is counterintuitive to what many people experience when they produce sentences in a second language. Certainly, for example, English speakers of Japanese who had been told initially that Japanese has a Subject + Object + Verb ordering would be amazed if

Krashen were to tell them that, in the production of sentences in their everyday lives, they were consciously aware of such an ordering. I feel certain that all second-language learners can cite such examples (of consciously learned rules becoming unconscious and automatic) from their own experience (if they can become aware of them!). Of course, there are times when second-language learners do become aware of applying grammatical rules in the construction of sentences. However, this may occur only in the early stage when the learner has not yet integrated that knowledge well enough.

If I may, I would like to approach this acquisition/ learning issue from a non-language but still quite relevant perspective. This involves the learning of arithmetic. Suppose I ask you now to divide 954 by 6, and to do it as quickly as possible. (You can do it on paper or in your head.)

Do you have the answer? Now, were you conscious of every step you took? I can ask you, according to one commonly used method of division, if you were aware that your first step was to begin by considering the single leftmost (not rightmost) digit of 954, which is 9? Then, were you aware of deciding that, since 6 is equal to or less than 9, you must subtract 9 and have 3 remaining? Were you aware that because the remainder was less than 6 you would write a 1 for the beginning of your answer? What did you then do with that 3? Were you conscious of having to place the next leftmost single digit of 954, which is 5, and then treat the two digits of 3 and 5 as 35? Next you divided 35 by 6 and got an answer of 5. But how did you do that? Were you conscious of dipping into the multiplication table $(1 \times 1 = 1, 1 \times 2 = 2, 1 \times 3 = 3 \ldots 6 \times 4 = 24, 6 \times 5 = 30, 6 \times 6 = 36)$, which you had memorized years and years earlier? You needed that knowledge to determine that the product of 30, which is produced by 6×5, will bring you closest to 35 without exceeding it; 24 would not be as close as 30, and 36 would exceed that number. Therefore, you selected 5 as an answer and you then placed that 5 to the rightmost of your answer of 1. You would then have 15 and be on your way to completing the answer.

Were you aware of all the steps that would bring you to the answer of 159? Not likely. Yet, all of these steps were taught to you explicitly in the classroom; through your teachers' explanation of the process, you 'learned' the process. Now, certainly, while the initial learning was formal and presented through explication, nevertheless, through time and practice the rules of the process became unconscious and automatic. Krashen's claim, therefore, that learning never becomes unconscious and automatic is one that cannot be upheld with regard to arithmetic knowledge. This being so, there is no reason to believe that a special case should be made for one particular kind of knowledge, language knowledge. It seems clear to me that much learning that is gained in a formal situation *can* become unconscious and automatic. Since Krashen's acquisition/ learning distinction is not a valid one, and since experience indicates that explicit learning can become unconscious, there is no good reason to suppose that teaching grammar by explication cannot be beneficial.

The Silent Way

The Silent Way, a method developed by Gattegno, is based on the radical notion that the classroom, especially the teacher, is to be as silent as possible. In contrast to other speech-based methods, the method virtually reverses the natural sequence in first-language learning, by having production precede comprehension. The teacher says little but rather encourages the students to talk. As might be expected, this is especially difficult and stress provoking since the students do not know how to say anything in the beginning. In this regard, alphabetic letters are often used to get students to speak. The teacher will point to letters (on 'Fidel' pronunciation charts) and by gesture indicate that students are to utter sounds. The teacher requires students to produce as much speech as possible, and as early as possible.

The teacher is required to use a certain set of physical objects, which Gattegno specifies. These consist of a number of coloured rods of different sizes, which, when used by the teacher, provide a situational context in which speech is produced. Initially, students are even encouraged to make nonsense sounds in the foreign language, some-what like the babbling of infants acquiring their first language. Then, as the instructor points to printed letters and encourages students to say them in sequence, an initial meaningful syllable is elicited. In the course of an hour or so of instruction, a student will probably have pronounced the correct word in the target language for 'rod' and a word for its colour. Then follow a number of expressions involving relationships, such as, 'The blue rod is next to the red rod', so that the students are able to describe the rod situation which the teacher has constructed. Such relationships can be extended to persons in the room, such as 'John is next to Mary'. The instructor does not generally model pronunciation, but waits for good pronunciation from someone in the class and lets that serve as a model.

The underlying approach to this method is said to be based on the 'creative' aspect of language learning, where learning is viewed as a process of discovery or creation on the part of the student. In essence, the use of induction on the part of the student is relied upon. The students are to induce the grammatical rules and structures which are inherent in the situations presented to them.

Some participants of Silent Way classes are enthusiastic about the method. However, a good many students do not react positively to the stress of being forced to produce speech. In this regard, the small groups required for the Silent Way (usually less than 15 per group) ensure that no one can hide from the teacher! Interestingly, the Silent Way, in contradistinction to the Natural Approach and Suggestopedia, assumes that some degree of stress and anxiety is conducive to learning. It seems to me that students will learn under either condition, so long as they are willing participants.

Suggestopedia

If one believes the claims made about Suggestopedia by its founder Georgi Lozanov, then it is the closest thing to the 'magic method' which everyone has been looking for in second-language teaching. Briefly, Suggestopedia purports to produce in the students an altered state of consciousness which is conducive to learning. This state, termed 'hypermnesia' (super memory) is brought on by certain relaxation techniques, including listening to certain passages of classical music (including Haydn). The music must be played at a specific tempo to enable it to induce the desired state of mental readiness. Furthermore, the learners must be provided with armchairs and pleasantly decorated rooms. As a result, according to the founder, in 24 days second-language learners can learn 1800 words, speak within the framework of a whole essential grammar, and read any text.

Teaching involves the presentation of dialogues and vocabulary which the student is to study and memorize. The materials are presented first in written and then spoken form, along with a translation of the written form. The materials are presented three times to the students. On the first presentation the students follow by reading. On the second and third, they just listen. It is on the third reading that the music is played, supposedly inducing hypermnesia and learning on the part of the student. In effect, Suggestopedia is little more than Grammar–Translation with music.

What can we say about the extraordinary claims of success which have been made by Lozanov and his small group of followers? There is certainly nothing wrong with the idea of memory enhancement. If a second-language teaching method comes along and claims, as does Suggestopedia, to greatly enhance memory by relaxation and music thereby allowing for an enormous amount of language to be acquired in just a matter of weeks, it should not be dismissed out of hand. The fact of the matter though is that almost 20 years after its introduction, the method, which has been given a fair try in many countries, still has offered no convincing evidence in support of its extravagant claims. Its only legacy seems to be that of some teachers playing music before they begin class in order to calm the students down.

11.4 Conclusions

It is safe to say that students will learn something from any method. No method is a total failure because, in all methods, students *are* exposed to the data of a second language and *are* given the opportunity to learn the language. It is also safe to say, to the disappointment of all, that there is no magic method. No method has yet been devised that will permit people over the age of 12 or so to learn a second language as effortlessly and as enjoyably as they did their native language. Still, teachers can do much to make the experience for a learner rewarding and enjoyable, whatever method is employed.

Unfortunately, no empirical research has been done which evaluates the comparative effectiveness of the teaching methods. It would be extremely difficult to do the kind of study that such a problem merits. To conduct a proper research study for each of the methods being tested: a variety of students must be matched in ability; a variety of teachers must be matched in language and personal abilities; and language tests must be available which validly measure the progress of students. These are but some of the problems. In addition, students would have to be studied for years in order to measure the long-term effects of learning. Little wonder, then, that such important research has not been done.

In judging the relative merits of teaching methods, one must consider goals. Just what is the purpose of having people learn a second language? If the ability to speak and understand a second language is the primary goal, then a speech-based method would be best for them. If, on the other hand, the ability to read and write is the primary goal, then Grammar–Translation should be the method of choice.

The goals of a nation are important in determining second-language teaching programmes in the school system. One country may wish to promote the study of reading and translation of scientific material from a second language, and would, therefore, wish to stress the knowledge that is gained through reading. In such a case, the Grammar–Translation may well be appropriate. Other countries, however, may regard communication through speech as the highest priority. As such, speech-based methods may be preferred providing, of course, that adequate finances are available for the specialized training of teachers in such methods and that the school system can afford teaching classes with small numbers of students. When large numbers of students are to be taught and few teachers are available, Grammer–Translation might well be chosen by default, since, practically speaking, no other choice is viable.

A teacher who can afford the luxury of selecting a method might well consider putting together a personal method of second-language teaching. With both speech and literacy as objectives, for example, one could adopt Communicative Language Teaching and then supplement it with physical activities (from Total Physical Response), pattern practice drills (from the Audiolingual Method) and explication and translation (from Grammar–Translation). Given the state of knowledge which we have today, an eclectic approach such as this might well be the most sensible path to follow.

11.5 Discussion questions

1. If you were to begin learning a new language, what method would you prefer to be taught by, and why?
2. How would you characterize the Communicative Language Teaching Method in terms of the five dimensions offered at the beginning of the chapter?
3. How has the Grammar–Translation Method managed to survive all of the attacks made on it, particularly from speech-based methods?
4. Why is a speech-based method generally more strenuous on a teacher than Grammar–Translation?
5. What ideas of Chomsky's brought down the Audiolingual Method?
6. Why may Total Physical Response be viewed as a contemporary version of the Direct Method?
7. Ask someone to divide 441 by 7 as quickly as possible. After they have finished, ask them what steps they were aware of while doing the problem. How does their answer bear on Krashen's Monitor Hypothesis?
8. Employing the various methods available, devise your own eclectic method. Give the rationale for your selection.
9. Outline a research study that would compare the effectiveness of the Grammar–Translation Method and Total Physical Response. What problems do you run up against?

Suggested readings

Asher, J. (1982) *Learning Another Language Through Actions: The Complete Teacher's Guide Book* (2nd edn) Los Gatos, CA: Sky Oaks Productions.

Gattegno, C. (1976) *The Common Sense of Teaching Foreign Languages*. New York: Educational Solutions.

Gregg, K. (1984). Krashen's Monitor and Occam's Razor. *Applied Linguistics*, **5**, 2, 79–100.

Krashen, S. D. and Terrell, T. D. (1983) *The Natural Approach: Language Acquisition in the Classroom*. Oxford: Pergamon.

Lozanov, G. (1979) *Suggestopedy and Outlines of Suggestopedy*. New York: Gordon & Breach Science Publishers.

Fries, C. C. and Fries, A. C. (1961) *Foundations for English Teaching*. Tokyo: Kenkyusha.

Palmer, H. and Palmer, D. (1925) *Language Through Actions*. Reprint edn. London: Longman Green (1959).

Richards, J. C. and Rodgers, T. S. (1986) *Approaches and Methods in Language Teaching*. Cambridge: Cambridge University Press.

Rivers, W. (1981) *Teaching Foreign Language Skills* (2nd edn) Chicago: University of Chicago Press.

Sauveur, L. (1878) *The Natural Method: Introduction to the Teaching of Ancient Languages*. New York: Holt.

Widdowson, H. G. (1978) *Teaching Language as Communication*. Oxford: Oxford University Press.

Yalden, J. (1983) *The Communicative Syllabus: Evolution, Design and Implementation*. Oxford: Pergamon.

Journals

Language Learning,
TESOL Quarterly

CHAPTER 12

Bilingualism and cognition

12.1 Varieties of bilinguals

To begin with, for the sake of clarification, it would be useful to consider just what the term 'bilingualism' includes. Most of us, without a second thought, would think of a bilingual as a person who is able to speak and understand two languages (languages like English and Russian) and for the most part, we would be right. That, beyond this, there might be 'varieties' of bilinguals is likely to strike many of us as odd. But, we should realize that there are people who know a *sign* language, too, such as British Sign Language or Swedish Sign Language, and these are true languages in their own right. Moreover, there are people who can read a second language fluently, even write it well, but who cannot speak or understand it to any significant degree. These people have not learned just reading (reading being founded on the acquisition of speech), but they have learned the language in the *written* mode. (For a justification of sign language and written language as genuine languages, see Chapter 4.)

Because language in all its complexity can be acquired through a variety of modalities – sound (speech), vision (writing) and visual motion (signs) – an adequate concept of a bilingual should allow for any of these realizations. Thus, we may say that a person is bilingual if he or she knows (1) more than one realization of language in the same modality, for example, two sound-based languages such as spoken English and spoken German, or two sign-based languages such as American Sign Language and Japanese Sign Language, or (2) two languages based on different modalities (spoken German and American Sign Language, for example).

There is no good reason to exclude any of these combinations from the label of bilingualism. So long as any discussion of bilingualism makes clear just what modality is being considered and how it is being considered, the setting of exclusionary standards is unjustified. However, because the languages that are mostly involved in research on bilingualism are speech-based, the discussion presented in this chapter will focus on the speech modality. Conclusions that are drawn for speech-based languages, however, may be generally extended to languages based on other modalities.

Proficiency in a language may be evaluated with respect to a variety of variables, including knowledge of syntax, vocabulary and pronunciation (signing or writing for non-speech). Researchers are not agreed on what level of proficiency concerning these variables is necessary to constitute a sufficient standard for knowing a language. Researchers establish their own criteria study by study. There is general agreement, however, by most contemporary theorists that the reading and writing of a language is not essential for the bilingual classification. Not to regard someone as bilingual who speaks two languages, but is illiterate in both, would be absurd.

On the other hand, we probably would not want to regard as bilingual, someone who knows two dialects of the same language, e.g. British Yorkshire English and American Midwestern English. While these dialects do differ in significant respects, the differences are not so great that linguists consider them separate languages. The accepted term *bidialectalism* seems to best describe this phenomenon. However, since bidialectalism does to some extent relate to bilingualism, the same concerns that are raised for bilingualism can be extended to bidialectalism.

12.2 Is bilingualism beneficial or detrimental?

Most people consider bilingualism as something good. For one thing, knowledge of another language enables people to communicate with members of other cultures in their own language. This, in turn, provides a means for furthering cooperation and understanding among nations and peoples.

This applies not only between countries but within countries where there is more than one prevalent or official language as in Switzerland or Canada. There are cases where an authoritarian regime (like that of North Korea) might wish to curb contact with other peoples by limiting the teaching of other languages, or, where an attempt is made to destroy a cultural group by forbidding the use of that group's language (like the former Soviet Union's ban on many languages). Such situations, however, are generally regarded as deplorable.

At a personal level, the pleasure and cultural benefits of bilingualism, too, are obvious. Who would *not* like to be able to travel around the world, to Paris, Moscow, Helsinki, or Tokyo, and be able to talk with the people there? What lovers of movies and theatre would *not* like to understand performances in the original language?

This being the case, where then is the controversy? How can one reasonably be against bilingualism? It's like being against Mom and apple pie, as an American might put it, and no one would admit to that.

Firstly, it must be said that some of the arguments are not against bilingualism itself but the *early* acquisition of the second language. It has been charged that acquiring a second language at an early age can be harmful in two main respects: linguistically (retarding the acquisition of the first or second language) and intellectually (retarding the development of thinking and such cognitive abilities as mathematics and reading).

Secondly, it must be said that the criticism that has been levelled against early bilingualism is primarily of another era, the early half of the twentieth century. That was a time when conceptions and experimental methodology involving language and intelligence were at a rather naive level and when the mood in America (where most of the research was done) was one of isolationism and a wariness of foreign influences. (See the Meyer case in Chapter 8 for a reflection of this attitude.) Sometimes the motivation was racist in nature.

The issue of effects is an important one and well worth consideration. What follows is what I consider to be the most important and representative research on the issue to date. (For more detailed coverage, the reader is referred to

Hakuta (1986), Taylor & Taylor (1990), and McLaughlin (1987).)

12.2.1 Effects on the development of language

As was noted above, the issue here is whether learning a second language at an early age, while the child is still in the process of acquiring the native or first language, has a negative effect on acquisition of the native language. There is a concern (not at all illogical) that bilingualism might somehow retard first- or second-language development so that, for example, a child raised with two languages might never really learn either language as well as would monolingual speakers of those languages.

Negative reports

The most well-known and influential piece of research for its time was that of Madorah Smith, back in the 1930s. Smith gathered comparative data in Iowa (where she did her graduate work) and in Hawaii on the language of pre-school children; the children were from a variety of ethnic and linguistic backgrounds. The Iowa children were essentially white and monolingually English while the Hawaii children were ethnically diverse (of Chinese, Filipino, Hawaiian, Japanese, Korean and Portuguese parentage) and bilingual, with English as one of their languages. Smith recorded sentences uttered by the children and evaluated the sentences in terms of standard usage in the languages. The principal finding was that the bilingual children from Hawaii had many more errors in their English speech than did their Iowa counterparts, which led Smith to conclude that bilingualism caused retardation in language development.

By defining errors the way she did, Smith could not help but come up with the results that she did. For, the children in Hawaii in general spoke a sort of English that was prevalent there, which was not the so-called 'correct' English spoken by the children from Iowa. Smith's bias is reminiscent of the later work of Bereiter, Engelmann and Basil Bernstein in the 1960s, who claimed that non-standard speakers of English (inner city blacks in the US and working-class whites in Britain) had poor language knowledge as compared to standard English speakers. The brilliant work of Labov and other linguistic researchers in the 1960s and 1970s, however, conclusively demonstrated that non-standard dialects of English are every bit as complex as standard dialects (Midwest speech in America, for example) and must be regarded as linguistically comparable. Smith's work has other serious methodological problems, too, particularly the inadequate matching of monolinguals and bilinguals in terms of their families' socio-economic and educational backgrounds.

Incidentally, I might mention in passing that when I was a graduate student at the University of Hawaii in the 1960s, I had sought Smith out in order to ask her some questions regarding bilingualism. I located her in a home for the aged (the King's Daughters Home) and found her to be as bright and spirited as she was reputed to be. Her opposition to early bilingualism, however, had remained unchanged.

Positive reports

More sophisticated investigations in comparing the linguistic skills of monolinguals and bilinguals have been done by Lambert and his associates in Canada, where English and French are the official languages. (French predominates in the province of Quebec while English predominates in the other provinces.) Many of the research studies have involved children in so-called 'language immersion' programmes. In these programmes, children are immersed, so to speak, in the second language, being exposed to a substantial amount of academic instruction and social interaction in that second language.

One long-term study by Bruck *et al.* (1976) with native English-speaking children in a French immersion programme found that by the fourth or fifth grade, the second-language French skills, including reading and writing, were almost as good as those of native French-speaking children. Importantly, all of this was achieved at no loss to their English native language development (as compared to a control group of English monolingual children). In addition, the immersion group did better than the English monolingual control group on creativity tests. In many cases, their mathematics and science scores were also higher. Similar research has strengthened these findings.

There is some question, however, as to the validity of these findings. Principally, this concerns whether the parents of the children may have in some way affected the outcome. For, even when the parents of the monolinguals and bilinguals are matched socio-economically and educationally, no control is allowed for the attitude and motivation of the parents regarding bilingualism. Perhaps parents who wish to be involved in a bilingual programme somehow would tend to provide a more advantageous home environment for their children, intellectually and linguistically, than would other parents. There is no way this issue can be resolved unless researchers are allowed to randomly assign children to monolingual or bilingual programmes regardless of the wishes of their parents.

Conclusion regarding effect on language

There is no evidence that early bilingualism has an adverse effect on language acquisition, be it in the first or second language. Recent work, moreover, even tends to show some beneficial effects for early bilingualism, although this work is not without methodological difficulties. After considering the entire body of research, it would be difficult today to find any reputable theorist who would conclude that early bilingualism itself causes negative linguistic effects. The worst that could be said is that the research concerning beneficial effects is inconclusive.

12.2.2 Effects on the development of intelligence

Does learning a second language at an early age, while the child is still in the process of acquiring the native or first language, have a negative effect on a child's intelligence, thinking ability, creativity or cognitive areas such as mathematics? Somehow, the burden of learning an additional language is considered to have an adverse effect on the child's abilities. As was the case in considering effects on the development of language, most early research tended to find a negative effect. The possibility that learning a second language could in some way have a positive effect on intelligence was not something that was considered viable until relatively recently.

Negative reports

In one of the earliest studies, Goddard (1917) gave the English language version of the Binet intelligence test to 30 recently arrived Jewish adult immigrants at Ellis Island. On the word-fluency portion of the test, it was found that less than half of the adult immigrants could provide 60 words, a figure much below the 200 words that 11-year-old American children could provide. Based on these results, Goddard classified 25 of the 30 Jews as 'feeble-minded'. (My father, who came from Russia, landed at Ellis Island and knew no English, could very well have been one of these!) Later, Goddard used such results to petition Congress to enact more restrictions limiting immigration to America.

Many more studies, whose methodology involved the use of English either as a direct measure of intelligence or as a medium for inquiry, were to follow. In fact, such faulty methodology was the direct cause of almost 50 years of negative results. Not surprisingly, immigrants and non-standard English speakers fared especially badly. It is rather distressing that such eminent psychological researchers as Brigham and Florence Goodenough also did not hesitate to conclude that foreigners, especially non-Nordic Europeans, were *inferior* in intelligence, as evidenced by their poor performance on intelligence tests administered in English.

It was only in the 1950s that psychologists seriously began to consider that knowledge of language was not a fair measure of intelligence and that the language content of many widely used intelligence tests was culturally biased. The more sophisticated psychological studies on language and intelligence in the 1960s and 1970s have attempted to improve on this situation.

Positive effects

Given the more knowledgeable views of language and intelligence that emerged, the methodology and interpretation of research studies greatly improved. The work of

Lambert in the early 1960s led the way in this regard. Unexpectedly, positive effects began to be found and such results have continued to be reported even to the present.

To date, one of the most impressive studies done has been that of Bain and Yu (1980). They compared monolingual and bilingual young children (between 6 to 8 months of age) in different parts of the world (Alberta, Canada, Alsace, France and Hong Kong). Linguistically, the children were bilingual in either English and French, or, English and Chinese. The children were raised either monolingually or bilingually by their parents under the guidance of the researchers. Families were recruited by advertising in local newsletters for parents who wished to volunteer in a monolingual and bilingual research study. The tests which Bain and Yu used involved puzzles and having to carry out verbal instructions. Some of the instructions were rather linguistically complex for a 4-year-old, e.g. the child was told, 'When the red light goes on, say "squeeze", and squeeze the ball'. By the time the children were around 4 years old, the results on some cognitive performance tests showed the bilinguals to be superior to the monolinguals, in addition to their having acquired two different languages.

Hakuta (1986) challenges these results on methodological grounds, claiming that the parents of the monolinguals and bilinguals could have been substantially different initially (bilingual parents having more advantageous beliefs and attitudes) and therefore could have biased the findings. (The same point was raised in a section above regarding the studies of Lambert and others on the effects of language.)

Of course, this is entirely possible. However, the fact that the parents of the monolinguals responded to the newspaper advertisement to be included in the language study, as had the parents of the bilinguals, serves to greatly reduce the possible effects of this variable. The monolingual parents must have been specially motivated out of concern for their children's language welfare or they would not have responded to the advertisement to participate in the study. It could be said, however, that even had the bilinguals validly outperformed the monolinguals on the tasks given, this might not have been a strong enough basis on which to presume a general and continuing intellectual superiority on their part. Broader measures of cognitive abilities along with later age follow-ups is what is needed.

Conclusion regarding effect on intelligence

Thus, we find that there is no evidence that early bilingualism will harm the intellectual or cognitive development of the child in any way. Not only that, but there is evidence, although not strong, that it may perhaps even benefit the child intellectually.

As for future research, given the view I expressed earlier (in Chapter 1) that thought and intellectual processing develop independently of language, I do not expect that researchers will ever be able to demonstrate that language affects intelligence in any important way. Unfortunately, because editors of scientific journals tend not to accept (for publication) research studies that do not result in statistically significant differences or correlations (called 'negative results' by experimentalists), substantial experimental evidence that would favour this view is not likely to be forthcoming.

12.2.3   Conclusion regarding effects of early bilingualism on language and intelligence

A consideration of the research evidence shows no harmful effects either regarding language (first or second) or intelligence. In fact, some research suggests there may even be beneficial effects. Given the advantages of knowing another language and of young children's propensity for speedy language acquisition, we must conclude that there is every reason to favour early bilingualism.

12.3   Simultaneous and sequential learning situations

There are essentially two conditions according to which a person may become bilingual: the two languages can be acquired at the same time or in sequence. The simultaneous learning of two languages occurs only with children, since in only the most abnormal of circumstances would a child when exposed to a language not learn it. On the other hand, sequential learning can occur with both children and adults; the second language can be learned in childhood or after the person has become an adult.

12.3.1 Simultaneous acquisition

There are two situations in which a child may acquire more than one language at the same time. One is when speakers of the different languages use only one language each when talking to the child. For example, a mother might speak only Spanish while the father might speak only English. The one parent using one language only situation ('1P–1L').

The other situation is when the same person uses two different languages while speaking to the child. For example, the mother and father use both Spanish and English when talking to the child. The one parent using two languages situation ('1P–2L').

It seems that children are so flexible that they can become bilingual in both languages by the age of 3 or 4 years, regardless of their language situation. Although evidence bearing on this issue is not available, it seems likely that the child in the 1P–1L situation will learn the two languages faster than the child in the 1P–2L situation simply because of consistency. On hearing some speech, the child would not have to puzzle over just which of the two sets of language knowledge is to be referred to. I do not think, however, that the difference in speed of acquisition between the 1P–1L and 1P–2L situations would be great; it would be only a matter of months, perhaps, before the 1P–2L child would eventually sort it all out.

On the other hand, it may be that 1P–2L children produce more mixed language sentences (the view of McLaughlin), where vocabulary and syntax of the different languages are used in the same sentence, e.g. 'Open the *reizoko*' (where *reizoko* is refrigerator in Japanese). Of course, in time the child will overcome the mixed input and get things right. Overall, it would seem that the 1P–1L situation is better since acquisition may be faster and less mixing might occur.

One of my favourite 1P–2L examples which I like to cite involves a friend who lives in the US. (The example is mentioned in another context in Chapter 8.) My friend's wife is a Japanese speaker, while he is an English speaker, although they know each other's language. From the time of the birth of their two sons, who are about three years apart in age, the mother spoke Japanese and the father spoke English to the children. To add to the situation, there was the live-in grandmother who spoke only Russian to the children. The result? By the age of 3, each of the boys, in turn, became trilingual in English, Japanese and Russian. Because the family lived in an English-speaking neighbour-hood (in Honolulu), English is what they used when they went outside to play.

Whether the bilingual child must be *conscious* of the existence of two languages in order to make progress in acquiring them is virtually impossible to determine. One cannot interrogate a 1- or 2-year-old on such a matter. However, once the child has acquired some degree of fluency in language, even very young children may indicate an awareness of knowing two languages. (For a considera-tion of the issue of consciousness in language learning, see Schmidt, 1990.) One Estonian–English bilingual child was only 2 years old when he expressed embarrassment on becoming aware that he had spoken in Estonian to his English monolingual cousin (Vihman, 1982). And, De Villiers and De Villiers (1978) cite hearing a 4-year-old say, 'I can speak Hebrew and English', to which his 5-year-old American friend responded with 'What's English?'! Perhaps the monolingual English-speaking child needed some knowledge of two languages before he would understand what a language is. Likewise, if a person saw things only in red (through rose-coloured glasses), you would not expect that person to be able to understand what is meant by colour. A contrast is essential for such a realization. (Relating to this point is the dolphin discussion in Chapter 3. Because the dolphins had learned language only in the imperative format (Bring this, Take that, etc.), and because they knew no other contrasting syntactic forms (declarative, question, etc.), it was argued that the dolphins could not know the syntactic form of the imperative.)

Before closing this section, I would advise parents (or

potential parents) who have bilingual abilities and have decided to raise their children in a bilingual situation to use the languages in the 1P–1L fashion right from the start. It is inadvisable to wait until the child is 1 or 2 years of age before introducing the second language. If such parents wait, they may not be able to carry out their plan. For, in the course of a year or two their use of one language will become so set that they will experience great psychological difficulty in changing to another. When a social relationship has been established with the child by means of one language right from birth, it will not be easy to switch to a different language.

12.3.2 Sequential acquisition

The sequential kind of bilingual situation occurs for a child when parents speak one language and the community at large speaks another. The parents could be immigrants, foreign residents or simply people who have moved from one part of a country to another part (from English-speaking Toronto to French-speaking Quebec City). The parents speak one language at home, which is different from the one which the child is exposed to outside the home. Clearly, sequential acquisition of the second language may take place at a variety of ages and under a variety of situations.

Consider, for example, an immigrant couple to America who come from China. They speak Chinese at home with their infant daughter. Then at the age of 3, the child starts attending an English-speaking nursery school. By the time the child is 4, she will be speaking English with her playmates and others while continuing to speak Chinese at home with her parents. Thus, the child learns two languages sequentially, i.e. where a second language is introduced after the first language has started being learned. Of course, some of the acquisition of the two languages will occur simultaneously. What is sequential is the different starting times for the introduction of each language.

In acquiring the second language, speed, proficiency and fluency will be determined by certain psychological and social variables. A detailed discussion of such variables is presented in Chapter 8, where child and adult acquisition of a second language are compared.

12.4 Transfer effect of L1 on L2 learning

12.4.1 Similarity of syntax, vocabulary and sound system

While linguists agree that no one language is more complex overall than any other language, and psycholinguists agree that no one language is easier to learn than any other language, nonetheless, not every *pair* of languages can be expected to be acquired at the same rate. For example, after having learned English, learning French will not be as difficult as learning Japanese. There are differences between English and French syntax but these differences are small in comparison to the monumental differences between the syntax of English and Japanese. Furthermore, there are significant similarities between English and French in terms of vocabulary. A learner would not be starting at zero as he or she would if learning Japanese. The Japanese speaker learning English is placed in a comparable position. Yet, acquisition of Korean by a Japanese speaker is rather easy because those syntaxes are very similar.

On the other hand, English speakers would not have as much trouble with Chinese syntax as they would with Japanese syntax because Chinese syntax is more similar to English. Yet, when it comes to the sound system, Chinese, with its tones, is so different from English and Japanese that the English speaker will find the Japanese sound system easier to handle.

Thus, we may conclude that the greater the similarity between two languages in terms of their syntax, vocabulary and sound system, the more rapid the rate of acquisition in the two languages. If we had to scale the importance of these variables, undoubtedly we would give syntax the greater weight. Good pronunciation or a wide vocabulary can hardly compensate for poor syntax. In this regard it is interesting to note that in its recent history America has had two foreign-born Secretaries of State, Kissinger and Brezinski, who speak English with accents (German and

Polish, respectively). In other respects, they excel in the English language. Good syntax with good vocabulary is the best duo combination for language success.

12.4.2 Facilitation, errors, interference, Second Language Strategy and First Language Strategy

Facilition

Given the considerations above, it is clear that the knowledge one has of one's first language may help or facilitate the learning of a second language. Even when two languages are very different, from both a linguistic and psycholinguistic processing viewpoint (producing and under-standing sentences), there is much facilitation. It is just that the facilitation is not as noticeable as are errors. It is easier to spot cases of errors than it is to spot instances of facilitation.

With cases where both languages have, for example, the article (as in English and French), gender (designation of nouns as masculine or feminine, as in French and Italian) and obligatory marking of nouns when plural, the occur-rence of positive transfer to the second language is rapid. Knowledge of the complexity of structure, morphology (word formation) and phonology (sound patterns) in one language cannot help but serve to facilitate acquisition of the other language, for the learner does not have to wonder about how to deal with language as he or she did in first-language learning. The second-language learner has already dealt with similar language problems in the first language, not only with regard to formal linguistic properties but also with respect to developing psycholinguistic strategies that are used in the process of producing and understanding sentences.

I believe that facilitation can be so great that, given the proper environment – where children are placed in a 'natural', not a 'classroom', situation (see Chapter 10 concerning details on this distinction) – a second language can be acquired more quickly than the first. This would explain the oft-observed phenomenon of young immigrant children around 4 or 5 years of age acquiring fluency in a second language in less than a year.

Errors, interference and second and first language strategies

Because errors are so easy to observe and are good indicators of a person's level of second-language knowledge, there have been many reliable studies done on errors. There is some confusion, however, when it comes to interpreting just what the cause of errors might be. In my opinion, only a minority of errors can be attributed to interference. Rather, most errors are the result of the application of what I shall call the 'First Language Strategy' and the 'Second Language Strategy'. These strategies are applied when relevant second-language knowledge is not yet known or incompletely learned.

Consider the following errors made by my Japanese freshman university students while writing answers to examination questions:

1. *Now Tom happy is.*
This sentence follows Japanese constituent order.

2. *Afterwards they ate the dinner.*
The article is improperly inserted before the mass noun 'dinner'. There is no previous reference to a specific 'dinner'.

For the sake of fairness, let us now consider an error commonly made by English speakers who are learning Japanese. The English speaker might well produce the following order of constituents in Japanese:

3. *John Mary met at the theatre yesterday.*
Here the Japanese Subject + Object + Verb constituent order is correct but the adverbials are improperly placed. They should be only at the beginning of the sentence, not at the end. Thus, 'Yesterday at the theatre John Mary met' is the proper form (Adverbial + Subject + Object + Verb).

Let us now discuss these sentences and the problems they raise.

#1 *Now Tom happy is* **Interference**

Because the student has had years of English and knows English word order rather well, it is likely that this is a case of interference. In the process of constructing the sentence, perhaps because of haste (native speakers too make errors in such circumstances), the Japanese order of constituents intruded on the process so as to cause the error.

#2 *Afterwards they ate the dinner* **Second-Language Strategy**

The student has to some extent learned the article rule and its application to types of nouns but perhaps mistakenly thought that 'dinner' here is a countable noun which requires the article. Another possibility is that because the student was unsure of the status of 'dinner', she employed what could be called an Article Insertion strategy. That is, when in doubt insert the article, because nouns taking the article are more frequent in the second language. Thus, this is the result of applying general knowledge of the second language to that second language – the Second-Language Strategy.

#3 *John Mary met at the theatre yesterday* **First-Language Strategy**

Supposing that the person did not know the English rule; this could well be an instance, not of interference, but of the result of using the First-Language Strategy, i.e., applying first language knowledge to the second. When second-language knowledge is lacking, this strategy is very useful. It is one that, I believe, all second-language learners automatically use and rely on, especially in conversational situations. Usually it is better to say something, even if wrong, than to say nothing. This strategy will allow for something to be said, based on knowledge of the first language.

12.4.3 The double trouble phenomenon

I am a native speaker of English. When I started to learn to speak Japanese, French (with which I hadn't been in contact since leaving Canada for the US 15 years earlier) came to mind when I tried to speak Japanese. When I later took a trip to France a few years later, my smattering of Japanese unexpectedly came to mind when I tried to speak French. Perhaps foreign languages all are tossed into the same bag in the mind before they get sorted out. (I wonder what would happen if I started to learn Chinese, as my wife would have me do!)

12.5 Discussion questions

1. What might be an unusual variety of bilingualism? Consider language acquisition modalities.
2. Why do you think childhood bilingualism and not adult bilingualism is studied for effects on language and intelligence?
3. Is early bilingualism harmful regarding language and intelligence?
4. Might there be harmful effects to children in the simultaneous acquisition of three languages? Four? Five?
5. What advice would you give parents who wish to raise their newborn baby bilingually?
6. What research would you like to see done on bilingualism?
7. What language factors would you consider in predicting whether one second language would be easier to learn than another second language? Give examples.
8. Give an example of your own for first language facilitation in learning a second language.
9. What is the 'First Language Strategy'? Give your own example of an error in a second language that could be caused by its operation.
10. Would a bilingual person necessarily make a good professional translator or interpreter?

Suggested readings

Bain, Bruce and Yu, Agnes (1980) Cognitive consequences of raising children bilingually: 'One parent, one language'. *Canadian Journal of Psychology*, **34**, 304–13.

Bruck, M., Lambert, W. E. and Tucker, G. R. (1976) Cognitive and attitudinal consequences of bilingual schooling: the St. Lambert project through grade six. *International Journal of Psycholinguistics*, **6**, 13–33.

De Villiers, J. G. and De Villiers, P. A. (1978) *Language Acquisition*. Cambridge, Mass.: Harvard University Press.

Goddard, H. H. (1917) Mental tests and the immigrant. *Journal of Delinquency*, **2**, 243–77.

Hakuta, Kenji (1986) *Mirror of Language: the Debate on Bilingualism.* New York: Basic Books.

Labov, William (1970) The logic of non-standard English. In James Alatis, (ed.), *Report of the Twentieth Annual Round Table Meeting on Linguistics and Language.* Washington, DC: Georgetown University Press, pp. 30–87.

McLaughlin, Barry (1987) *Theories of Second-Language Learning.* London: Edward Arnold.

Padillo, A. M., Chen, A., Duran, R., Hakuta, K., Lambert, W., Lindholm, K. J. and Tucker, G. R. (1991) The English-Only Movement. *American Psychologist*, **46**, 2, 120–30.

Schmidt, Richard (1990) The role of consciousness in second language learning. *Applied Linguistics*, **11**, 2, 17–46.

Smith, Madorah (1939) Some light on the problem of bilingualism as found from a study of the progress in mastery of English, among pre-school children of non-American ancestry in Hawaii. *Genetic Psychology Monographs*, **21**, 119–284.

Taylor, Insup and Taylor, Martin (1990) *Psycholinguistics: Learning and Using Language.* Englewood Cliffs, NJ: Prentice-Hall.

Vihman, M. M. (1982) The acquisition of morphology by a bilingual child: A whole-word approach. *Applied Psycholinguistics*, **3**, 141–60.

Author Index

Subject Index